THE
ART OF
LEADERSHIP
IN WAR

Recent Titles in
Contributions in Military History
SERIES EDITOR: THOMAS E. GRIESS

The General: Robert L. Bullard and Officership in the United States
Army, 1881–1925
Allan R. Millet

The Twenty-First Missouri: From Home Guard to Union Regiment
Leslie Anders

The Politics of the Second Front: American Military Planning and
Diplomacy in Coalition Warfare, 1941–1943
Mark A. Stoler

The Anatomy of a Small War: The Soviet-Japanese Struggle for
Changkufeng/Khasan, 1938
Alvin D. Coox

Reconsiderations on the Revolutionary War: Selected Essays
Don Higginbotham, editor

The Leavenworth Schools and the Old Army: Education,
Professionalism, and the Officer Corps of the United States Army,
1881–1918
Timothy K. Nenninger

In Peace and War: Interpretations of American Naval History,
1775–1978
Kenneth J. Hagan, editor

Pacifying the Plains: General Alfred Terry and the Decline of the Sioux,
1866–1890
John W. Bailey

Divided and Conquered: The French High Command and the Defeat of the
West, 1940
Jeffery A. Gunsburg

The Army and Civil Disorder: Federal Military Intervention in Labor
Disputes, 1877–1900
Jerry M. Cooper

History of the Art of War: Within the Framework of Political History,
The Germans
Hans Delbrück, translated by Walter J. Renfroe, Jr.

John Horsfield

THE ART OF LEADERSHIP IN WAR

The Royal Navy
From the Age of Nelson
to the End of World War II

Contributions in Military History, Number 21

GREENWOOD PRESS

WESTPORT, CONNECTICUT • LONDON, ENGLAND

Library of Congress Cataloging in Publication Data

Horsfield, John.
    The art of leadership in war.

    (Contributions in military history; no. 21
ISSN 0084–9251)
    Bibliography: p.
    Includes index.
    1. Leadership. 2. Admirals—Great Britain.
3. Great Britain. Navy—History. I. Title.
II. Series.
VB205.G7H67   359   79–54059
ISBN 0–313–20919–7

Library of Congress Catalog Card Number: 79–54059
ISBN: 0–313–20919–7
ISSN: 0084–9251

First published in 1980

Greenwood Press
A division of Congressional Information Service, Inc.
88 Post Road West, Westport, Connecticut 06881

Printed in the United States of America

10 9 8 7 6 5 4 3 2 1

359
H

CONTENTS

Illustrations   *vii*

Acknowledgments   *ix*

Introduction   *xi*

1 Early Writings on Leadership   3

2 Naval Leadership: Some Distinctive Features   12

3 The Eighteenth Century: The Making of a
   Tradition   22

4 St. Vincent: The Sailor Who Did *Not* Fall
   from Grace with the Sea   47

5 Nelson: A Hero's Life and Death   62

6 Collingwood: The Stoic   76

7 The Age of Nelson—Also Taking Part—
   Lesser Mortals   82

8 The Long Victorian Peace   91

9 Entering the War   104

10 Jellicoe and Jutland   111

1

11 After the Great War: Beatty and Keyes   125

12 Interlude between the Wars   143

13 Cunningham: The Lessons of the Great War
    Learned and the Search for Another Nelson
    Concluded   148

14 Recessional: Admirals All for England's Sake!   159

    Notes   *171*

    Bibliography   *207*

    Index   *233*

ILLUSTRATIONS

Old Style Recruiting! Painting by A. Johnston   26

Visit of George III to Lord Howe's Flagship   38

Portrait of St. Vincent by F. Cotes   43

Portrait of St. Vincent by Sir William Beechey   44

John Bull Taking a Luncheon by J. Gillray   63

Sir Sidney Smith by J. Eckstein   83

Portrait of Vice-Admiral Sir George Tryon   97

Admiral Jellicoe and Admiral De Bon, 1917   112

A Composite Picture of World War I Naval Officers   126

Sir Roger Keyes and Sir Ian Hamilton at Gallipoli
Day Ceremonies   135

Sir Andrew Cunningham Broadcasting his "All's Well"
Message   149

ACKNOWLEDGMENTS

I am grateful to Arthur Marder, who suggested that I write on the topic of British naval leadership and whose advice was the sine qua non of this work.

I am also grateful to Henry Cord Meyer and Jon S. Jacobson for their helpful suggestions, to Roger Berry, Head of Special Collections at the University of California, Irvine, and Natalie Korp for their indispensable assistance in preparation of this study.

I owe much to my family and friends for their interest in my writing. And, finally, I would like to thank the many correspondents in the United States and the United Kingdom who have provided me with information and comments on the subject.

Further acknowledgment of particular assistance received is given in the notes at the end of this work.

INTRODUCTION

This book makes a chronological and selective study of British naval leadership over two centuries to see whether there are any common and continuing elements in the style and nature of that leadership that transcend historical periods. I examine the way that notable admirals such as Nelson[1] and Jellicoe[2] exercised leadership in action at crucial times in their careers and in the fortunes of Britain. I look at the relationship of such leaders with their political and naval masters and their professional relationship with subordinates. Despite my concentration on the highest echelons of command, I do not necessarily subscribe to the view that everything depends on the leader, that is, that the history of the leader is the only significant history. Marshal Foch's view that great results in war are due to the commander, and that without a commander, no battle, no victory, is possible, ignores the fact that lions are sometimes led by donkeys. The omission of lesser men and lower ranks here is not to belittle their contribution to victory—or defeat.

Bearing in mind, therefore, the contributions of followers as well as leaders, this study is written in the belief that a closer examination of the methods of well-known naval leaders is worth making, and that this examination should try to keep a fair balance between consideration of the general nature of naval leadership and the varying demands of different situations and different wars. This study does not aim to be one of tactical and strategical skills, although these features of leadership are mentioned in a general sense, as they throw light on personal qualities. I am concerned with admirals in action, not desk-bound admirals, except insofar as naval administrators have had a decisive part to play in the selection and encouragement of those who led in battle.

The study of naval leadership from the point of view of British experience is particularly rewarding because of the plethora of battles in which the Royal Navy took part. The earl of Orrery[3] wrote in 1677 of the Romans, "Their trade was War. I thank God ours is not." This comforting disclaimer of an interest in war is shared by many British people, who regard themselves as essentially peace loving. But the evidence of history suggests a different kind of experience. Britain has participated in more wars than any other major power since the fifteenth century, and most of them were naval as well as land wars.[4] In the twentieth century, to keep up the record, the British Empire was in the two world wars for longer than any other power—a record that can be regarded only with mixed feelings. There is certainly plenty of action to consider. With this background of frequency and intensity of involvement in war, I emphasize in this study the value of a continuing tradition.

Considering the modern cult of a search for instant success and instant excellence, it behoves us to bear in mind the value of tradition, that is, the continual blending of old and new experience. Tradition in this sense is not necessarily reactionary. The attainment of quality is not an instant overnight process, as the lords and masters of our contemporary institutions should remember. Sir Andrew Cunningham,[5] the great British admiral of the Second World War, effectively made this point when he said, "It takes three years to build a ship and three centuries to build a tradition."

In the creation and continuance of a venerated British naval tradition, successful admirals such as Hawke[6] or Cunningham have obviously had much more to contribute than the unsuccessful or disastrous ones such as John Byng[7] and Tryon.[8] Even so, in a negative way, as Voltaire aptly pointed out regarding Byng's execution, a man's failure might be a lesson to others.

In this survey I concentrate on renown rather than notoriety and familiar faces rather than more obscure individuals. St. Vincent,[9] Nelson, Collingwood,[10] Jellicoe, Beatty,[11] Keyes,[12] and Cunningham receive special attention. All were successful leaders, but the inference should not be drawn from this selection that only successful leadership is worthy of study; though admittedly it makes for a more cheerful pursuit than the study of failure, which has had students of its own.[13]

I have not attempted to create or even test a general theory of leadership. This effort has so far proved to be an exercise in the chimerical as will be seen in the survey of writing on leadership in the first chapter. I believe the meaning of the concept of leadership evolves from a thoughtful consideration of events and personalities of the period under study, rather than by an initial and premature attempt to define limits of the concept. I have made general comments on the leadership of the period surveyed and incidental comment, at the start of the study, on the distinctive features of naval as compared with military leadership. The subject of comparative naval and military leadership in contrasting nations is also interesting, and I make passing comment on French naval leadership in the eighteenth century. However, I have limited myself to a national theme—the Royal Navy during two centuries of history—and have concentrated on a single, albeit very important, aspect of its history.

In focusing on this theme of naval leadership, my method has been to estimate the significance and effectiveness of the selected naval leaders by means of a series of questions. I have asked these questions in the belief that the exercise of naval leadership is very much a test of the whole man, of the exercise of so many aspects of personality. Yet a man must always be considered in relation to his fellow officers and to the men who serve under him. I have thus been concerned with human relations as well as tradition.

The questions I ask are these: first: What were the relations of the admiral to his superiors, to his colleagues, and to the men? second: What was his attitude to change? Did he venerate tradition? Did he show initiative? Was he an innovator? third: What was his general sense of strategy and tactics—tactics in particular? fourth: What were his administrative abilities as related to the conduct of war? and fifth: Were there any aspects of his personal background, social or domestic, that affected his leadership? This study, in addition to being concerned with purely professional attributes and performance, is also concerned with the public persona of a naval leader. What were his relations with the Admiralty, with politicians? Indeed, I consider his relations with the wider, nonprofessional world insofar as it had a bearing on naval leadership.

I consider my approach to be an empirical one. My conclusions evolved naturally in the course of this study and were not made a priori at its inception. I go into these conclusions at greater length in the final chapter. However, it is appropriate for the reader to have a sense of these conclusions at the outset, even though this work is interpretative and the substance must be digested before the conclusions can be fully appreciated.

In my search for common and continuing elements in British naval leadership, I have been able to detect three main aspects. These aspects may be appropriately called the *variable*, pertaining to the changing times, the *particular*, pertaining to a national tradition peculiar to the Royal Navy, and the *universal*, pertaining to the qualities of personality and organization that seem relevant to any age or any century.

In the concluding chapter I also reflect on the perennial questions that are of great concern to any writer on leadership. I consider the questions of whether leadership is an innate quality or whether it can be taught. I consider the significance of the contribution of individual leaders in comparison with mass effort. Although I will not anticipate my conclusions on these questions now, in my survey of naval leadership I do attempt to keep a level head and try not to project infallible recipes.

I frequently pause during this study to comment on the passing social and cultural background to events, when aspects of the ethos of the time are of particular relevance to the phenomenon of naval leadership. The second, third, and eighth chapters in particular contain comments of this nature. Leadership can be considered in a vacuum no more than any other aspect of history. It is both a manifestation of culture and society.

Before considering the selected naval leaders, I give an introductory survey of other writings on the subject of leadership to set my theme and approach in perspective in an intellectual and cultural sense. I also use the survey to give the reader a more acute sense of the problems that leadership studies raise.

THE
ART OF
LEADERSHIP
IN WAR

chapter **1**

EARLY WRITINGS ON LEADERSHIP

The word *leadership*[1] was not frequently used until the middle of the nineteenth century, that is, in the sense of a "capacity for leading." The concept of course is far older than the word. Pre-Industrial Revolution society paid great attention to rank as the authority for the exercise of leadership. Indeed, in the Middle Ages, kings, of whom St. Louis[2] was a shining example, exercised not only military leadership, administrative and judicial authority, but sacred power as well. With the Industrial and American and French revolutions, the emphasis in leadership lay in tested personal qualities, a competitive situation with the recognition of individual ability rather than privileged position.[3]

The nineteenth-and twentieth-century development of professionalism in so many walks of life created an interest in the concept of training for leadership and in the nature of successful or effective leadership. Professionalism in this sense might be defined as the self-conscious, organized exercise of a particular skill or art according to accepted standards and techniques. This growing interest in leadership led to a spate of books on the subject, and attempts were made to define the concept more rigorously. Thomas Carlyle, in his *Heroes and Hero Worship* and in his writings on Oliver Cromwell and Frederick the Great, was obviously obsessed by the theme of leadership.

In nineteenth-century culture there had been a pervasive interest in the role of the great man or hero. By the end of that century there was an attempt to apply the intellectual approach of the natural sciences to the theme of leadership. It was thought that if the scientific method of inquiry could be applied to the history of man's leadership, a science of leadership could be formulated. Man in the present could then be tested against these ascertained leadership qualities and his future performance predicted. Hence we have the social science approach to the question of leadership.

A useful way to classify the large and varied literature on leadership would be to note first this social science approach and then to look at what may be called the classical approach taken by both historians and more purely military writers. I define the classical approach as generalized and impressionistic writings from historical evidence. This approach has emphasized that leadership is an art rather than a science and has not attempted to make any statistical test of its conclusions. It has produced writing that is by implication predictive, for it states the best elements of leadership for a recommendation of future performance, while emphasizing the uncertainty of human nature and human relationships.

Many writers use this classical approach. For example, Wavell[4] and Captain Roskill[5] might be described as both academic and military in purpose, writing works of a historical nature while also seeking to inculcate the lessons of successful leadership in the minds of entrants into the naval and military professions. There may be no difference in method and manner between a writer in the *Naval Review*[6] commenting on leadership for purely professional reasons and a historian commenting on past wars. However, the first writer may be compiling an article or text for action, and the second one merely contributing a reflection on the past with no utilitarian purpose in mind.

Looking at the first kind of leadership writing—social scientific— we see that in the twentieth century, when the principal body of work has been produced, sociologists have tended to see no necessary distinction in kind between professional civilian management and professional military leadership.[7] They have asked three fundamental questions: First, are there distinct leadership traits that, exhibited by one person, can be applied to every situation from a Sunday school outing to the Götterdämmerung? After all, a person who can cope with the Götterdämmerung might not be able to cope with the exigencies of a Sunday school outing and vice versa. Or to draw on a historical example, a Napoleon in Spain fighting a national uprising might find a more difficult kind of challenge than a Napoleon in northern Italy. A second question is whether so-called leadership qualities are innate or can they be taught? That is, is leadership merely a form of acquired skill rather than an inherent character trait? Third, can leadership ability or potential leadership performance be predicted, whether, for example, it be by academic-type testing in the lecture room or by artificially contrived situations on the assault course?[8]

Until the end of the First World War there was a widespread belief among social scientists, which was eagerly adopted by the combatant governments, that leadership qualities in an individual could be objectively tested and when discerned could predict that person's future performance in either a civilian or military situation.[9] Modern society with the advent of mass war was demanding guarantees that money spent on training leaders would not be wasted on the wrong caliber of person. The military employed the methods of the social scientists for training and testing purposes, but in contrast retained the very elitist assumptions the social scientists were challenging. Most of the modern writing by military or naval authors on leadership still shows little sign of acceptance of, or even exposure to, the social scientist's doubts regarding the notion of abstract leadership qualities.

The growing use of leadership tests in the United States, Europe, and the British Empire was paralleled by the growing use of educational intelligence tests which led to the vogue for talking in terms of intelligence quotients.[10] However, doubts about the validity of leadership and intelligence testing sprang up among social scientists long before any diminution in the use of these methods. Leadership testing abounded in the Second World War among the Axis and Allied powers, even though the assumptions on which it was based were under increasing challenge. By the end of the war, the prevailing view among social scientists was that there was no officer type, that there was indeed no leader type at all. Leadership was not an innate quality. It was concluded that leadership effectiveness depended on the way a particular person in a particular situation answered the demands of that situation. It was the relationship between group and personality at a particular moment. Effective leadership in such circumstances was not related to either training or experience. Within a group facing challenge or the accomplishment of a task, leadership might shift as the demands of the situation shifted, with the torch of leadership going from hand to hand as each person made the most effective response. Therefore the denoting or predicting of leadership performance by use of artificial situations was not a certain way of predicting anything. The artificial form of testing omitted by necessity the fluctuations of situation and risk that only war itself could provide. A traditionalist might agree with this social science view that war can only be taught by war.

The social scientists also had to face the problem of institutional leadership. Here, with the admiral, the general, or the bishop, the authority of the leader did not in actual practice move or fluctuate according to the vagaries of the situation. Leadership or command could continue to be exercised in an unfavorable situation with poor performance. In this situation, whether a nominal leader was a true leader was a matter of judgment. Some social scientists distinguished between what they called a leader such as President Lincoln, who had charismatic qualities, and a "headman" such as President Harding, who did not. James MacGregor Burns has distinguished between transforming leadership such as that of Lenin, which helps make followers into leaders, and transactional leadership, which is that of the customary bargain-making party leader.[11] Institutional leadership has its own particular inner variations, styles, successes, tensions, and failures. In this role a leader may acquire respect or trust in one situation where he is adept in exercising leadership and employ the confidence so gained in another situation where he is not so confident. The duke of Wellington's[12] leadership in war and peace is an example. Wellington transferred his role of leadership from one institution, the army, to another, the civil government. This change of situation might be said to give rise to a transferability of competence, in a very hit-or-miss situation.

Whether or not social scientists have favored or deplored the concept of objective testing of leadership or have seen the development of leadership as innate or environmental (generally favoring the environmental), they are at least united in their distaste for the list of inherent and abstract qualities, such as courage and loyalty, recited by more traditional or classical writers on leadership like Roskill. These lists have often seemed little more than a reverse catalog of the seven deadly sins—denoting the hero image of the writer. Such traditional writers have often drawn a picture of the ideal leader that is almost too good to be true, and they seem to have forgotten the obvious—that training for leadership in war is essentially preparation for killing the enemy. Indeed, these traditional writers have dodged the question of realistic leadership synthesis by making no distinction between qualities especially relevant to the military-leadership situation and those anyone would cultivate in pursuit of the good life.

Despite the apparent onset of a new or radical approach to the issue of leadership, social scientists have not themselves produced any synthesis. They have merely challenged the old assumptions of innate qualities. Their present thinking on the issue recognizes this frustration or impasse. All the social scientists can say is that particular situations demand and affect the exercise of different kinds of leadership. However, they have tended to neglect or avoid in their analysis what may be called the long-term leadership situation. Nelson's conflict with the French from 1795 to 1805 may be looked at from one angle as one leadership experience containing different leadership situations within it, affecting and modifying one another. Each incident of leadership in that period could not be analyzed without being related to what went before. Yet a social scientist may well consider such a relatively long period as too long and too complex for a valid study.

At least in their emphasis on particularity, the social scientists are not too far removed from the traditional concern of the historian, who so often describes and interprets particular events where leadership may arise and does not attempt to make a universal synthesis of the concept. Again and again social scientists have a familiar message which the historian should remember; that is, the leader must be seen in relationship to the rest of the pack. Caesar can no more be regarded as distinct from the Roman Republic than Napoleon is from the Revolution. We are thus continually reminded by social scientists of the pitfalls of elitist thinking where the leader is considered in isolation from the led.

At present, then, the sociological approach to the question of leadership has reached a commonsense if tentative conclusion, that is, an acceptance of the particularity and uncertain nature of the subject.

It is not a satisfactory situation for the social scientist, but at least it means that for the time being the social scientist and the historian are not on divergent paths—even if the fact of the situation may be temporary and accidental. The social scientist yearns for certainty and objectivity. The more traditional academic and military historian sometimes too readily takes for granted a certainty of values, for example, that loyalty is essential for effective naval leadership. Indiscriminate loyalty may indeed dangerously narrow vision and encourage delusion of self or others. Effective leadership thus appears to be the exercise of experience and relevant traits in particular and changing situations. The study of leadership and indeed the exercise of leadership itself thus remain matters of art, rather than science, and uncertain matters at that.

However, it is not true that past leadership has no real effect on present and future situations. For example, the British naval success during much of the eighteenth century meant that the French were essentially on the defensive in most of the naval wars of that period. Villeneuve[13] had a sense of inferiority because of Nelson's previous successes, and this was shared by the French minister of marine, Decrès,[14] who had been a serving officer present at Nelson's annihilation of the French fleet at the Battle of the Nile. Past successes or past failures can thus be a psychological asset or disadvantage in future engagements. Styles of leadership may be very much products of past experience or may arise from a misunderstanding of the past. Battle experience may give confidence in facing a new situation, but it may give no insight into changing conditions of warfare.

In the area of classical or traditional writing on leadership, as early as 1759 John Moncreiff[15] published, in his *Three Dialogues on the Navy*, a discussion of what would later be called the theme of naval leadership. The *Naval Chronicle*[16] frequently published material on this theme, as it did in 1801 when it published an *Essay on the Duty of a Captain*. But it was in the midnineteenth century and thereafter that every naval and military historian, every assertive and superannuated general or admiral, had something to say on the subject. All of them produced lists of admirable leadership qualities that are generally beyond criticism. To select just a few significant names; Mahan[17] saw different types of naval leadership. Sir John Fisher[18] had six principles of naval leadership. Henderson,[19] Richmond,[20] and Roskill wrote about it. Professor Arthur Marder[21] saw twelve leadership traits. Omar Bradley[22] and Montgomery[23] pontificated, and General Hackett[24] and Brigadier Sir John Smyth[25] ratiocinated. Captain Bennett,[26] the naval historian and writer, saw in his *Nelson the Commander* (1972) fifteen leadership qualities. The *Naval Review* and the professional military journals[27] have turned to the theme again and again. Indeed, recent articles on leadership in the *Naval Review* might well have appeared in earlier periods with their emphasis on loyalty, good humor, and drive and their description of a leader as someone who is admired. The official pamphlet on leadership published by the Royal Naval College has much the same traditional tone. It is sound and well meaning, but the phraseology is unedifying. All of the writing is instructive in tone and all of the writers speak from experience or reflection. Many of the checklists of leadership qualities have elements in common. Moral courage, professionalism, and confidence in subordinates are frequently listed. The reader is reassured by what the lists have in common but inevitably disconcerted by their varying length and content. He ends up with the feeling that these writers are all saying the same thing over and over again in different words, and that much of it is obvious.

In this rapidly growing mass of literature concerning required leadership qualities, several focuses stand out. Richmond emphasized—and this was the paramount theme of his life—the need for an educated officer. Edward Brenton in 1838,[28] Montgomery and Roskill more recently, have insisted on the importance of the spiritual or moral factor. One obtains from them a composite picture similar to that of Thomas Arnold's[29] ideal schoolmaster—a Christian and a gentleman with an essential humility. But where does that leave Napoleon, who was hardly a Christian, not a gentleman, had contempt for his subordinates, and certainly revealed no humility? There seems to be confusion here between what may be appealing qualities in a leader and a recipe for successful leadership. They are not always the same thing. Genghis Khan was a successful leader in war but presumably might not pass Roskill's moral test.

Roskill stands out in what may be called the moral and classical approach, and with the encouragement and approval of the Royal Navy, he has written generally on naval leadership. drawing widely on his wealth of professional naval experience and historical knowledge. He sees a sense of style and moral principles—above all, moral principles—as being the determining factor in the highest forms of naval leadership. He gives us a skillfully mixed cocktail of the required elements, as culled from different leaders, such as Nelson's humanity and Wavell's integrity. It is very much of the traditional type of writing on leadership and deserves the respect due to a significant naval historian. But the generalizations can be breathtaking, as they are with all makers of lists, and perhaps he might have effectively looked at fewer leaders in a more concentrated way, for nothing quite fits everyone in every situation. For example, clarity of communication is a valuable leadership attribute according to Roskill, and so it is. But Oliver Cromwell[30] and Howe,[31] who were military and naval giants, were not conspicuous for the clarity of their thought and instruction; yet they were highly successful leaders despite their verbal contortions and confusion. Would clarity have made them more successful?

What position on the question of leadership can emerge from this critique of writing on the subject? I am not purporting to present a new synthesis of the social scientific and the classical writing approaches with regard to the reasons for successful leadership. Yet my labors have produced something bigger than the proverbial mouse, for I do submit that what has been written on leadership could have been done better by the historian.

This does not mean that general statements about leadership cannot be made at all. But they should be made with greater caution and attention to background than hitherto. I do not mean that character responses such as loyalty are irrelevant, only that they are meaningless if disassociated from the culture and situation in which they are exercised. This case history on British naval leadership is, then, meant in many ways as a cautionary tale—a cautionary tale for all writers or would-be writers on leadership.

The conclusion from all of this is that a sense of period, chronology, and cultural background must be kept to the forefront in considering naval and military leadership; otherwise we are here with Caesar, there with Napoleon, and somewhere else with Marshal Zhukov,[32] slipping effortlessly, but in a not very informative way, on a historical magic carpet or random package tour.

The purpose of this study of British naval leadership is to keep in mind the importance of chronology and a sense of the past and to show how a leader is often influenced by past leaders or past tradition and may attempt to imitate past glories in a new historical situation. This study also shows that at its highest level, and in particular in the theaters of war such as the Mediterranean, British naval leadership has required the exercise of political and social as well as more purely professional skills.

chapter 2

NAVAL LEADERSHIP: SOME DISTINCTIVE FEATURES

The first question to ask in employing the term *naval leadership* is whether there are any features that distinguish naval leadership from purely military command. Gibbon believed that the separation of the naval and military professions was both the effect and cause of modern improvements in the science of navigation and war. In British naval history, however, the full separation of these roles did not come until the eighteenth century. Prince Rupert,[1] Blake,[2] and Monk[3] had all moved from military to naval command in the seventeenth century with no great problem arising from the change of element. In the eighteenth century and afterwards there remained "amphibious" admirals such as Sir Sidney Smith[4] who were at home fighting on land or at sea.

Yet several circumstances—in particular the physical situation and condition, the tighter control in the navy, and an earlier sense of career professionalism in the navy than the army—all differentiate the role and manner of leadership in the two services.[5]

Despite the relatively late differentiation of military and naval roles, the different situations of life on board ship and life on land, including the greater proximity of leaders and followers at sea, have led to a traditionally closer rapport between officers and men in the navy than in the army. The loneliness and the pains and joys of leadership were experienced in particularly exquisite form at sea. It was a little world in which the captain was king. For some individuals, their command competency in relative isolation at sea may have diminished their ability to deal with people on an equal level in the more complex situation on land. Collingwood believed that everything that happened on a ship was the responsibility of the captain. When there was mutiny on board, it must be the fault of the officers. Indeed, the captains were concerned with everything down to the minutiae of everyday life. For example, Captain Duff in his standing orders for *HMS Mars* in 1804[6] gave detailed instructions regarding the routine of the ship's cook, saying that as soon as dinner or breakfast was ready he was to bring some of it aft to the officers—and what the ship's cook did was important for everyone's survival!

Peter Cullen,[7] the naval surgeon, writing his thoughts on naval discipline in 1800, stated that:

The duty of a sea life is very different from that of the military one. For promptitude in obeying orders may be the only safety of a ship or of a fleet. . . . A seaman looks up to his officers, as a son to his father, whom he knows to be more wise, more experienced and more skillful than he possibly can be, because scientifically taught.

Certainly an element of filial feeling among the men can be detected, and this form of relationship could sometimes be extended to that between the admiral and his captains. "They are my children," Nelson wrote of his captains. Anonymous missives praising Nelson and his captains were wont to be circulated. Writing to his wife on June 15, 1797, Nelson pointed out an incident of this nature:

A few nights ago a Paper was dropped on the quarter deck, of which this is a copy—"Success attend Admiral Nelson! God bless Captain Miller! We thank them for the officers they have placed over us. We are happy and comfortable, and will shed every drop of blood in our veins to support them, and the name of Theseus shall be immortalized as high as the Captain's. SHIP'S COMPANY."[8]

In the First World War similar effusions greeted Admiral Jellicoe and lamented his departure from the Admiralty in January 1918. Thus in a telegram the Tenth Submarine Flotilla expressed its regrets in this fashion:

Dear Sir John:

We heard with regret of your retirement and would wish to hear of what was the cause, you know of course that we have implicit trust in you and please do not take it lying down, we want you back d'ont take any notice of Arm-chair critics, what do they know of our want(s?) and desires. . . . you are our Idol and one who we would follow to Death . . . you have shown us the way to possess ourselves in patience you have always been one with us in our sports and you the Man we want.[9]

The tone may sound adolescent and fulsome to a later, more skeptical generation, but the sentiment was deeply felt.

A ship's captain by definition had always been preoccupied with details of life on his ship, at least for his own self-preservation. A captain who later became an admiral retained this habit. In the mid-eighteenth century we see for the first time a sense among admirals and captains of concern for improvement of the men's conditions, beyond mere preservation of the crew and the fleet. (I examine this development at length in the next chapter.) Admiral Vernon,[10] in the first half of the eighteenth century, was concerned about excessive drinking and the moral qualities of the men; Jellicoe, in the First World War, with their recreation. Army colonels and generals were not oblivious to the fate of their men, but no affectionate effusions greeted Wellington or Haig.[11] Apart from not fitting the role of the benevolent father figure, they were too remote. Wellington might ride along the front of his massed army; Haig could not do even that with armies of unparalleled size. Lord Moran,[12] in recollecting his First World War service, catches this sense of superior officer remoteness in describing a formal visit by the French General Nivelle,[13] in anticipation of which there had been much preparation amidst the Flanders mud: "He did not leave the duck-boards, he appeared to be in great haste and hardly noticed the men, stopping only to shake hands with the Colonels of the Battalions."[14] Mud produced some fine poetry in the First World War, but it is not a favorable environment for the growth of hero worship. In contrast, naval life at sea, whether or not in action, had a particularly omnipresent quality. Everyone was part of an especially concentrated experience in a physically limited space. Geographical remoteness and social distance at least in a personal if not class sense were impossible in this situation.

The stress of the situation at sea for those in responsibility took its toll. It is worth noting that British naval history from the middle of the eighteenth century presents a remarkably lengthy and distinguished sick list of admirals. Was it merely the extra tension of prolonged life at sea, the noise of the cannon intermingled with the relentless sound of the waves? Or was it, less heroically, due to the age and promotional structure of the profession, where so often seniority if not ripeness was everything? Was it a profession about which one might say, once an admiral always an admiral—almost, that is? In the case of Admiral Provo Wallis in the nineteenth century, we do indeed almost get a glimpse of eternity, for he served for eighty-eight years in the navy and died at the age of over 100 as an Admiral of the Fleet. The navy revealed the physical and nervous tension of leadership, but it also took its toll of lesser men. It was calculated that, in the Nelson era, insanity in the navy occurred at a rate seven times higher than it did in civilian life. Dr. Gilbert Blane,[15] who produced these figures, suggested that the chief reason was the number of head injuries incurred, often arising from drunkenness—the beams of the old ships were certainly low—but there were grave injuries also caused by shock and blast.[16]

The leaders of the navy, amidst their complaining and complaints, felt martyrdom was inevitable. Rodney[17] was prey to illness and doctors, as was Viscount Hood.[18] Both Rodney and Hood were far from well at their great victory, the Battle of the Saints, in 1782. St. Vincent, who lived to be eighty-eight, clamored for recall home and envisaged an imminent end for himself many times while he was at sea. In his old age he continued to be afflicted by medical advice and was himself an amateur doctor at heart. The standard of medical treatment at the time was at best uncertain as we see by the letter of Admiral Sir Henry Nicholls to Admiral Pole on June 10, 1824: "I am very sorry to find you in the hands of Dr. Sandamore, as he very near killed me."[19] Admiral Nicholls's subsequent tale is a medical horror story regarding the near fatal qualities of Dr. Sandamore's physic.

With Nelson we have the greatest sailor and the greatest invalid. He had some reason to be so, with his record of wounds in battle, but by no means were all his miseries due to the scars of battle. His frequent sense of ill-being was at times psychosomatic. He wrote that his activity of mind was too much for his puny constitution. He himself once declared that, "I feel sick when not active," and the duke of Clarence[20] said of Nelson as early as 1787 that he was more in need of a nurse than a wife. Although this is the condition of many single men, it was a particularly appropriate comment to make of Nelson. He had a morbid desire for death in battle and anticipated his own death before every major action in which he participated. He also had a curious habit of carrying a coffin (presented to him by Ben Hallowell[21]) in his cabin.[22] He at least was at one with the morbid strain of the Romantic Age.

To close this somber theme, we have Collingwood and Jellicoe. Collingwood was a paragon of self-immolation. "I am not ill, but weak and nervous, and shall think seriously in going home, for the service I am on requires more strength of body and mind that I have left me in my old age,"[23] he wrote on August 25, 1808. He was ultimately carried off his ship in 1810, a dying man. In the twentieth century Jellicoe was the epitome of the suffering servant, pessimistic and afflicted by sundry distressing although not crippling ailments such as boils and piles, while presiding in some discomfort over a frustrated fleet in a gray sea.

The physical conditions of service had, then, a contribution to make to the stress of leadership. Throughout the period of this study, the professional orthodoxy of opinion was to wish to be in one's ship rather than in the relatively comfortable haven of the Admiralty. An admiral, whatever his inner misgivings, has to appear publicly to want to be at sea, just as an academic has to appear to want to be at his research or in the lecture room. But to be a long time at sea, whether cruising or blockading, especially in difficult seas such as those off the coast of Cadiz, could be a sore physical and mental test, particularly in the eighteenth century, before the age of comfort. Hawke gave some sense of this trial when he wrote:

When I was ordered to the Mediterranean, I had just returned from a long cruise to the Westward. Since my embarking at Portsmouth, I have not slept one night out of the ship, or scarce ever set my foot on shore, all of which have so impaired my health that I must beg the favour of their Lordships to indulge me with leave to be on shore some time for the re-establishment of it.[24]

Out of this conventional embracing of stress came tension, even neuroticism. The last word on this theme is left to Chatfield[25] who wrote to Dudley Pound[26] in 1937, "If you want to rise to the top you must take a reasonable amount of care of yourself."[27] As it was, both

Pound and Chatfield were afflicted by that professional hazard of gunnery officers—impaired hearing—with Pound being even deafer than Chatfield.

A further difference applicable to the British navy as opposed to the army was the theoretically tighter nature of Admiralty control over the activities and conduct of subordinates. The Admiralty throughout these two centuries of naval history supervised, nominally at any rate, the strategy in all theaters of action and the regular disposition of the fleet, and was also concerned with the minutiae of the seaman's life. One must emphasize the word nominally since, in the eighteenth century, one of the two secretaries of state guided strategy, especially in the days of Pitt the elder[28] and orders were from the king in council as transmitted by the secretary of state (even if the Admiralty might issue them). A Royal Navy captain had more supervision of his everyday conduct than had an army company commander or battalion colonel. He had not only his own admiral to cope with, but the Admiralty. The Admiralty not only saw him in relation to his colleagues in the same fleet, but in relation to fellow superior officers in other fleets in other seas. Yet the actual picture must not be distorted. Especially in the emergencies of the eighteenth and early nineteenth centuries, the admiral, whatever command theory might have been, had de facto greater scope in far-off stations for the exercise of individual judgment. Admiralty instructions, because of the remoteness of distance and the time lag in receiving them, were often merely essays in speculation as far as the immediate situation was concerned. It was said, for example, of Rodney's conduct at Cartagena [Carthagena]: "Sir George trusting to the resources of his mind and to his own judgment and discretion, preferred acting on his own responsibility, (as he was ever accustomed to do) to the tardy and less direct mode of sending home for instructions."[29] Yet this scope for individual discretion was not always accidental. It could arise from a good relationship of trust as in the case of the extraordinary confidence Lord Barham[30] at the Admiralty had in Nelson at sea; for example, Barham trusted Nelson to make good dispositions of the fleet.

More modern technology was to bring theoretical and actual practice closer with the speeding up of messages. A form of telegraph was used in 1797 between London and Portsmouth during the Naval Mutinies. Now communication has improved so much that the First Sea Lord can pick up a phone and give an order personally to almost any British warship captain anywhere in the world. The exercise of discretion that depended on personal authority declined as the years went on, although it still had the backing of tradition and history. In the eighteenth and much of the nineteeth centuries, the Admiralty claimed far greater detailed control of its service than did the War Office. By the twentieth century the Admiralty and War Office chains of command moved closer to one another in style, and both could not only claim control but exercise control, in a general sense, of distant operations.

A final difference is that in the Royal Navy there developed much earlier than in the army a tradition of career professionalism. "That glorious profession,"[31] as George III called the navy in entrusting the education of the young duke of Clarence to Hood. Like any true father, George III, as well as giving a compliment, wanted Clarence to have the correct kit and clothes with him when he joined the navy and asked Hood if he would write down a list of things required to assist the king in sending his son to sea.

We see evidence of this conscious sense of professionalism in the frequent discussion of essential qualities of leadership in the holding of a naval commission. The quality of naval leadership and the assessment of naval success were central themes of the *Naval Chronicle* at the end of the eighteenth century. The duties of a ship's captain were recited again and again as in a litany. During the spring of 1805 no less a person than the First Lord of the Admiralty, Barham, set out a list of qualities that were required of the officer put in charge of cruisers, convoys, and so on:

He should be deeply skilled in practical professional knowledge, so as to know, from a sloop to a first-rate, what each is capable of performing, the time it will take to fit her, the service she is capable of performing, and what time it is necessary to perform it in.[32]

There was much greater professional self-confidence in the navy at a much earlier date than in the army. Why was this true? Naval officers went into the navy at a much earlier age than army officers went into the army. There was much more to learn in the navy. Napoleon had a hint of this when he said that one is born with the proper qualities of commanding an army, whereas the necessary qualities of commanding a fleet can be acquired only with experience. The aristocracy provided many naval and military officers. With a shortage of sinecures, the professions were attractive in satisfying the virtually unsatiable hunger for suitable places for young men of good families.[33] Younger sons would go into the navy and would tend to regard it as more of a profession than a passing educational experience in the school of life. Their older brothers would go into the army, while they waited to inherit the title and the estates. Although there was a good deal of patronage regarding naval entry, commissions were not purchased, as they were in the army. Whereas the French army saw a rapid and deliberate spread of professionalism in the modern sense in the 1780s and 1790s, the British army, lacking any social upheaval such as the French experienced at that time, developed much more slowly. Another sign of a burgeoning sense of a naval profession was that, between wars, rising naval officers such as Richard Kempenfelt[34] and St. Vincent went abroad to France or Russia, not only to learn the language but to look at shipbuilding. There was also a greater sense of a unified profession in the navy than in the army, since the navy for obvious reasons did not have the diversity of the army with its sense of regimental solidarity, Finally, navigational skills had to be acquired by everyone in the navy. Hence there was a common professional corpus of knowledge. It took much longer to make a navy than an army officer. These factors, then— physical conditions, the tighter nature of control in the navy at an earlier period than the army, and an earlier sense of career professionalism—all made naval leadership, especially in the eighteenth century, a more demanding and self-conscious profession than was that of army leadership.

What about the demands made on an admiral as opposed to a captain or lower ranking officer? Since the eighteenth century, a great deal has been written about the navy as a profession and a career and how to become and be a good officer. There is plenty of advice even on how to become a good captain. But it is interesting, if not surprising, that there are few recipes in memoirs or booklets on how to become and to be a good admiral—not much more in fact than on how to become and be a good follower! William Falconer wrote, in 1771, on the duties and responsibilities of an admiral in his *An Universal Dictionary of Marine*,[35] and Commander Russell Grenfell in 1937 published *The Art of the Admiral*. But Falconer's comments are too brief, and although Grenfell's work does have a promising title, it is a routine mixture of comment and generalization.

Is the relative sparsity of work on this theme due to the attainment and exercise of the highest rank being regarded as a self-evident process? Or was it regarded as too arcane an operation to be revealed to the masses? More seriously, are different qualities required to be an admiral than a captain? Or is the question merely one of the widening of the range of activity? Marshal Saxe,[36] the great French general, once remarked, "I have known very good colonels become very bad generals."[37] As high an authority on war as Clausewitz wondered why many a bold sublieutenant became a cautious commander. St. Vincent himself said in writing to Evan Nepean,[38] secretary of the Admiralty, ". . . many a man who had gained credit in a frigate had made a bad figure in the command of a line of Battle Ships."[39] He particularly noted Duckworth[40] as not having the qualities required for the superior position, commenting that, "Duckworth will not shine in a higher sphere than the command of a division." A much more recent comment in the military sphere has come from Field Marshal Montgomery, who declared that every officer had his own ceiling rank, beyond which he should not be permitted to rise, particularly in wartime.

A rare general comment on the qualities required of a flag officer came from Admiral Henderson, who listed five qualities: strategical, tactical, administrative, professional qualification, and physical.[41] He said that Nelson had the first two in marked degree, but it was the combination of Nelson and St. Vincent that brought Britain naval ascendancy. Despite this comment, no pamphlet has been offered on how to be a flag officer and no school has been established for admirals per se. Historically, the assumption has been that certain qualities make a good junior naval officer—add to those qualities experience, performance, luck, and, in the eighteenth century, connection, and you have an admiral!

Certain features, then, differentiate the demands and conditions of naval and military leadership and these characteristics have arisen from the different histories of the two services. However, the two services did not require completely different qualities for the exercise of leadership. It was rather the different physical and historical circumstances and demands that accentuated the different tendencies in manner of leadership between the services.

Tradition had a significant part to play, too, in the exercise of naval leadership, and it is on the eighteenth century that we shall now concentrate to see how a successful British naval tradition evolved.

chapter **3**

THE EIGHTEENTH CENTURY: THE MAKING OF A TRADITION

The second half of the eighteenth century was, taking into account all aspects of life, the most creative age in British history. Among the glories of an age that included Adam Smith's economics, Wordsworth's poetry, and the Industrial Revolution was the finest generation of British naval leaders. History is indeed a seamless garment, for the growing wealth of Britain made possible the large navy of St. Vincent and Nelson's day, and in return the navy of Nelson protected British commercial hegemony.[1]

The fifty-year period from the middle of the eighteenth century developed a tradition of confident naval leadership in action and of all-round excellence, which reached its culmination in the achievements of Nelson. Even the major naval setback of the American revolutionary war did not reverse this apparently inexorable trend of improvement. Indeed, except for the disconcerting intervention of the French, the American Revolution might be regarded as an inter-family feud, for both sides in the naval aspect of the revolutionary war were said to have been largely composed of one another's deserters!

To understand the confidence of Nelson and his contemporaries, we shall first look at the diverse favorable background developments in the second half of the eighteenth century which enabled British naval leadership to forge so far ahead of its French and Spanish equivalent, and then, secondly, trace the evolution and development of such confident leadership by reference to the careers of Anson,[2] Vernon, Hawke, Rodney, Hood and Howe, the lineal naval forbears of St. Vincent, Nelson and their generation.

In the middle of the eighteenth century French and Spanish warships were better built than British warships, and by the end of the century Russian ships were also regarded as better constructed. British navigation in this period had made great progress in the fields of chronometers, hydrography, and surveying, as revealed in the work of Captain Cook,[3] Flinders,[4] and Bass,[5] and in the realm of gunnery with the work of Sir Charles Douglas.[6] But British shipbuilding suffered from pre-Industrial Revolution rigid and monopolistic practices. The shipbuilders, the particular trades associated with them, and the timber suppliers were all wedded to age-old practices of family involvement from father to son and of corruption and overcharging the government. Whereas the French were conducting scientific research into shipbuilding, improvements in British shipbuilding were few and far between. Copper bottoming was one of the few significant improvements, but shipbuilding in Britain remained in a technical backwater, compared with the revolutionary changes elsewhere in British industry. So it could still be said at the end of the eighteenth century that the best of all British sea vessels was a captured French ship with an English crew.

However, in the field of manpower and in the attitudes of officers toward discipline and the general welfare of the men, there was a significant improvement in the Royal Navy. It was an era of great difficulty in the manning of crews for frequent wars as well as an era of great stress, with the mutinies of 1797 and the disciplinary reverberations after these traumatic events. Yet, in general, leadership attitudes were changing, and it was noted that there was a better type of officer in the Royal Navy by 1800 than in 1750.

What were the causes of this change? Why were British crews by the time of the Napoleonic wars so much better than French or Spanish crews? In the preparation of men for action, the British had greater battle experience, more time at sea, and greater experience in gunnery, and discipline was more severe than it was in the French and Spanish navies. Often, of course, the superiority owed a lot to the qualities of a particular commander-in-chief. (I look at particular commanders later in this chapter.) A good leader is good for morale. But general and pervasive factors had a part to play, too.

The general tendencies of the age that assisted in the British naval advance were better medical services; an increasing sense of human-itarianism and even on occasions evangelicalism among leading naval officers; a rising sense of the need for economic efficiency, a trend often linked with utilitarianism; and an improved administrative ethos at the Admiralty.

In questions of health and medical services, this was a crucial era. A captain had always hoped for a healthy crew. William Falconer wrote in 1771 that "the health, order and discipline of his people are not less the objects of his [the Admiral's] consideration that the condition and quality of his ships." Early in the next century Nelson himself remarked: "The great thing is health and you will agree with me that it is easier for an officer to keep men healthy than for a Surgeon to save them.'"[7] It is the second half of the eighteenth century that we first see the leading officers of the Royal Navy not only attempting improvements in the health of the men but also succeeding. The losses in men before the era of improved health had been appalling. In Anson's famous circumnavigation of 1740–44—a voyage that in many ways was a springboard for British naval improvement—of the 1,955 seamen who originally embarked for the expedition, 1,951 died of disease. In the Seven Years War a calculation was made that 1,512 seamen were lost in action and 133,708 were lost by disease or were missing.[8] The main causes of this harvest of death were scurvy, yellow fever, and typhus. Naval leaders were greatly interested in trying to eliminate these scourges. Rodney patronized Dr. Gilbert Blane, and Howe patronized Dr. Thomas Trotter.[9] By 1815, with the work of these two physicians and a third, Dr. James Lind,[10] scurvy, the main seafarers' ailment, was under control as far as the Royal Navy was concerned, although the Merchant Navy was much behind in such health matters.

In 1754 Dr. Lind published his *Treatise of the Scurvy*. His findings and advice took years to get general acceptance, although individual admirals and captains adopted his ideas. In 1795 the recom-mendations of Dr. Blane and Dr. Trotter were accepted and there was a regular issue of lemon juice ordered in 1799. The medical statistics showed a significant improvement. At the start of the American war, the rate of sickness was 1.0 in 2.4, and by the end of the Napoleonic War it was 1.0 in 10.7.

There was a general improvement in health and hygiene measures, no doubt stimulated by the difficulty of getting replacement crews. French ships were better built but dirtier, and the health of their men was neglected. On French ships the Catholic practice of keeping dead bodies on ship and not burying them at sea was hardly conducive to seaboard wholesomeness. The British navy was the first to attempt what we now call a public health service with free medical treatment, even free for venereal disease after 1795. In the French navy, on the other hand, pay was stopped whenever men went into the hospital or were under medical care. It is not speculation to say that at the end of the century the enthusiasm of Nelson's crews was not only due to excellent personal leadership, but due to the fact that because of better health care the men were fitter and healthier. The navy had come a long way since 1741 when the Cartagena expedition had to be abandoned because of disease.

The second main new feature was an increasing sense of humanitarianism in naval leadership. Comment was made at the time on the higher character and finer feelings of a   significant number of the officers. This may have come partly from the spirit of enlightenment of the age, but also from the increasing sensibility and the growth of the evangelical movement in the Church of England. Many of the leading officers of course came from the class that produced the squirearchy and the Anglican clergy. We must, however, get the trend in perspective. As long as the pressing of men continued, and there were some very "hot" presses in the 1790s,[11] it was little exaggeration to describe the lower deck of a British man-of-war as akin to a slave ship. As Daniel Baugh observed with respect to an earlier period, the navy spent more in trying to prevent desertions than in trying to raise morale.[12] It was recruitment by kidnapping. Captain Edward Thompson said the navy contained the scum of the universe and the collected filth of gaols. As James Nugent, who on February 23, 1763, received three hundred lashes, would no doubt have agreed, service for most men in the Royal Navy of the eighteenth century was hardly voluntary. If anything, the actual conditions of service with the hot presses and inflation may have become temporarily harsher in 1790s. Inflation diminished the value of the men's little and late pay.

Old Style Recruiting! The Pressgang Seizing a Waterman on Tower Hill on the Morning of His Wedding Day. A. Johnson (Courtesy Radio Times Hulton Picture Library)

Wages had remained at the same level as they had been in the seventeenth century and no one seriously thought of raising them as a means of easing the manning problems. Yet in this somewhat cheerless scene there were signs of more enlightened times. These signs were diverse: Anson and Hawke had tried to stop profanity on their ships—a rather unrealistic aim, one might guess. There was a concerted attempt by the serving officers to see that wages were paid more regularly. In 1806 running the gauntlet was abolished, although flogging remained. Attempts to provide a more varied diet on board ship and to attack the problem of drunkenness were successful. The gradual introduction of uniforms depended on the individual initiative of the captains, and this innovation had a very good effect on the welfare of the men. Such clothing was often better and more hygienic than the haphazard and inappropriate clothing that seamen had been accustomed to wearing.

Humanitarianism and the not infrequent displays of religious zeal should not be mistaken for mildness or lack of formal discipline. But there was an attempt by naval leaders like Howe, followed by St. Vincent and Nelson, to see the men as individuals, not merely as cannon fodder. The greatest practical step forward in both discipline and good relations with the men—an all-round physical and psychological step forward—was made by Howe, who introduced divisions. Divisions were lead by the lieutenants and they were further broken down into squadrons under midshipmen. With a division, men were compelled to parade regularly under a lieutenant who was responsible for their general supervision. At these parades clothing could be inspected and an immediate firsthand appreciation secured of the health and welfare of the crew. This innovation was particularly approved by the naval medical reformers. Howe and other leaders of his ilk made a real attempt to get to know the men's names and make sure that hard-luck cases got some form of provision made by the authorities at home. Thus a great and permanent step forward was made in manpower management. These naval improvements were paralleled elsewhere in civilian life by the attacks in England on the gin trade and the slave trade. Other aspects of this humanitarian spirit can be seen in the urban revival of the Church of England and in the spread of methodism. On a metaphysical level it can be seen in the agonizings of the Romantic lyricists such as Wordsworth and Blake.[13] The *Zeitgeist* was a great stimulus to naval improvement.

Different in tone, but even more efficient in performance, was utilitarianism.[14] The utilitarians, increasingly influential in the last quarter of the eighteenth and the beginning of the nineteenth centuries, did not advocate increased government, but they did insist that government should be efficient and economical. If individuals may have been motivated by religious or humanitarian instincts, the Admiralty as an institution was more influenced by economic strictures. There was abroad in Britain a spirit of economic reform. The utilitarian writers were associated with this movement or sometimes were leaders of it in attacks on old abuses. For the utilitarians, sickness and unnecessary deaths were affronts, because they were wasteful and uneconomical. For Adam Smith, David Ricardo, Thomas Malthus, Jeremy Bentham,[15] and James Mill, all utilitarians, manpower was a form of wealth. Maximizing production and saving manpower were essential to the development of the Industrial Revolution. The utilitarian movement from Bentham to Edwin Chadwick hailed improvements in health as improvement in economic efficiency.

An interesting example of the close relationship of the economic spirit and naval improvement can be seen in the work of Bentham and his younger brother Sir Samuel.[16] The latter worked for many years with the Russian navy. He was much influenced by his older brother's utilitarianism and its associated ideas of efficient reform. In 1795 Sir Samuel returned to Britain and devoted himself to improving naval administration, with particular reference to dockyards and shipbuilding. The utilitarians wanted to modernize prisons, workhouses, and men-of-war! One practical example of the link between efficiency and health was the introduction by Sir Samuel of the first steam engine into Portsmouth dockyard. This resulted in the mass production of blocks for the rigging and a subsequent decrease in ruptures.[17] The constant replacement of crews through disease and administrative incompetence had been a great waste finanically. In this battle for efficiency were not only Admiralty administrators but, as we shall see, active, fighting admirals such as St. Vincent. The disorder that had been such a feature of the earlier eighteenth-century navy was giving way in the second half of the century to a more rational order of things.

In the 1790s the improvement of naval administration accelerated. There were the great figures of Spencer[18] and later Barham as First

Lords. But in a much earlier period Anson, and at a lower level of authority Thomas Corbett[19] and Nepean, had a part to play. Constant interaction is evident between superior naval administration and superior naval leadership in action. Spencer set going Nelson's Nile campaign, and Barham, Nelson's Trafalgar campaign. The most decisive exercise of British naval leadership at sea needed a better administrative framework on land. The trend towards more effective administration had been manifest ever since Anson went to the Admiralty.

An improved sense of economy and efficiency, medical and hygienic improvements, a better system of control of the men with the advent of divisions, a concerted attempt at improvements at every level of naval procedure and administration—all made a favorable backdrop for the dazzling leadership success of the Nelson era. It is in the work of individual talent, meanwhile, that one can see the professional linear ancestry of Nelson.

In British naval leadership in action, the decade of the 1750s is a turning point. The decade included both the bad naval practices of the previous half century and an anticipation of a better future. In the first half of the eighteenth century the British navy had been hidebound in its approach to action. An orthodoxy prevailed that ships should line up opposite number to enemy opposite number and fire broadside at the enemy equivalent. This *in-line* or *line-ahead* approach, as it was called, had become moribund. It envisaged, indeed virtually necessitated, action of approximately equally sized combatant fleets. Between the Battle of Barfleur in 1692 and the Battle of the Saints in 1782, there was no really great British naval victory in a stand-up fight. Anson at Finesterre in 1747 and Hawke at Quiberon Bay in 1759 got nearest to a victory of the kind that became frequent at the turn of the century.

A nadir had been reached with the Mathews[20] and Lestock[21] fiasco at Toulon in 1744. Neither admiral worked well with the other, and after failure to master the French fleet, Mathews, the commander, was accused by Lestock, the subordinate, of actually breaking Admiralty instructions by attempting a chase that would have broken the line-ahead formation. In the action Lestock had refused to follow Mathews. The subsequent courts-martial of both admirals, as a result of which both were found innocent of improper conduct, was an occasion for an outburst of political acrimony. The furor created by the incident led to the in-line orthodoxy being reinforced rather than diminished. As David Hannay has so well put it, "The Fighting Orders reinforced by the sentence on Admiral Mathews had apparently established the belief that to miss beating the enemy was a misfortune, but to disorder the line for the purpose of beating him was a crime unbecoming an officer and a gentleman."[22] Lestock had preserved and Mathews had broken the line. Hence it might be said that, by the conventions of the day, Lestock had had a naval victory of sorts.

The naval scandal of the 1750s was the execution of Byng in 1757 for his alleged refusal or reluctance to engage the enemy. The whole incident led to unfavorable comment throughout Europe and can only be compared in odium to the incident of Frederick William I's barbarous treatment of his son a few decades before.[23] Byng plaintively asserted at his trial that instead of his retreating from the French and Spanish fleets, they retreated from him, and he did not pursue them.[24] Voltaire, who had more than a passing interest in all English matters and in Byng's fate did not succeed in saving Byng by his arguments. The trial, where many of the judges expected an ultimate act of mercy as far as the execution of the sentence was concerned, was as mishandled as the Minorcan campaign that was its origin. Political considerations prevailed ultimately over professional judgment, although in fairness it must be said that this was neither the first nor the last time when these were factors in a court-martial and execution of sentence.

The period to the end of the 1750s abounded with tactical uncertainty. Expeditions were launched as part of a grand strategy and then floundered or stagnated when the principles could not agree on how to meet their objectives. There was frequent resort to councils of war, either among the admirals themselves or with the military commanders of joint navy and army expeditions. Councils of war were not bad in themselves, serving in the eighteenth century the role that planning meetings might do today. But as St. Vincent once said, they could be cloaks for cowards. Thus Admiral Vernon's expedition at Panama in 1739 and Hawke's in 1757 off the coast of Brittany stagnated while an on-the-spot debate on tactics was held. In the 1757 expedition Hawke tried to use all the force of his character to persuade Sir John

Mordaunt,[25] the military commander, to take the initiative. It was to no avail. So often the council of war was a front for leadership afraid to take responsibility, rather than a search for agreed solutions.

Yet already at the darkest hour the dawn was coming. Signs of revival had already been apparent before the middle year of the century. The revival of the navy can be linked with Vernon, Anson, Hawke, Rodney, Hood, and Howe. They developed a tradition of devotion to duty, a tradition of talent and intellect. It was a tradition of victory, in fact. An emphasis on individuals is appropriate because the Admiralty as an institution was not responsible in the eighteenth century for the direction of naval strategy and only marginally responsible for the conduct of naval operations. The king and his ministers directed these matters. The First Lord in the eighteenth century was often a naval officer and a lot depended on the political connections of individual admirals.[26]

Vernon was very much a sailor of an older generation, who received that supreme accolade of English culture in becoming a popular inn sign. He was a political as well as naval figure. He was an autocratic, brilliant, but irascible, man whose energies were often taken up with that all too frequent source of dissension at the time—prize money disputes. His career ended on a controversial note. He clashed in 1746 with the First Lord, the duke of Bedford,[27] over his publication of correspondence with the Admiralty Board and was struck off the list of flag officers. In Vernon's general correspondence we see a new and reforming note presaging improvement. For example, he wrote to the duke of Newcastle[28] on November 15, 1742, in an attempt to stop defalcations, "being persuaded your grace, will take care, to preserve the property of the Crown from thus becoming a prey, to those in the immediate service of the Crown."[29] This was a text the eighteenth-century navy needed to take to heart. Vernon had the concern of a reformer and bombarded the duke of Newcastle with letters suggesting improvements.

In addition to being concerned for the welfare of his men, Vernon was equally solicitous for them whether they were in the navy or the army. In the War of the Austrian Succession he insisted that the forces from the American colonies be treated as well as the rest and not made to feel apart. He was determined to reduce drunkenness by limiting the number of punch houses in Port Royal, Jamaica—hence Vernon's grog, a mixture of rum and water as a substitute for straight rum. He urged that there be better hospital facilities in Jamaica. Like Anson and Hawke he was concerned with what must have been in practice more futile and unrealistic campaigns. Thus he attempted to reduce blasphemy and swearing on board his ships. In so attempting, he shared the contemporary zeal for reformation of morals and manners, in an era that saw the rise of methodism. One doubts his ability to change morals and manners, but that such a notable admiral was bent on actively improving the living standards of the ordinary seaman was a good omen for the future.

Anson, the second major figure, made a reputation throughout Europe with his voyage around the world, 1740–44, in which he and most of his original crew successfully survived all vicissitudes. Despite his fame, his personality is elusive. Thus Sir Charles Hanbury[30] said that Anson had been around the world, but never in it. However, a man is better judged by his deeds than by the marriages he makes. While First Lord of the Admiralty from 1751–62, Anson was the best naval administrator since Samuel Pepys in the 1670s. He had impeccable connections. He married the daughter of the Lord Chancellor Hardwicke[31] and was the nephew of another Lord Chancellor, the earl of Macclesfield.[32] His luck was proverbial. The capture of the Spanish treasure galleon off Manila in 1743 made his fortunes in more ways than one. But he was also famed for his sound judgment and modesty. On the technical side of naval leadership he continued Vernon's policy of supplementing the Naval Instructions to give more flexibility and encourage a positive approach to action.

In the formation of a tradition of British naval leadership, Anson was a key figure in the encouragement of rising talent. In selecting officers he always depended on personal knowledge he had gained as an active seaman. Under his regime Augustus Keppel,[33] Sir Charles, Saunders,[34] Howe, and Philip Saumarez[35] were all rapidly promoted. Saunders, Saumarez, and Keppel had been with him on his round-the-world expedition. Having been on that expedition with Anson was a great advantage in an officer's career. Like St. Vincent, later in the century, Anson had a discerning eye for up and coming talent and St. Vincent himself received his first commission as a lieutenant from Anson. Anson's greatest immediate contribution to British naval success was his organization of Hawke's expedition in 1759. In it he was indefatigable in his attention to details. He selected the choicest flag officers—Hawke, Boscawen,[36] Keppel, and Saunders. With Pitt, who on the military side promoted Wolfe[37] and was an excellent strategist, the two made an ideal strategic and administrative combination. Anson had also worked well with the duke of Bedford.

Alfred Mahan, in his work *Types of Naval Officers*, couples Hawke with Nelson.[38] Despite Mahan's praise of Hawke and despite the advocacy of later writers such as Ruddock Mackay,[39] it is difficult to get a vivid sense of the man. His piety, belief in Christian marriage, and humanitarianism are attractive traits, but he was not given to dramatic gestures and he has failed to capture the imagination of later writers.

Hawke's professional reputation has perhaps unfairly suffered because of his lack of political judgment and his political indiscretion. Yet he had as a patron no less than George II after his impressive conduct at Toulon. Later in his career Hawke and Pitt fell out and this set back Hawke's career. But because of the nature of their command and its ramifications with political considerations, leading admirals have always had to exercise a large measure of political judgment, especially in the eighteenth century.

Otherwise, Hawke's professional leadership was first-rate and the qualities he showed presaged Nelson. His orders were models of clarity, and the word *beauty* has even been applied to them. One must bear in mind that the exercise of orders at the time had the additional complication of signaling problems. Hawke had a fine grasp of tactical thought and had a habit of constant discussion of tactical and other matters with his subordinate officers. Above all he had a willingness to take a calculated risk and believed in getting up close to the enemy and attacking. All these qualities are rightly regarded as particularly Nelsonic. His written alteration of Article XIII of the Fighting Instructions has a forecast of Nelson:

As soon as the Admiral shall hoist a Red Flag on the Flag Staff at the Fore Topmasthead, and fire a gun, every ship in the Fleet is to use their utmost endeavour to engage the enemy *as close as possible, and therefore on no account to fire until they shall be within pistol shot.*[40]

Hawke, like Nelson, paid close attention to the health of his men, and he could make the most of poor ships and poor crews. It has been said that his command of the *Berwick* in 1743 was a remarkable achievement, showing his skill as an outstanding commander with a most unprepossessing crew.

Howe, Keppel, and Rodney all served under Hawke, and his influence upon them was obvious, especially in the field of offensive action. This Hawke-type wresting of the initiative was repeated in the work of many other officers and led to the crippling of French and Spanish naval power by the end of the eighteenth century.

Rodney, the next great naval leader, is a decisive figure in two aspects of naval leadership: in the tactical, in his maneuver of breaking the enemy line, and in the hygiene and health of the men, in his patronage of Dr. Gilbert Blane.

In an oligarchic and caste-ridden age Rodney appears to have gone too far, even for the times, in his manifest hauteur. He claimed to be the favorite admiral of George III, and his nepotism was blatant even for the standards of the age. His son was a post captain at the age of fifteen. As so often happens with those who take on a seignorial mien, things had a disconcerting habit of going wrong, even if in the material sense fortune favored the brave, and Rodney never received the slightest wound in action in his long naval career. However, he did have his fair share of the trials and tribulations of life. At times the mask of self-control slipped, as for example when on March 15, 1781, he wrote of his own bad health and how he would not remain longer on a leaky ship.[41] Rodney was a martyr to gout, and his mind always had other preoccupations as well as the king's business. These preoccupations were usually the state of his own health and his financial problems. Like Mr. Micawber in the field of finance, Rodney always hoped something would turn up, perhaps a governorship of Jamaica, which would solve his financial problems once and for all. Insolvency was always waiting in the wings for him—although this was not an unusual experience for an eighteenth-century aristocrat. It is ironic that at one crucial time it was a Frenchman, the Maréchal de Biron,[42] who came to Rodney's rescue and enabled him to leave his debtor's retreat in Paris and return to England. This incident is another sign of the homogeneity of interest among eighteenth-century European aristocracy. At least a Frenchman helped to save Rodney, whereas Voltaire in his interventions failed to save Byng from a fate worse than debt.

Rodney's professional career is full of disputes. In 1781 he quarreled in a high-handed way with the merchants of Eustatius, trying to inject a little patriotism in their outlook and make some financial gain for himself. They had been trading with the enemy, and he confiscated their merchandise. He wrote to General Cunninghame, the governor of Barbados, on February 17, 1781: "France, Holland and America, will most severely feel the blow that has been given them, and English merchants who forgetting the duty they owe their King and country were base enough for lucrative motives to support the enemies of Great Britain, will for their treason greatly merit their ruin."[43] Unfortunately, although he sent the confiscated material back to officialdom in England, much of it was seized by the French en route, and Rodney had merely stirred up hostility and litigation in England arising from his arbitrary action. Rodney shows a combination of old-style aristocratic and autocratic temperament with the new-style professionalism. At least he was the most successful British commander in the American revolutionary war. He had firm views on military as well as naval questions, and of the military leaders on both sides during that war, he believed that Benedict Arnold was the only man who really knew what he was doing.

In the West Indies in 1781, he was joined by Hood, a better man at human relations than Rodney, and the inspirer of Nelson, although Hood lacked Nelson's affectionate nature. This was a clear case of mismarriage of talent, and the relationship of Rodney and Hood was not an easy one. Rodney as the commander made courtly, almost suspiciously fulsome, suggestions about policy to Hood. Neither gifted admiral was satisfied with the other. Hood although himself of good birth, resented Rodney's airs and regarded him as lacking in energy. James Grenville[44] sympathized at home with Hood's misgivings about Rodney. On December 22, 1781, Grenville wrote, "I will only say that the reappointment of Sir George Rodney has not come as of surprise and disappointment to your particular friends alone."[45]

Yet despite all the quarrels and irritations, physical and political, at the Battle of the Saints in 1782, the French line was broken and there was a resounding victory. More has been written about this battle than any other victory under sail except for Trafalgar. The cult of the line ahead had at last started to lose its sway. At Martinique in 1781 Rodney had appeared to attempt to break the enemy line, but much of his fleet, attached to the old orthodoxy, does not appear to have realized what his intentions were, with some resulting confusion. Who could claim to be parent of the idea of breaking the line? Critics of Rodney asserted that it was not his idea at all at the Battle of the Saints. There was a brisk controversy in the nineteenth century on the issue when Sir Howard Douglas,[46] the son of Rodney's fleet captain, Sir Charles Douglas, asserted that the idea of breaking the line originated with his father who had had to force it on Rodney. Moreover, Sir Howard alleged that Rodney's intervention in calling off the fight prematurely had deprived Britain of an even greater victory. Hood, who had a low view of Sir Charles's battle capacity, also made this criticism of Rodney's conduct of the battle, claiming that the French fleet escaped annihiliation because Rodney was unwilling to take risks.

However, Rodney had his defenders. He had secured the position of physician at St. Thomas's Hospital for Dr. Gilbert Blane. Blane, who at Rodney's invitation was physician to the fleet, had been beside him throughout the battle. Blane, not too unexpectedly, came to Rodney's defense and asserted it was Rodney's idea to break the enemy line. But success has a thousand parents, and there was another claimant as the originator of the concept. This was John Clerk, Esq., of Eldin,[47] the writer on naval tactics and the great advocate of breaking the line and attacker of the old line-ahead notion. Clerk asserted that it was he who had inspired Rodney. Rodney rose above, or rather remained above, the controversy and graciously acknowledged the value of Clerk's thesis without necessarily subscribing to its determining role in the actual battle. Evidence seems to support the claim of Sir Howard that Sir Charles gave Rodney the suggestion. The validity of Clerk's claim seems unlikely. Whether the success at the Battle of the Saints was due to an impromptu response or a deliberate plan is an unresolved question, but at any rate, with Rodney the era of prevaricating councils of war and indecisive engagement had ended.[48]

Hood's name has been irrevocably linked with Rodney at the Battle of the Saints, but he was also one of the most successful commanders in his own right in the early part of the French revolutionary wars, as in his success at Toulon in 1793. Nelson and the duke of Clarence thought highly of him. Nelson believed that Hood was equally great in all situations in which an admiral could be placed. But it was not all success. He had not, as we have seen, worked well with Rodney. Nor did he work well with Graves[49] off the American coast—hence the failure at Chesapeake Bay in 1781, a political disaster for Britain. As Horace Walpole sourly commented on the failure of Graves and Hood, ". . . Lord Hawke is dead and does not seem to have bequeathed his mantle to anyone."[50] Still, apart from this Hood has always had a good press.

Hood's personal influence on his subordinates is shown in a warmly worded and deeply felt letter that Isaac Coffin[51] wrote to him on December 19, 1782: ". . . and now My Lord permit me to thank you a thousand times for your kindness to me in getting me to the Height of my Profession, after having behaved so very ill, that the bare Recollection makes me shudder. . . ."[52]

The final significant contribution to the development of a tradition of naval leadership before the St. Vincent-Nelson era was Howe. Black Dick,[53] they called him—an ominous sounding sobriquet. But it merely described the physical trait of a strongly marked and dark countenance, for he certainly was mild enough in manner. Horace Walpole in an oft-quoted phrase said Howe never made a friendship but at the cannon's mouth.[54] He was not as voluble as St. Vincent and Nelson, nor did he have great quickness of mind. But his victory on June 1, 1794, over the French fleet off the coast of Brittany sealed his reputation with the profession and the public. He was sixty-nine at the time, perhaps a little late in life to have a military masterpiece. By this victory he made as an orthodoxy of his generation the concept of breaking the enemy's line and concentrating the maximum amount of force on part of it. Hawke had originally introduced Howe to George III, a symbolic act of continuity, and Hawke ensured the advance of Howe's career. Like Hawke before him and St. Vincent after him, Howe was to be a First Lord of the Admiralty and he was also to be an Admiral of the Fleet as St. Vincent was. Despite all this professional elevation, he was kind and considerate to junior officers. He was not an egotist in a profession where egotism flourished. He was also an apostle of new signaling tactics—an unusual interest for a man whose verbal instructions baffled subordinates by their obscurity. Yet he was a most thoughtful tactician. He also bore public criticism with equanimity. As he blockaded off the coast of France in 1793, he kept his

Visit of George III to Lord Howe's flagship (Courtesy National Maritime Museum)

ships well provisioned and preserved the health and good humor of his men. By his movements he improved the seamanship of the men and the discipline of the fleet. No one ruffled him except perhaps Alexander Hood[55] (subsequently Lord Bridport). Bridport's lax leadership contributed to the disciplinary problems of 1797.

In tactics and discipline, St. Vincent was to be a disciple of Howe, although not an emulator, as we shall see, of his manner. It was always said that Howe was *suaviter in modo* and St. Vincent *fortiter in re*.[56] So the tradition was passed on from Hawke to Howe and Howe to St. Vincent. Howe was the only officer whose reputation was high enough with both government and men in the mutinies of 1797 to be able to act as an intermediary—a channel of complaint and appeasement. He was regarded as the Grand Old Man of the Fleet, even grander in his time than St. Vincent.

Thus we have the progress from Anson and Hawke to Rodney, Viscount Hood, and Howe, and we have seen a rising standard of leadership evolving from the contribution of gifted individuals and the favorable trends noted earlier in this chapter. However, it would be wrong to see an effortless and continuously successful story of improvement in morale, in aggressive intent, and in leadership ethos in general. The aristocratic structure of the fleet and the oligarchic nature of the leadership reflected the civilian society of the time. The jobbery in the placing of officers and the political considerations regarding appointments took their toll on internal discipline. The notable and the less notable naval leaders had to cope continually with the problem of insubordination and professional incapacity in more junior ranks, and lack of cooperation in higher ones, and sometimes they contributed their own particular brand of chaos as well. The pursuit of prize money might conflict with the pursuit of strategic objective. In Vernon's time, officers left their posts for no good reason. Boredom and personal discomfort no doubt got the better of the quest for fame. No uniform brand of officer was produced despite the improving trend. Even if there was a greater sense of professionalism as time went on, the navy still had its fair share of sadistic officers such as Captain Pigot of the *Hermione*, who so maddened his crew that they rose up and murdered him and his officers.[57] On a less somber note, there were eccentric officers like Sir Thomas Pakenham[58] or characters such as "Mad" Montagu,[59] who on occasions had his men dressed in the strangest uniforms. There were sexual adventurers, too, like Augustus Hervey,[60] the navy's answer to Casanova, whose amours included princesses, duchesses, marchese, countesses, the wife of a doge of Venice, the wife of a French *fermier general* of taxes, artists' models, publicans' daughters, nuns, actresses, singers, and dancers. His most elevated sexual adventure was when the duchess of Cadaval, then the only lady of rank in the Portuguese peerage, had him kidnapped to satisfy her desires.[61] Men such as Hervey were not part of the world of serious ethical intention and professional dedication, which was coming into its own as the century progressed.

Not until the austere work of St. Vincent had taken its toll and permeated all ranks could it reasonably be said that orders when given would be obeyed. The great mutinies of the men in 1797 have received much historical comment, but there were continual malfunctions of the navy due to dissonance among higher ranks. Gentlemen were gentlement and apt to go their own sweet way in the interpretation of orders. However, things were never as bad as they were in the thirteenth century, when on one ignoble occasion King John led out the fleet he had summoned and none of his barons followed.[62]

Unlike the admirals of the First and Second World wars, the naval leaders of the eighteenth century could not count on the automatic execution of orders. Rodney complained to Hood of "how little the young officers know their Duty and how much they are wanting in their respect due to their Senior Officers."[63] Rodney's relations with his officers were never very smooth. But Howe had a similar experience at the battle of June, 1, 1794, when the inexperience and incapacity of many of the commanders was commented on, and Howe's orders were undoubtedly not carried into effect by the choice or incapacity to execute them of a very large portion of his fleet. Only seven of Howe's twenty-six ships succeeded in piercing the enemy's line. Sir Edward Codrington,[64] whose keen eyesight as a very young man made him a special lookout at that battle, remarked on how little Howe was served by his officers compared to Nelson.[65]

Even Nelson was irritated by the troublesome incapacity or overweening insistence on rights by junior officers, and he denounced improper and inappropriate requests for courts-martial when he was in the West Indies in 1787. As late as Admiral Cochrane's[66] time in 1810, there were still examples of gross inadequacy among officers, as, for example, the crass incompetence of the Hon. Captain Warwick

Lake, who abandoned part of his crew on a desert island, Sombrero, in the West Indies. Cochrane reprimanded him and sent him to take the men off the island, but they had already been rescued by an American ship and had landed in the United States.

Codrington's own description of the limitations of naval education when he was first in the navy in the 1780s may explain the shortcomings of some of the officers. His daughter Lady Bourchier wrote that her father spent nine years as a midshipman in the 1780s, and "I have repeatedly heard him say, that during those nine years (so important for the formation of character) he was never invited to open a book nor received a word of advice or instruction, except professional, from anyone."[67] All depended on the quality of the instructing captain. Howe's problem was that he could not always communicate his high standards to others. In this respect, his forbearance did him a disservice. St. Vincent by sheer force of character, Nelson by communicative genius, and Collingwood by dedicated professionalism were to obviate this pervasive problem of command.

Other features of the Royal Navy, while adding to its diversity and attractiveness, were more particular to the eighteenth century and did not become part of the mainstream of the modern navy tradition. The naval world of the eighteenth century was never single-minded and professional. Anson, Rodney, Keppel, and St. Vincent, to name but a few, were also politicians of varying success. Anson made a reputation in administration and, as we have seen, had both the ear and daughter of Hardwicke. St. Vincent was the best seaman who became First Lord, but was not as successful in his energetic wrath in that office as one might have expected. Indeed, his robust—overrobust— exercise of that office was regarded as the chief cause of the downfall of Addington's ministry.[68] Still, the First Lordship was not at this period the perquisite of an unalloyed politician. The involvement of the admirals in the world of Westminster may have led to naval disputes with a political basis, as in the notorious case of the Whig Keppel and the Tory Hugh Palliser.[69] Palliser was second-in-command under Keppel in 1778 in an indecisive action off Ushant against the French. The quarrels of Keppel and Palliser weakened the British effort. Subsequently, Palliser accused Keppel of allowing the French to escape. Keppel was acquitted by court-martial amid massive Whig demonstrations of jubilation.

Yet looking far ahead to another age, it might be said that this conventional penchant in the eighteenth century for the political life at least mitigated against the existence of the kind of political ingenuousness or diffidence that a Jellicoe was to reveal in the twentieth century. Nor must it be said that diplomatic, social, and political skills and interest were unrelated to naval leadership in the eighteenth century. Especially in the Mediterranean or farther east, with the geographical remoteness of Admiralty control and the increasing size and complexity of British commitments and responsibilities, an admiral had to have a political and diplomatic skill at least equivalent to that of a British minister abroad—perhaps even more, considering the example of Lord Albemarle,[70] the British ambassador in Paris in 1749, who unfortunately appears to have deliberately avoided meeting French people! Indeed, in the cases of Collingwood and Keith,[71] the British naval commander-in-chief had more of the stature of a British minister abroad or an under secretary of state. Thus we can see that this public role was of great importance to the proper exercise of naval leadership. Since the eighteenth century the political demands made on naval leaders have diminished but not completely disappeared, as can be seen in the career of Sir Andrew Cunningham. In the eighteenth and early nineteenth centuries the political sense of an admiral could be crucial to the proper exercise of his authority.

The eighteenth century was a world, too, where prize money disputes and promotional intrigues could take by modern standards inordinate, indeed unjustifiable, time. Still, "time is money," and Anson and Saunders, for example, made enormous fortunes out of the institution of prize money. One might say that flag rank at sea almost assured a fortune. Additional income could be generated by carrying freight, a practice that continued until 1914. There were on occasions bonanza days in the eighteenth-century navy, when it seemed that the sky was the limit. Keppel's expressions, or rather reputed expressions, at the siege of Havana in 1762 give us a sense of the time. He is reputed to have declaimed:

The purser will give every brave fellow a can of punch, to drink prosperity to Old England, and then we will go about our business with spirit. We shall be as rich as Jews. The place is paved with gold, which the lubberly Dons have gathered for us. Old England for ever! is the word and the day is ours.[72]

Keppel as commodore is said to have made over 20,000 pounds from the attack. It was all in the family, so to speak, for his brother the earl of Albemarle,[73] the military commander, made over 100,000 pounds, as did Admiral Sir George Pocock,[74] the naval commander.[75] Add to this pot hunting the clamor for sinecures and titles, and we have an impression of thrust and freewheeling enterprise in the eighteenth-century navy.

The rapid expansion of the navy, its increased activity, and the frequency of its actions brought problems as well as dividends, especially in relation to manning the lower deck discipline. This element of unrest, which culminated in the mutinies of 1797, is considered in the following chapter in an assessment of the leadership of St. Vincent.

Despite all the chronic problems, fine individual leadership and diverse favorable trends ensured a continual increase in the standard of naval leadership in the last quarter of the eighteenth century—the making of a tradition, in fact.

In contrast, France, which had larger and better designed ships in the eighteenth century, fell behind in tactics and morale. There had been a fine French officers corps developed under Choiseul[76] that served in the American Revolutionary war. The performances of Pierre de Suffren,[77] de Guichen,[78] and de Grasse[79] compared well with their English counterparts. Then revolutions and social unrest weakened the esprit de corps of the French navy, while Brest and Toulon, the chief naval bases, were Royalist danger points. The capture of French ships at Toulon by Hood in 1793 was a terrible blow to the French navy. The Convention then showed more zeal than judgment in its efforts to catch up with England. Like the American effort in Vietnam, the watchword for the Convention was spend, spend, spend, but it showed little naval sense. Its approach was to call for more ships and more guns, but it had no answer to the better if harsher discipline in British ships and the greater care of British officers for their men. Although the French ships had more guns, they had little practice in using them.

The Spanish fleet was in an even worse situation. The bravery of Spanish officers was proverbial, but the Spanish navy was fundamentally weak in manpower, spirit, and material. Its men were not well trained.

The frequent wars against France and Spain contributed both to battle experience and a continuity of battle experience for the navy of Nelson's time of the kind which the Royal Navy was so greatly to lack in 1914. But the greatest battle or fighting innovation of the second

Growing old in the service. Portrait of St. Vincent by F. Cotes
(Courtesy National Portrait Gallery)

Portrait of St. Vincent by Sir William Beechey (Courtesy National Maritime Museum)

half of the eighteenth century in the Royal Navy was the reintroduction of initiative. Talent was often given its head, especially in the years 1790–1810. This was the other side of the coin, then, to the element of insubordination and the incapacity of the mediocre. There was a growing emphasis on the surprise element in naval warfare. Great successes justified the breaking of the old orthodoxy of the line ahead, and it came to be believed that if the policy of getting close up to the French were followed, they would inevitably be beaten.

Thus the climate was favorable for the exercise of the individual genius of Nelson, indeed for the work of the great trinity of admirals—St. Vincent, Nelson, and Collingwood.

chapter 4

ST. VINCENT: THE SAILOR WHO DID *NOT* FALL FROM GRACE WITH THE SEA

In our study of British naval leadership we reach a relatively early peak of excellence with the work of St. Vincent and Nelson. Although what came afterward was not completely a dying fall, the standards set by these two leaders were never to be excelled. One can go further and say that the contribution of St. Vincent and Nelson was crucial to the attainment of the unchallenged British naval supremacy that was achieved by the time of Nelson's death in 1805 and retained for over one hundred years thereafter. Between them, they possessed all the characteristics that illustrate successful naval leadership. For example, in the field of tactics Nelson was masterly, whereas St. Vincent's work was the foundation of the reputation of the British navy for good order and discipline. The equation has been made that Nelson plus St. Vincent equaled Napoleon, the equation rather underestimates the total capacity of the first two.

St. Vincent and Nelson present interesting contrasts of style and character that were recognized in their own day. As Nelson said, "Where I would take a penknife St. Vincent takes a hatchet."[1] Nelson was the charismatic leader, a figure of inspiration and affection, yet wayward at times. St. Vincent was the heroic worker, indefatigable in his energy and full of common sense. Both admirals contributed to each other's success. St. Vincent by his guidance and encouragement eased the way for Nelson's achievements. Nelson supported St. Vincent's harsh enforcement of discipline and acted as his main striking force in the Mediterranean.

St. Vincent did not, except for the battle that gave him his title, have great fighting experience as a commander-in-chief, although he had much battle experience at a more junior level. But the quality of his leadership merits close attention not only for his example, but for the influence, benevolent or baneful, he had on the careers of others. With his stentorian voice, he was like some fiercesome headmaster of the sea. "I must go to sea with Sir John Jervis," said Sir Edward Berry.[2] "If there is anything good in me, it is he will discover it."[3] St. Vincent was a seminal and pivotal figure and, like Anson, a great encourager of the best talent. He himself had been influenced early in his career by Anson and Sir Charles Saunders. He had been given his commission by Anson and promoted to the *Porcupine* by Saunders. St. Vincent was not the only professional influence on Nelson. Sir Peter Parker[4] and Viscount Hood had relatively greater influence on Nelson's career, when he was a less experienced officer. However, St. Vincent let Nelson use his own initiative, when Nelson was at the height of his powers.

St. Vincent's method of leadership was robust. He was rigid, at times going to the point of brutality in his discipline. Yet he could show the human element at the appropriate moment. He could on occasion play the role of the benevolent father figure, as in his friendly treatment of Sir Thomas Fremantle[5] and his wife to be, Elizabeth Wynne.[6] Courting couples or newlyweds need to be treated with care, and St. Vincent was not always unsympathetic to human frailty. It was noted that he was very partial to kisses, even if he always thought that as far as the navy was concerned, marriage put a man at a professional disadvantage.

St. Vincent's personality is revealed in his vigorous style of writing, which is second only to that of Lord Fisher of Kilverstone in its color of expression. St. Vincent's refusal to mince words in the late eighteenth and early nineteenth centuries makes for good reading in the twentieth century. His correspondence with Sir Evan Nepean gave vent to his prejudices and predilections, and his obsessional belief, all too often justified by experience and events, that the discipline of officers and men was of an unacceptable standard. He was the greatest figure in the preservation of some semblance of order in the dangerous year 1797 and in the restoration and preservation of naval discipline in subsequent years. It might have been said about Britain's sailors after St. Vincent that they were like Gibbon's Roman soldiers who feared their own officers more than the enemy.

St. Vincent was not a soothing influence among senior officers. He made little secret of his favorites: Sir Thomas Troubridge,[7] Pellew,[8] and Nelson. Troubridge, above all, found his favor, and when St. Vincent went to the Admiralty to be First Lord, he took Troubridge with him as his chief assistant. Indeed, he considered Troubridge to be the greatest seaman that England had produced, but the premature loss of Troubridge meant that this view was not put to the full test of events. St. Vincent never recovered from Troubridge's loss. Those whom St. Vincent disliked, for instance, Sir John Orde,[9] received humiliating treatment. St. Vincent's own parsimonious upbringing gave him some sense of social self-deprivation and made him bristle at the aristocratic airs of many of his fellow admirals.

St. Vincent did not change his manner when he became First Lord of the Admiralty under Addington in 1801–04. He treated the Navy Board and the dockyard contractors just as he had treated the Channel Fleet—"tilting at dockyards," the process might be called. Here was another Augean stable for his Herculean effort. At a time when it cost 13,600 pounds to repair a ship and only 12,000 pounds to build a new one, critical questions needed to be asked. St. Vincent's economical spirit was roused. Unfortunately, he tried to do everything at once. Here, the vested interests fought back. The timber contractors, the shipbuilders, and even the Medical Board raised an anti-St. Vincent clamor. St. Vincent's reforming zeal was seen by many opponents, including Pitt the younger,[10] as destructive of the war effort when ships were so urgently needed. Pitt made a stinging attack on St. Vincent: "I did believe that his name, in whatever naval capacity, was a tower of strength, but I am apt to think that between his Lordship as a commander at sea, and his Lordship as First Lord of the Admiralty, there is a wide difference."[11]

The result of St. Vincent's efforts was uproar and the fall of the Addington ministry. As St. Vincent said, he had friends when he went into the Admiralty and none when he came out. The young Sir William Parker,[12] writing to his father on September 7, 1801, commented: "The noble Earl is here much disliked, everybody *rife* for turning him out of the Admiralty. I fancy he adheres too strictly to his duty for them and I believe there are some who would not be sorry to have him confined as a *madman*."[13] Such is the thorny path of the institutional reformer. St. Vincent was a very old-fashioned Whig—one might say the devil's answer to Dr. Johnson. He was appalled at the notion of democracy and yet no respecter of vested institutions fallen into decay.

Although St. Vincent was not to be an unmitigated success at the Admiralty, in the great naval action of his life—the Battle of St. Vincent[14] in February 1797—he showed the highest qualities of leadership. As in 1941 with Sir Andrew Cunningham, so in 1797 with St. Vincent, England sorely needed a victory, and St. Vincent provided one. In February 1797 he was about to lead a fleet into battle for the first time. He was not found wanting. In this battle he was luckier in his success than Jellicoe, who had a similar experience of a great naval engagement at Jutland in 1916 with no previous experience in action as a commander-in-chief.

However, St. Vincent had earlier shown high quality in the action in 1792, in which the *Foudroyant* fought the *Pégase* off Brest, and in the close and continuous blockade of French bases, a concept evolved by Hawke. Even before the Battle of St. Vincent, however, St. Vincent had been informed that he would be made a peer of the realm for his Mediterranean services. So the battle was the culmination of a period of high-quality offensive service at sea.

In the battle of 1797, St. Vincent showed no hesitation in attacking the Spanish fleet against all odds.[15] He favored bold action and he showed absolute confidence in the unanimity, zeal, and bravery of the squadron under his command. His fleet gave an excellent display of orderly conduct and regular maneuver, except, that is, for Nelson. Nelson's surprise attack on the Spanish ships *St. Nicholas* and *San Josef*, in itself a tactical masterpiece, was a *coup de foudre*, quite unforseen by his own commander-in-chief, but readily approved after the event. Nelson at the Battle of St. Vincent sealed himself in his commander-in-chief's affections. St. Vincent, the unsparing critic of so many, was unsparing in praise of Nelson over the years. For example, St. Vincent wrote to Nelson on May 31, 1801, "All agree there is but one Nelson. . . ."[16] As it turned out, one Nelson was enough to secure British naval hegemony. Writing to his brother in February 1797, Collingwood described the incident that was to make the fame and fortune of both Nelson and St. Vincent: "Commodore Nelson boarded and took sword in hand and (what may never happen again) received the submission and swords of the Officers on the quarter deck of the first rate the *San Josef*, while one of his seamen made a bundle of them, with as much composure as if he had been tying faggots. . . ."[17]

In St. Vincent's orders we get the impression of meticulous concentration on detail and vigorous carrying out of policy. He gave rebukes with great force, when all was not quite to his taste—when all was not quite "Sir Garnet,"[18] in later military parlance. For example, on October 21, 1800, he sent a verbal rocket to Captain Monkton of the *Mars* and the officer of the watch because of the way in which they had pushed through two other ships:

The very unofficer and unseamanlike manner the Mars, was conducted this morning, by pushing through the Ville de Paris and Barfleur, those ships being at the time in very close order, thereby obliging the Barfleur to lay all aback to avoid running on board the Mars, obliges the Commander-in-Chief publickly to reprimand Captain Monkton, and the Officer of the Watch, and strictly to forbid the like conduct in future.[19]

Everything had to be just so in St. Vincent's world.

We see him at his most effective in the 1797 mutinies and at his most acrimonious in his treatment of Sir John Orde. In these two incidents St. Vincent showed himself at his best in his assertion of authority, a necessary quality of leadership, and at his most controversial in his failure to secure good feeling among his most senior subordinates. In this latter respect he lacked the warmth of Nelson's charismatic leadership.

Lecturing in 1931 at Greenwich Naval College, Commander W. G. Tennant[20] said that the men are and always have been reliable except for a few weeks in 1797. This was an unfortunate remark to make in what was to be the year of the Invergordon Mutiny.[21] The disputes in 1797 and 1931 were fundamentally about pay, the first showing disciplinary problems caused by inflation; the second, caused by deflation. Not too surprisingly, both were years of great national financial trouble.

In the second half of the eighteenth century the physical chances of a seaman surviving increased with a successful attack on scurvy, but there was not a similar financial improvement. The seaman's remuneration remained the same. Wages were low and late. As early as 1780 Hood wrote to his brother that, "The poor devils of seamen are so turned from ship to ship without the smallest consideration to them, that there is not a possibility of denying them justice especially their wages."[22] The long periods at sea, the shortage of suitable manpower, and the lack of continuity of manning led to unrest. The most popular of admirals had problems in keeping their manpower. Thus Keppel on September 28, 1778, warned his captains, "It is strongly enjoined to you whilst in Port to take every Method to avoid the Desertion of your People and tho', it would be cruel to deprive them having some liberty on Shore, yet I would recommend its being done under very prudish restrictions."[23] Keppel was always a realist with an economical frame of mind, as when at Spithead on May 27, 1778, he ordered a diminution of gun salutes because of the large size of the fleet and the frequent coming and going of notables.[24]

The behavior of the seamen was a continual problem so often linked to the question of payment of wages, especially that of their regularity of payment. Thus in 1787 Howe wrote to Hood about the possibility of trouble if there was obstruction to the payment of the wages of Nelson's men.[25] Howe was also worried about discipline in general in 1794, when he criticized "Captains who kept their men as prisoners on board when they came into harbour while they themselves spent a great deal of time on shore, leaving the command of their ships to subordinate officers."[26]

From the experience of authority over the years, the mutinies that occurred at Spithead and the Nore in the spring of 1797 cannot have been completely unexpected, but the extent of the trouble certainly was. The navy in the period 1792–1802 suffered all kinds of stresses that can arise in an institution from rapid expansion. In these ten years the navy expanded from 16,000 men to 135,000, many of whom were recruited by the press gangs in very hot presses. The Admiralty had had more particular and immediate warnings of impending trouble. Rear-Admiral Philip Patton[27] wrote to the First Lord, Earl Spencer, on December 8, 1797,[28] after the mutinies, reminding him that he had put into his hand a paper of April 1795 warning him of the danger of general mutiny and had also sent warnings to Pitt and Henry Dundas.[29] In Patton's view, low pay was the main reason for trouble. Merchant seamen were able to command 40 shillings a month, but navy men could only command 22 shillings. Patton asked how good seamen could be expected to stay in Royal Navy ships for that kind of pay. He also thought an improvement in the quality of petty officers was needed.

The Spithead mutineers in April 1797, being more reasonable and deferential than the subsequent Nore mutineers, had sent their pleas by way of petition for better conditions to Howe, who, as they were not individually signed, ignored them. He afterwards said that he regretted doing this, but had no option because of improper procedures. Howe was regarded as Father of the Fleet and was trusted by both men and government. His readiness to parley with the men, once the mutiny had reached its peak, seemed to some to make the whole world upside down. As Admiral Lord Gardner[30] wrote to Admiral Sir Charles Pole[31] on May 17, 1797: "... I understand from the Lieut of the Watch that Lord Howe is coming off with the Union Flag flying in the bow of His Boat, with the Spokesmen of the Fleet attending him; Good God, can this be true, or am I dreaming. . . ."[32] He was not! The Spithead mutineers had the government by the throat, and their demands were acceded to. Fifty-nine unpopular officers were dismissed, and the whole affair ended with a gala celebration organized by the men at which Howe and his wife were the guests of honor.

The Nore Mutiny later in that spring was a violent and not so successful uprising. But the results of both mutinies were a great blow to the exercise of authority in the navy, and it was left to St. Vincent, above all, to have the hard task of restoring order and preventing the spread of disaffection in the Mediterranean.

St. Vincent, even before the mutinies, regretted that there were so few captains with vigor of character and knowledge of seamen. It seemed that few could emulate St. Vincent's consistent assertion of order in small and great things. Writing from his flagship the *Ville de Paris* on May 21, 1797,[33] he deplored the fact that so few admirals and other officers had stayed on board their ships. He especially disapproved of the conduct of Lord Seymour[34] and George Berkeley[35] and said there were many others like them. St. Vincent's strength was his omnipresence. He was always close at hand and, as he slept very little, up and about as well. He was up at 4 A.M. Some indeed said 2 A.M.! His interview hours were from 5 A.M. to 7 A.M. Another virtue was that he always had an interest in the problems of the individual seaman.

How did he preserve order in the Mediterranean Fleet from May 1797 to July 1798? It was by sheer brutal exercise of authority. Hangings there were, even on a Sunday, despite the protests of Sir Robert Calder[36] and Vice-Admiral Thompson,[37] who objected to the profanation of the Sabbath. Nelson fully supported St. Vincent, and here we see the ruthless side of Nelson's nature, as when he wrote to Calder: "Had it been Christmas Day instead of Sunday I would have executed them."[38] New and possibly unreliable crews were put in moral and physical quarantine from the rest of the fleet until their discipline, situation, and disposition were better known. St. Vincent made quite sure where the loyalty lay and then struck down on pockets of disloyalty with a heavy hand, not wasting words with officers who favored leniency.

The policy succeeded, and in due course, in 1799, he applied the same methods to the Channel Fleet, employing an unaccustomed severity that pleased neither officers nor men. Neither in the Mediterranean Fleet nor with the Channel Fleet did St. Vincent have an easy task. His letter to Nepean on July 4, 1797, reflects the problems he faced: "We have had some awkward sensations in this squadron; one on board the *Irresistable*, I am assured by Rear-Admiral Nelson is fully settled. The *Diadem*, spiritedly commanded has a dirty blackguard Crew, who have gone lengths, but are kept down with a tight hand."[39]

It would be wrong to see St. Vincent as nothing more than a martinet. He himself realized how unpopular he was. "Why do they send me the mutinous ships?" he complained. "Do they think I will be hangman to the Fleet?"[40] Indeed, he had some humanitarian instincts. He was opposed to the slave trade. It affronted his Whig principles. In contrast, Nelson supported it, since he believed the trade encouraged and gave scope for the development of British seamen. St. Vincent was not merely an overblown and more successful version of Captain Bligh.[41] He evoked loyalty, although hardly affection. His self-confidence in the righteousness of his measures stiffened the fiber of weaker brethren.

St. Vincent's rigorous standards meant that he was not easily satisfied in matters of discipline. Indeed, the discontent among the men
persisted during the rest of 1797, after the mutinies, and for some
months after that year, although not on the same scale. St. Vincent
sustained the theme of the need for continual severity for many years
after 1797. Others corroborated his view of the strain of restlessness
in the fleet. Writing to Admiral Pole in 1797 regarding the poor physical condition of the men in some ships, where they suffered from
scurvy and lacked shoes, Captain Payne commented, "In God's
name what can we be about? Have our Rulers, or *Miss* Rulers, forgotten that Seamen are Men, and that they are wounded by the same ill
treatment that affects others of their species. The whole fleet conceive themselves to be outlaw'd, and Woe to the man, that once ex-
cites them! again. . . ."[42] St. Vincent continued his complaints. On
November 4, 1797,[43] he referred in a letter to the very small remains
of discipline and order in the service. On January 28, 1798,[44] he
lamented the amount of time the men had been allowed to pass in port
since Howe's victory of the Glorious First of June in 1793. There was
the additional problem of discontent arising from the United Irishmen movement.[45] The alarm this caused can be seen in the General
Order of Sir Richard King,[46] commander-in-chief at Plymouth, on
August 29, 1798:

the Captains and Commanders of HM Ships and Vessels at this Port, are
hereby required and directed to point out to their Crews the enormity of the
Crime of which these desperate Men are guilty of being engaged as United
Irishmen in the Rebellion . . . their Lordships are confident all Seamen will
show that the place of their Birth can make no difference in their love for their
Country.[47]

St. Vincent, not mincing words over this problem, wrote on June 30,
1800, ". . . there cannot be doubt that the Irish in the Fleet who are to a
man incorrigable Villains, have been continually at work to bring
about another mutiny. . . ."[48]

It was not only the men who received the opprobrium of St. Vincent. On January 2, 1802,[49] he foresaw very soon an end to discipline
in the navy. Certain admirals like Robert Man[50] and Sir George
Young[51] he castigated as men who never knew what discipline was

and never would acquire it. In St. Vincent's view there was always more to do in disciplinary matters, in civil as well as naval and military life. In 1812 he saw the whole of society falling apart, "I do not like the Signs of the Times, which forbode a convulsion, Respect for the higher orders is rapidly on the decline. . . ."[52]

However, the higher orders of St. Vincent did not always see eye to eye. Sir John Orde and St. Vincent had a most notorious quarrel—the strange case of Sir John Orde, it might be called. This incident illustrates both the style of St. Vincent's leadership and the important issue in leadership of getting the goodwill and cooperation of subordinates. St. Vincent's manner tended to arouse antagonisms, especially with a person like Sir John Orde, who has been described as a fustian fire-eater.[53]

Orde was an officer senior to Nelson and under the command of St. Vincent in the Mediterranean in 1798. Collingwood, who also served in the Mediterranean at that time, speculated about the clash of personalities and decided that St. Vincent had a social jealousy of Orde:

He treated Sir John Orde very ill—I never could discover what was the cause, but when two proud Dons meet—it is not altogether difficult to find a cause of difference—I believe Sir John Orde is as zealous in the publick service as himself—but in his manner and stile of living there was a magnificence that the Chief was perhaps jealous of, and in a very unprecedented way he sent him home.[54]

Despite the quarrel, Orde's material state flourished, and on April 1, 1805, Nelson wrote to him, "for by reports you will be the richest Admiral that ever England saw."[55]

In the winter and spring of 1798, St. Vincent had publicly treated Orde in conventionally flattering terms, but St. Vincent regarded Orde, of whom he himself did not approve, and Nelson, of whom he did approve, as being for very different reasons sources of discontent among the senior officers. On February 19, 1798, St. Vincent wrote to Nepean, "There is such a universal prejudice taken against Sir John Orde by all the Captains of this Fleet that it is really painful to place them under his orders. . . ."[56] Later in the same year, on June 19, in a much-quoted letter St. Vincent was to write to the same correspondent, "There is such a faction against Nelson here, that I wish you would order all the admirals above him to England or elsewhere immediately—the service cannot go on, unless you do this."[57] Nelson's talents and the favors of St. Vincent aroused the envy of more than Orde. Yet Orde had reason to think he had been lured into a false sense of security by St. Vincent. Just before St. Vincent was criticizing him to Nepean, Sir John Orde wrote to Lady Orde on January 19, 1798, "PS. Lord St. Vincent continues all goodness to me. He is a wonderful Officer and man."[58] Again, on February 24, 1798, he wrote, "The confidence of Lord St. Vincent in leaving me here at the moment I feel very flattering."[59] Finally, on March 20, 1798, he stated, "Lord St. Vincent continues to be very kind and I doubt not we shall remain on friendly terms."[60]

Nelson was appointed to lead a separate squadron in the Mediterranean—the appointment that led to the Battle of the Nile on August 1, 1798. This appointment was too much for Orde, who felt he had been passed over and wrote complaining about this to Spencer, the First Lord of the Admiralty. St. Vincent thereupon ordered Orde home in a highly arbitrary fashion in August 1798 and rebuked him for his communication with the Admiralty. This action did not find favor with the Admiralty, and they rebuked St. Vincent in return on October 13, 1798, with these words:"... they are therefore pleased to direct that you do not in future send home any Flag officer that may be under your command without receiving instructions from their Lordships so to do, unless some very strong and some very peculiar circumstances make it absolutely necessary."[61]

Nelson, writing to Orde long after the event, in July 1801,[62] implied that his appointment in 1798 was not an act of favoritism on the part of St. Vincent, but a decision made at the Admiralty long before he, Nelson, was actually sent on his mission.

The departure of Orde did not diminish St. Vincent's indignation. St. Vincent referred to him on September 6, 1798, as "this strange man" who had taken a "litigious and inquisitional turn."[63] Later in the year St. Vincent denounced Orde again: "Neither you, or any of his nautical acquaintance, can be ignorant that he is not a practical Seaman, neither has he reach of Sea understanding, ever to become a Tactician; his abilities as Governor of a Colony, I have no doubt are transcendent."[64]

But Sir John Orde, former governor of Dominica, was a grandee who would not turn the other cheek. He wrote to the Admiralty of St.

Vincent:"... having in my opinion acted unbecoming the character of an officer, by treating me in a manner unsuitable to my rank, between the 17th May and 29th August 1798, both days inclusive."[65] Orde agitated for a court-martial for himself and challenged St. Vincent to a duel, which George III personally forbade. Orde then circulated the correspondence between himself and St. Vincent, putting forward his point of view of the quarrel to his influential and professional friends. The replies from those circulated, and other letters of sympathy sent to him, are interesting not only for their implicit view of Orde and St. Vincent, but for the light they throw on the writers of the replies themselves, and for the concept of naval leadership at the time the issue was raised. In the replies received by Orde, there was much wringing of hand and vague sympathy, but reluctance to intervene and help. It was generally felt that St. Vincent had exceeded the limits of accepted conduct, but nothing could be done.

Bridport, as might be expected, sat on the fence. He had trouble enough already presiding over the Channel Fleet. Sir John Duckworth, no favorite of St. Vincent, favored Orde's cause, but thought that Orde had not employed his usual discernment. Duckworth thought that, anyway, St. Vincent would be protected for political reasons. James Saumarez[66] said Orde's experience had been shared by others, and Collingwood described service under St. Vincent as "a fine school of humility,"[67] adding,". . . but when I consider what others have suffer'd I ought not to complain." Coming from the long suffering Collingwood, these are powerful words indeed. The Mediterranean was a cruel sea.

St. Vincent was an issue in Orde's correspondence for years to come. The Tory radical William Cobbett's[68] comment to Orde on December 28, 1802, regarding the Whig St. Vincent at the Admiralty, was succinct: "The Bashaw Presbyterian has unfortunately the power of tormenting others now, of all ranks and degrees."[69]

But it is the replies of Howe[70] and Hood[71] that raised the general question of naval authority. Orde's indignation lay in the personal treatment he had suffered rather than in any attack by him on the Admiralty system. But the issue led Howe and Hood to make more general points, no doubt in an effort to assuage Orde's personal pique. Howe thought that particular men had to be employed for particular occasions, but said that as this kind of quarrel had happened so frequently, there could be a more uniform system whereby both higher and lower officers could be instructed in their particular duties. Hood thought that the less Orde said on the subject the better, and that the Admiralty had the authority to direct a commander-in-chief abroad to detach any particular flag officer under his command with any given number of ships on any service whatever.

We are here at the crossroads—the new professionalism is in the ascendancy, but the old administrative vagueness lingers on and touches it. Men like Orde could argue with good precedent that seniority and position in themselves could be the decisive factors for appointment, rather than the view that considered merit and performance could alone determine selection. Orde felt he had a vested claim to preferment over Nelson, and in so doing manifested an older view of the importance of seniority and social degree that had flourished earlier in the eighteenth century. Orde never gave in and he was still complaining of this and other slights in February 1811.[72] But the cause célèbre had deteriorated or ossified into an *idée fixe*. Orde's defeat was a symbol of the new order in naval affairs, for as much as St. Vincent may have posed as a *laudator temporis acti*[73] in social matters, he was no respecter of persons in professional situations. He very much anticipated the naval wave of the future, with its unswerving acceptance of the decisions of high authority and its loss of aristocratic pretensions about policy, although not its renunciation of an aristocratic style of personal living.

In modern parlance, St. Vincent's trenchant views and outspoken prejudices could be counterproductive. In no way could the leading admirals at the end of the eighteenth century, as opposed to Nelson's captains, be called a happy band of brothers.[74] Collingwood referred with feeling to his experiences in the Mediterranean, writing to his brother on December 14, 1798, when he made the bleak comment:

> The station I left was latterly rather disagreeable—the strange innovations which the Chief made in all the ordinary modes of discipline, and the high hand with which he carried himself towards some officers, made it very unpleasant to all—for my part I had the good fortune to keep clear of all disputes—nor do I know he ever said an uncivil thing to me or of me—and that is a very singular case—for very few escaped the asperity of his temper.[75]

Peter Cullen from a humbler position commented:

Earl St. Vincent, one of our best admirals, was haughty and imperious, rigidly and unnecessarily strict, on many occasions, in carrying on duty, which made him very much disliked by his captains and officers. Many others fulfilled their Commands in a more agreeable and equally efficient manner. For instance Lord Nelson, Lord Duncan[76] etc. etc. without his severity.[77]

Collingwood also commented on St. Vincent's favoritism, mentioning in the same letter to his brother, as last quoted, the real and purported reason why he himself was not sent to reinforce Nelson:

... the reason he would assign was the infirm state of my ship—the true reason was that my going would have interfered with the command of his great favourite Capt. Troubridge—who is junior to me—and who he meant should be second to Nelson—but Nelson having no such partiality kept Sir James Saumarez with him—and so the Chief was doubly defeated—for Sir James and he were on the worst terms possible.[78]

We certainly have a good recipe for unhappiness on the Mediterranean station. Take Orde's touchiness, add the profound jealousy that Nelson's ascendancy evoked, add mutinous and discontented men, and then complete the picture with the customary prize money disputes and St. Vincent's quarrelsome disposition and favoritism. A pie of pique indeed!

Fortunately, St. Vincent showed an element of self-knowledge, a greater self-knowledge than, say, his successor of a later century, Sir John Fisher, who also had the same sharpness of comment. Writing to Nepean on November 7, 1793, he said, "My Zeal, I confess, outruns my discretion."[79] On August 29, 1796, he wrote, "You and I, and in truth the whole profession are Hero-Makers, and nothing so common among us, as to say this, that and t'other man is a great Officer, when we really have few [great] Officers on the list of Admirals."[80] In the same letter he went on to state his preferences. He sang the merits of Troubridge. Nelson, he admitted, he could not avoid making an established commodore whether he liked it or not. On October 4, 1796,[81] he actually listed the post captains he valued highly—Nelson at the head, with Troubridge, Samuel Hood, Sir Thomas Fremantle, and Sir George Cockburn and others.[82] There was thus a nursery of admirals.

In St. Vincent's black books over the years, in descending order of merit, were Duckworth, Sir Hyde Parker,[83] Sir Sidney Smith, and

Orde. He thought Duckworth's abilities were limited, but that he had the redeeming feature of being a good trainer of midshipmen. St. Vincent regarded Sir Sidney Smith's judgment as not worth a pin, and over the years almost exhausted his store of epithets in describing him, consigning him apparently to a limbo only a little higher than Sir John Orde. There was thus very much an out-group of admirals, outside the inner, charmed circle (and I consider them briefly later).

St. Vincent's robust leadership was invaluable against the French, invaluable in the assertion of discipline, in steadying the navy in the trauma of 1797, but controversial when it came to a question of a sense of fairness and harmony among his colleagues, and when he attempted much needed reform ashore. His career reminds us that successful leadership qualities and experience in one sphere cannot always have the same effectiveness in others.

chapter 5

NELSON: A HERO'S LIFE AND DEATH

In Nelson, the second of the three great naval figures of the era—St. Vincent, Nelson, and Collingwood—we find a conspicuous but misleading example of leadership. The example is conspicuous because of Nelson's genius and misleading because it is very difficult to emulate a genius. The word *genius* itself may be unhelpful. Spenser Wilkinson,[1] the percipient military writer, thought so and took Mahan to task for applying the word *genius* to Nelson, saying that it has always seemed a bad definition to explain greatness by genius. Wilkinson added that *genius* was a synonym for *miracle* and amounted to abandoning the problem of explanation. Be that as it may, since Nelson's death the British navy has, not surprisingly, yearned for another Nelson and has been ever ready to anticipate another Nelson in lesser men among future generations. It is the combination in Nelson of so many personal qualities relevant to successful naval action that is so unusual. At times this search for another Nelson has taken on an almost mystical quality, like that of the search for the Holy Grail and the vigil for King Arthur's or Frederick Barbarossa's return.[2]

A word favored in the last thirty years in relation to leadership is charisma, and it would be correct to apply this to Nelson. He was charismatic in his life, and language concerning him during his life

A feast of victory! John Bull taking a luncheon by J. Gillray (Courtesy National Maritime Museum)

(and after his death), has, on occasion, succumbed to a state of mindless hyperbole. He caught the imagination of his fellow officers and men, and with the Battle of St. Vincent, the imagination of the British public as well—a public that satiated itself on the details of his life and in its own particularly morbid way on those of his death and funeral.

The tendency has been either to criticize in moralistic terms Nelson's sexual escapades and in particular his liason with Lady Hamilton[3] or to omit mention of them by a tactful or embarrassed silence, as if this side of his life were totally unrelated to his professional performance or should be regarded like the dark side of the moon in the prespace era. To do either one of these things is to make a very artificial distinction between professional and private life. The characteristics of a person are of one piece. The attractions of Nelson for and to women were just one aspect of an attractive personality, which endeared itself to many of his professional colleagues and subordinates and helped to make him such an effective leader. Nelson attracted even people such as Collingwood, who seemed to most to be immune to, or impervious to, fellow feeling. Like President John F. Kennedy, with his alleged revolving door of air stewardesses, or Lloyd George, who could charm a bird off a tree, Nelson attracted both men and women. Lady Spencer wrote, for example, of Nelson's uncouth appearance after losing an arm, but concluded by saying that when he spoke, his wonderful mind broke forth and he riveted her whole attention.[4]

Nelson's striking appearance and the confidence of his speech and argument made him dominate the encounter in his sole and accidental meeting with Wellington.[5] Wellington was a little bewildered by it all, but impressed nonetheless. The duke of Clarence, commenting on his own first meeting with Nelson, gives us a vivid impression of the man and his appearance: ". . . for I had never seen anything like it before, nor could I imagine who he was, nor what he came about. . . . There was something irresistibly pleasing in his address and conversation; and an enthusiasm when speaking on professional subjects that shewed he was no common being."[6] This meeting was the start of a lifelong friendship between Nelson and Clarence, during which the duke did Nelson the singular and princely honor of giving away his bride.

In all the welter of praise and notoriety surrounding Nelson, can the essence of his leadership qualities be refined and explained? No man is without critics, and even Nelson has suffered criticism about several aspects of both his life and leadership—his personal morality, his voracious appetite for fame and honor, and his vanity. He tended to be irritated with officers, James Saumarez for one, who did not always jump with enthusiasm for his ideas. Saumarez was a fine captain and later a fine admiral, and Nelson had a high opinion of him. But Saumarez did not always respond to the energy and enthusiasm of Nelson. Saumarez was said to have a pedagogical and unimaginative streak, which made him rather an outsider in Nelson's famous band of captains. At the battle of the Nile in 1798 he was second-in-command, but after the battle he received from Nelson what can only be interpreted as a slight: ". . . Captain Ball came on deck and interrupted the conversation by observing, 'Nelson says there is to be no second-in-command; *we are all alike in his despatches.'* "[7]

Another feature of Nelson's life, his administrative ability, has been left an open question, as he did not live long enough to have it proved or disproved in any great scenario.

His lack of professional discipline has been pointed out, particularly in the case of his service under Hotham,[8] Keith, and Sir Hyde Parker. Certainly Nelson was very fortunate to have been assisted in his career by sympathetic or compliant superiors, who shielded him from the dangers of allegations of insubordination arising from his langueurs or more frequently his idiosyncratic interpretation of Admiralty orders. Thus not the least part of St. Vincent's contribution to the national cause was not only what he did for England, but what he did for Nelson in shielding him from disapproval by superiors. Nelson himself was quite explicit about his own view of obedience. Writing to Lord Spencer on November 6, 1799, he commented:

Much as I approve of strict obedience to orders—even to a court martial to enquire whether the object justified the measure—yet to say that an officer is never, for any object, to alter his orders, is what I cannot comprehend. The circumstances of this war so often vary, that an Officer has almost every moment to consider—what would my superiors direct, did they know what is passing under my nose? The great object of the war is—*Down, down with the French!*[9]

To assist St. Vincent—in the support of Nelson, that is—was Lady Hamilton. One school of thought, of which Fisher (a lady killer himself in his time) was a delighted member, saw Lady Hamilton as fulfilling an important role not only in a physical but in a psychological way. She ministered to Nelson's self-esteem with all the facility and skill of one who already had much experience in fluttering around the candle of fame.

Sir Robert Calder was not the only one shocked by Nelson's individualistic unorthodoxy. He said, ironically no doubt, that Nelson deserved to be punished for the Battle of the Nile, because it was in contradiction to the practice of all former battles. One of the Mediterranean captains was to observe wryly to Nelson when St. Vincent came into the Mediterranean, "You did just as you pleased in Lord Hood's time, the same in Admiral Hotham's and now again with Sir John Jervis. It makes no difference to you who is commander-in-chief."[10] It would be fair to say that Nelson reported that he returned a pretty strong answer to these words.

But it is not enough to throw up our hands, overwhelmed by the achievement, and suggest with the poet that though others abide our questions, thou Nelson art free.[11] Many of Nelson's qualities are recipes for successful naval leadership in any era. The later nineteenth and the twentieth centuries, which have made of Nelson a cult figure, also recognized essential qualities of great leadership and tried with varying success to emulate them.

The setting was indeed favorable for Nelson's talents. There had been, as we have seen, a rapid decline of the French and Spanish fleets, and Napoleon's preoccupations were military rather than naval. Napoleon looked at naval matters in a military way, and British seamen often remarked how Napoleon treated naval strategy as a branch of land warfare, with the same possibilities of exact timing and calculated paces of march. Napoleon seemed to disregard the hazards of wind and weather. Never at a loss for an epithet or an excuse, he had something to say of his own fleet. "I have a hundred ships of the line and yet I have not a navy,"[12] he admitted.

Nelson himself had made a respected reputation relatively early in his career. As a result of this he had a good chance of independence of action and authority when he was at the height of his powers. He was supported in the exercise of his talents by the encouragement and experience of St. Vincent. In Nelson's career there is a particularly remarkable amalgam of attractive personal qualities and inspired professionalism.

The four main features of Nelson's leadership are his success as a leader of men, his tactical brilliance, his realism and willingness to delegate, and his aggressive spirit. He aroused enthusiasm for his personality and his naval outlook among both captains and the men. He had an extraordinary facility for inspiring the men under his command, first with confidence in himself and then with a desire to emulate him. At Trafalgar only six of about thirty captains had served under him previously, but the acquaintance of each one was soon made by Nelson, and their enthusiasm was immediately aroused. Thus Thomas Fremantle wrote in October 1805, "The arrival of Lord Nelson here has given us fresh life, and Spirits."[13] Above all, Nelson could arouse enthusiasm for action. The men believed he meant business and that ultimately by his triumphs the war would end sooner and they would go home. Among most of his contemporaries, he alone could man a ship without a press gang. Yet he always had a firm sense of realism about what could and could not be done. Faced with the problem of women on ships, he did not try to set impossible standards:

To Admiral Sir John Jervis.
My dear Sir,
The history of women was brought forward, I remember, in the Channel Fleet last War. I know not if your Ship was an exception, but I will venture to say, not an Honourable but had plenty of them; and they will always do as they please. Orders are not for them—at least, I never yet knew one who obeyed.
Your most faithful.
Horatio Nelson[14]

Rank and success never changed Nelson. He cared for his officers and men and was seen by others to care—a remarkable achievement in a formal age. His captains must have been comforted and encouraged by the fact that Nelson gave them every possible form of moral backing. He had always believed in supporting the dignity of the service. Earlier in his career, in February 1785, he had written: ". . . but my best endeavours, however deficient they may be, shall always be exercised in supporting the dignity of my brother Captains. . . ."[15] He put his beliefs into action in later years in the Mediterranean when he ably supported the honor of his captains against accusations of corruption made by Charles Lock, the British consul general in Naples.

In a period when a captain was very much *in loco parentis* to the midshipmen, Nelson was very compassionate in the exercise of his duties. Some idea of Nelson's sensitivity and sense of occasion may be gleaned from his letter to Evan Davis of Swansea in the summer of 1794: "From the nature of our profession we hold life by a more precarious tenure than many others, but when we fall, we trust it is to the benefit of our country. So fell your Son by a cannon ball under my immediate command at the Siege of Bastia. I had taken him on shore with me, for his abilities and attention to duty."[16]

Nelson's attention to his midshipmen was exemplary. If their health was affected, he immediately sent them home to convalesce. His influence on so many was profound at a time when training in the navy was essentially training by example. But his care extended to all ranks, and contemporaries commented on his uncommon attention to the personal comforts and welfare of the men under his command.

Nelson, as we have seen, did not lack for jealous rivals, but his popularity and close rapport with his subordinates made for ease of understanding, which ensured a favorable atmosphere for the execution of orders and the easy communication of ideas.

Despite his personal popularity and enjoyment of that popularity, it would be wrong to see Nelson as always amiable and the soul of humanitarianism. Those with charisma often have a steely edge. Although it is said that Nelson ruled by love, not fear, there is still a touch of the lash about his command. We have already seen that Nelson preferred the continuance of the slave trade to any possible decline in British seamanship. In the regime of Nelson and Sir Thomas Hardy,[17] there was frequent use of the cat-o'-nine-tails. Nelson's unreserved backing for St. Vincent in 1797–98 suggests that he might very well have taken the same harsh line if he had been faced with the same responsibilities.

The second significant feature of Nelson's genius (and despite Spenser Wilkinson's reservations, Nelson deserved the epithet) was the brilliance of his tactical perception and ability to communicate that perception rapidly. He had the gift of making his captains think it was their own ideas they were being encouraged to execute. If we may mention the two names in the same breath, Nelson was Napoleonic in the clarity and prescience of his signals and instructions. His tactical genius was displayed at the Battle of St. Vincent when he saw the essential weakness of the enemy center, and at the Battle of the Nile when he judged there was room for the entry of his ships at Aboukir. At the Nile he perceived that where there was room for one of the enemy's vessels to swing, there was room for a British ship to anchor. Because of his rapport with his captains, Nelson could rapidly and decisively unite his fleet to a common purpose. Thus he made the situation absolutely clear to his captains before the Battle of the Nile, as Captain Berry reported:

With the masterly ideas of their Admiral, therefore, on the subject of Naval tactics every one of the Captains of his Squadron was most thoroughly acquainted; and upon surveying the situations of the Enemy they could ascertain with precision what were the ideas and intentions of their Commander, without the aid of any further instructions.[18]

Nelson had explained fully to his subordinates what his schemes and intentions were, and he trusted them to do their best to carry them out. The council of war has fallen into disfavor because of its associations with failure, but Nelson before each of his battles assembled his captains, often to a dinner gathering, to ensure that all were one with his ideas.

With Nelson there was none of the controversy of Rodney, the obscurity of Howe, or the hectoring of a St. Vincent, In a memorable phrase, Collingwood said at Trafalgar, "I wish Nelson would stop signalling as we know well enough what to do." Nelson's fleet was well prepared. One gets the impression that many of the captains under his leadership performed above themselves. Howe praised Nelson over the conduct of the Nile and talked of the "eminently distinguished conduct of *each* of the captains of his squadron."[19] This contrasts well with the very variable performance of Howe's own captains at the Glorious First of June.

Nelson's third great quality was his realistic sense of the uncertainty of battle and his willingness to give discretion to subordinates and delegate authority when necessary. This quality may at first seem surprising in a person like Nelson, who had such love of fame, such monstrous self-esteen, and such great self-confidence. Nelson believed in the role of chance in human affairs, as in his famous message to Collingwood on October 9, 1805: "Something must be left to chance, nothing is sure in a Sea Fight. . . ."[20] Or as he said in a letter the year before: "In Sea affairs, nothing is impossible and nothing is improbable."[21] Indeed, there was no pattern to his great victories. Each triumph was the seizing of opportunities in a particular situation. Nelson never tried to fight yesteryears' battles.

With this grant of discretion and his willingness to delegate, Nelson was never overwhelmed with detail, as Jellicoe was in the First World War. In the reaction that set in against the authoritarian nature of First World War naval leadership, lecturers and commentators such as A. C. Dewar,[22] K. G. B. Dewar,[23] and Sir Herbert Richmond referred to Nelson's example for inspiration.

Nelson's fourth great quality was his personification of the aggressive spirit. It is this aspect of his leadership that is so often referred to as the "Nelson touch." In it there was the seizing of opportunity in a way that disconcerted the enemy, the determination to get close to the enemy, the use of the surprise factor, and, when the advantage was gained, not merely the defeat but the annihilation of the enemy. Nelson paid tribute to one of his mentors, Captain Locker,[24] for helping to inculcate this attitude in him, "To you, my dear friend I owe much of my success. It was you who taught me, 'Lay a Frenchman close, and you will beat him.' "[25] An example of Nelson's attitude is his comment on the battle plan to Sir Richard Keats[26] in the September before Trafalgar: "I think it will surprise and confound the enemy. They won't know what I am about. It will bring on a pell mell battle and that is what I want."[27] Nelson personally exposed himself to danger in battle in an unparalleled way. He did not always succeed: The Santa Cruz expedition in July 1797 and the Boulogne expedition in May 1801 were failures. However, his personal audacity and the audacity of his tactical appreciation do not mean that he was reckless in his orders or even attempted or allowed his subordinates to take unnecessary risks. This reminds us that great commanders are not wasteful of the lives of their men. Field Marshal Montgomery was equally parsimonious with respect to human life, although he lacked some of the essentials of the "Nelson touch," especially in his lack of the instinct for annihilation of the enemy.[28]

Nelson's instructions to Robert Pettet, captain of His Majesty's sloop *Termagent*, is an example of cautious stipulation in sending Pettet to an area where there was great uncertainty:

From the uncertainty of the present state of affairs the greatest Caution is needed in Entering the Tagus and in communicating with Lisbon as it is impossible to say what the Intentions of the Portuguese navy may be, you will therefore do so with the utmost care and circumspection that HM Sloop under Your Command may not be brought into any unpleasant Situation from want of due regard for the necessary precaution.[29]

Nelson made a similar careful calculation of the risks before the Battle of Trafalgar. What to later admiring generations might seem strokes of genius were so often examples of that kind of genius that takes infinite pain. As was said by his early biographers Rev. James Clarke and John M'Arthur, regarding Nelson's albeit unsuccessful attack on Santa Cruz in July 1797, "The experience and the cautious mind of Nelson endeavouring to anticipate every possible obstacle appear throughout the whole of these Orders and Regulations."[30] Nelson had the measure of the French and Spanish opposition from earlier experience and made his judgment accordingly.

One of the main alleged limitations of Nelson's place in the naval pantheon has been that he was never called upon, or never lived long enough to exercise, political or strategical authority. Thus it is asserted that his qualities were never put to the test in the widest of all fields. Yet his service in the Mediterranean did give him scope for the professional exercise of his diplomatic sense and political capacity. For example, in the years 1804–5 he was dealing with consuls, foreign governments, and ministers, even with the pope himself. The evidence gives a favorable, although not always successful, picture.

Often there was a fortunate coincidence in his close relations with Lady Hamilton and the Queen of Naples,[31] and the dictates of British policy. His relations with the court of Naples show a man of political and personal confidence, although not always correct political judgment, who could inspire and activate both the British minister Sir William Hamilton[32] and the court. As to Naples itself, Nelson had no high opinion, seeing it as ". . . a country of fiddlers and poets, whores and scoundrels."[33] By word and deed Nelson stiffened resolution against Napoleon, although he vastly miscalculated the determination of the Directory and the ability of the king of Naples to resist. Like Sir Sidney Smith, Nelson had no hesitation in entering into political matters, whatever the risk to his reputation, and he was a notable figure in his own right in the organization of opposition to Napoleon in the Italian peninsula. In July 1799 Nelson defended his disobedience of Keith's instructions by saying, "I have no scruple in deciding that it is better to save the kingdom of Naples and lose Minorca than to risk the kingdom of Naples to save Minorca."[34]

As far as strategy was concerned, he was never called on to exercise it in the grand manner. But in his letters to Sir Gilbert Elliot[35] in 1794 and 1796 regarding Corsica, Toulon, and Northern Italy, and to Hugh Elliot[36] in 1803 regarding the Sicilies, we see an ability to consider political naval and military factors in an incisive and lucid appreciation.[37]

Earlier, Nelson's advice to Hood and St. Vincent regarding combined operations on land and sea had been successful, as in the case of Corsica. In 1801, in his assessment of the Baltic situation, Nelson concluded that the Danes could be discounted and British efforts concentrated on Sweden and Russia—a correct judgment that his superior Sir Hyde Parker could not grasp. Nelson showed a fertility of ideas in organizing opposition to Napoleon, which suggests that he would have been quite at home, as Sir Sidney Smith was, in organizing operations on land—a successful amphibious admiral, in fact.

Above all, Nelson had the great quality of imaginative optimism, a Churchillian frame of mind, but with a sounder tactical approach than Churchill had. Nelson has this optimism, despite a personal morbidity that made him feel each battle would be his last. Nelson was not infallible—no man is, certainly no admiral is—but he had an ability to see a way out of a naval or diplomatic impasse.

Effective professional leadership is also concerned with attitude to superiors in rank and how far that relationship encourages or inhibits the use of initiative in leadership. In Nelson's relations with his superiors he had a fine sense of self-preservation—he knew how far to go. Liberties could be taken with lesser men but not with his patron St. Vincent.

Nelson had always dared to do the unorthodox thing—to risk disobedience. As we have seen, in 1800 he would not obey Keith's order to attack Minorca. He said it was not a danger to British interests, and he was right. Another conspicuous example of Nelson's insubordination was when he ordered a subordinate to ignore the commander-in-chief, Orde, and leave the Mediterranean. On this occasion he brought disobedience to a fine art when he instructed Captain Parker[38] in Hardy's presence in the following manner: "Sir John Orde remains at the entrance of the Straits and takes my frigates from me, and sends them away in some other direction from what I wish. I cannot even get my despatches home. You must contrive to get to the westward and go into Lisbon and avoid his ships." Endorsed on the back of Parker's orders in Parker's handwriting was:

Private instructions from Lord Viscount Nelson delivered to me with his Lordship's orders of 30th December, 1804, to proceed to Lisbon with despatches, at the time the Squadron under Vice-Admiral John Orde was cruizing off Cadiz, and not allowing the ships under Lord Nelson's orders to pass the Straits of Gibraltar.[39]

Nelson was a very difficult subordinate for his less idiosyncratic superiors such as Keith, Hotham, and Sir Hyde Parker, although at Copenhagen, despite the legend to the contrary, Parker gave Nelson an excellent tactical option and freedom of choice about whether or not to attack the Danes. All of this is a far cry from the late Victorian and early twentieth-century cult of obedience and veneration of seniority.

As far as St. Vincent himself was concerned, Nelson did have formal legal disputes with him over prize money, and he wrote to his agent, Alexander Davison,[40] on February 17, 1801: ". . . but the earl has wrote me the moment he came from the king a very flattering letter, asking for my support so I shall support him as a Great Sea Officer but was he forty times as Great I will not suffer him to rob me with Impunity. . . ."[41]

Nelson won the action against St. Vincent in which Keith had joined him as a third party. Yet despite these brave words, Nelson realized there was a limit to his various skirmishes with authority, and he wrote on October 9, 1801, "I must submit for I do not wish to quarrel with the very great folks of the Admiralty."[42] His relations with St. Vincent were always important, and earlier in his career Nelson, like lesser men, had to eat humble pie at St. Vincent's table and recognize his own imperfections. Writing to St. Vincent from the *Vanguard* on May 31, 1798 (a letter continued on June 15), Nelson commented that "the accidents which have happened to the *Vanguard* were a just punishment for my consummate vanity I must humble acknowledge, and kiss the rod which chastized me. I hope it has made me a better officer as I believe it has made me a better man."[43] However the rod that Nelson referred to here was an even greater authority than St. Vincent—the Almighty, no less.

After the Battle of St. Vincent, Nelson had acquired such a famous reputation that he could risk skirmishes with those like Keith without any risk of permanent damage to his career. Nelson's wearing of an order granted to him by the sultan of Turkey, as a result of the Battle of the Nile, upset George III, but Nelson had friends in the Royal Family, especially the duke of Clarence.

Nelson's individual genius was recognized at such an early stage by those who ultimately mattered—like Spencer, the First Lord who sent him to the Nile, and Barham, the First Lord at the time of Trafalgar—that he could take liberties with the command structure that no man in the British navy, before or since, has been able to do. Nelson was very much aware of his special position, exploiting it to the advantage of Britain, although not to the good humor of his colleagues.

It is not the function of this study to act as an advocate of Nelson; he needs none. The attributes of his leadership are clear even to a nuclear age, where materiel takes such mental energy and so many resources to develop, and the human aspects of an outstanding leader so often seem submerged in a technological background.

Yet to put Nelson in perspective it must be said that, although he was the greatest fighting admiral in British history, he never had as large a proportion of the fleet under his control as Jellicoe had. Moreover, Nelson lived in an age of rising British power, fueled by the Industrial Revolution, where often Britain was taking the technical, financial, and diplomatic initiative. In the twentieth century Britain was in an age of decline, reacting to rather than guiding events, although the symptoms were more often latent than overt in the First World War. Britain was a nation acting fundamentally on the defensive in the twentieth century, and, appropriately enough, she got her defensive admiral in Jellicoe. The man cannot be divorced from the background. Nelson's achievements were encouraged by the world surge of British power.

Nelson then had the particular qualities of leadership that are for all time—the confidence of his officers and men to an unparalleled extent, combined with decisiveness and clarity of exposition, brilliant tactical insight, and the offensive spirit, which evinced itself in surprise and the seizing and retention of the initiative.

Against the personality and fighting record of this extraordinary man, all British naval officers must be ultimately judged. It has been the privilege and misfortune of many otherwise outstanding naval leaders that comparison with Nelson has given them a rather lackluster glow.

chapter 6

COLLINGWOOD:
THE STOIC

Along with St. Vincent and Nelson, the third of the great trinity of admirals in the Nelson era is Collingwood. Even though Collingwood may appear diminuendo to St. Vincent's fortissimo and Nelson's crescendo, he was after all the most important admiral in active service between the death of Nelson in 1805 and Jellicoe's assumption of the Grand Fleet command in 1914.

Just as Nelson appealed to the heroic and the morbid of the age of Romanticism so did Collingwood appeal to the aspect of Romanticism that accentuated self-abnegation and duty. Alfred de Vigny,[1] the nineteenth-century French Romantic writer, selected Collingwood as a living embodiment of the heroic qualities in his reflective work on the military virtues, *Servitude et Grandeur Militaires* (1835). In these stories a Captain Renaud, who had spent some time as a prisoner of war on Collingwood's ship, reminisced about Collingwood: "At his feet I had learnt all about the sufferings caused by the exile of war, and how far a sense of Duty can triumph in a great heart."[2] He also says of Collingwood, "This imposing Roman life left me crushed by its elevation and touched by its simplicity, even after I had only looked for a single day upon it in all its grave, thoughtful simplicity."[3]

Collingwood was indeed an admiral's admiral, competent in all aspects, mediocre in none. He is a model of self-restraint, a gentleman, above all, in a gentlemen's age. He was a gentleman in the sense that Field Marshal Montgomery's father was to define the species: "You come of a family of gentlemen. You know that word does not signify mere outward retirement. It tells of a refined and noble mind to which anything dishonourable or mean or abhorrent is abhorrent or unworthy."[4] Collingwood was thought to be one of the few not corrupted by the hunt for prize money. He spoke of the spirit of money with contempt. Yet like many gentlemen of the day, he was always mindful of his worth and possessions. He treated the question of his place in the world with great seriousness, and when he died his free estate was valued at 163,743 pounds sterling.

Collingwood had none of the erratic personal and social habits, prejudices, or lapses of self-discipline that Nelson had, and none of the thunders and threats of St. Vincent. Despite Collingwood's reserve, his letters to his family reveal his frustrations and physical trials. It is interesting that from Rodney to Nelson and from Collingwood to Beatty and Sir Andrew Cunningham, letters home have proved an invaluable psychological release for admirals at sea, inevitably somewhat isolated both by geography and rank. Collingwood, with his relentless sense of duty, wore himself to death in the Mediterranean. He led the blockade of Cadiz on a lee shore with dangerous shoals, an operation that had earlier broken the health of St. Vincent. During 1793-1810 Collingwood was in England but one year. In the Mediterranean he never appointed a first captain or Captain of the Fleet. There is with him a sense of functional isolation. So like Jellicoe in 1914–16, who could not delegate, he was desk-bound and worked himself to a standstill. This was his greatest failing.

Collingwood was not a favorite of St. Vincent, although Sir Peter Parker had favored him as well as Nelson. But St. Vincent had no doubt of Collingwood's merit, and Collingwood kept his criticism of St. Vincent to himself.

The duke of Clarence, no mean judge of naval men, who knew Collingwood well, thought him equally great in judgment and abilities to Nelson and having the advantage of a better education. Collingwood was indeed a greater reader than Nelson, although Nelson himself could hardly be described as lacking an inquiring mind. Perhaps the two men reflect the differences in caliber of the grammar schools at Newcastle-upon-Tyne and Burnham. Clarence's view may contain an element of royal exaggeration, but it shows the regard that well-informed men had for Collingwood. Collingwood would certainly have passed with flying colors Richmond's test of an educated officer. One can safely speculate that a good deal of Collingwood's practical naval education came from his great friendship with Nelson, for he observed in commenting on the death of Nelson, ". . . since the year (17)73 we have been on the terms of the greatest intimacy—chance has thrown us very much together in service . . . and on many occasions we have acted in concert—there is scarce a Naval subject that has not been the subject of our discussion. . . ."[5]

Collingwood was a keen disciplinarian. He never knew how to unbend with the men, but he was both dedicated and successful in caring for them and their confidence. He loved mankind in general rather than man in particular. But his lack of personal warmth attracted unfavorable comment. The future Admiral Sir George Elliot,[6] looking back at service under Collingwood, remarked:

I was very many years in company with him and always considered him a selfish old bear. That he was brave, stubborn persevering and determined a officer as was known everyone acknowledged; but he had few if any friends and no admirers. In body and mind he was iron, and very cold iron—in heart I believe the same, except one small soft corner accessible only to his family.[7]

After Nelson's death there seemed only one other outside Collingwood's family who received his affection, his dog Bounce.

Collingwood abhorred corporal punishment and was very reluctant to employ it—a factor differentiating him from Nelson and Hardy. The record of the health of his men was abnormally good. His flagship usually had a complement of eight hundred men and went on one occasion one and one-half years without getting into port. During the whole of that time there were never more than six, generally no more than four, on the sick list. Like St. Vincent, Collingwood, as a matter of professional duty, aimed at getting to know the men as individuals and believed that it was important to get to know the men's names.

Collingwood's humanitarianism extended to treatment of the enemy. His careful attention to the welfare of the Spanish wounded and prisoners after Trafalgar assisted the reputation of England with Spain and was a consequent asset to the subsequent Peninsular War. Collingwood was ascetic, not imbibing wine and spirits. He himself never permitted bad language in others or used it himself. These features of behavior remind us once more that there was a streak of reforming zeal about the admirals of the eighteenth and early nineteenth centuries that goes from Admiral Vernon's grog to Augustus Keppel, who was a humanitarian, and Collingwood and James Saumarez, who played a leading part in the establishment of Sunday schools.[8]

Collingwood's record in action was notable. He played a significant part in the Glorious First of June, when he assumed command in place of wounded officers who were senior to him. At Trafalgar he was given the leading offensive position at the head of the column by Nelson and perfectly executed the plan. After Nelson's death, although he was not immune from criticism for his performance, he ably concluded the Trafalgar campaign in difficult weather and thereafter blockaded Toulon and preserved Sicily from French-inspired attacks.

Yet Collingwood never quite achieved the battle reputation of St. Vincent and Nelson. He failed to bring the French fleet to action, and when the French Admiral Ganteaume[9] did come out, Collingwood failed to find him for lack of information. There is no doubt that if Collingwood had discovered Ganteaume, he would have had a great victory. Collingwood did not have Nelson's same sense of amphibious strategy, but his mission in the Mediterranean to deny it to French naval power, was ultimately successful.

Like Nelson, Collingwood did not approve of rash schemes and unnecessary heroics. Like other admirals of the time, he had a cross to bear in having Sir Sidney Smith under his command on occasion. (I will have more to say about Smith later.) Collingwood had an excellent appreciation and apprehension of risks and disapproved of poor judgment in these matters. An example of this attitude can be seen in his letter to Vice-Admiral Thornborough from the *Ocean*, off Syracuse on October 18, 1807:

The practice of detaching boats on a distant service out of the protection of the ship, is a cruel thing to gallant young officers, who do not like to return, even when their judgment dictates to them that they ought. They are enterprises highly injudicious to the public service because they disable the ship from performing her real duty; and they are discouraging to the men, because they shew even to those of the least observation that they are schemes not directed by judgment.[10]

After Trafalgar the Mediterranean became like an English lake, although the French fleet was by no means physically destroyed and piracy remained prevalent. Collingwood presided over English fortunes there and showed his third outstanding quality, a political sense, which displayed itself in his skill as a negotiator. In this he was superior to Nelson, being less prone to personal predilections. He kept the court at Naples at arms' length, taking a more comprehensive view of the demands of the Mediterranean than Nelson had, and was three years in charge of that theater of war before he paid a personal visit to the king of Naples.

The role of naval leadership in the Mediterranean was not like that in the Channel. The commander of the Mediterranean fleet, exercising British power in a mobile way, had a complex role to fulfill. He had to keep in touch both with the home government and with British representatives over a wide area, at time when communications from Britain were often late. Collingwood fulfilled St. Vincent's dictum that the Mediterranean required an officer of splendor. It was a lake of potentates ranging from the Dey of Algiers and the Bey of Tunis to the sultan, the pope, and the Austrian government. Collingwood was the only British representative in the area who could contemplate the Mediterranean as a whole, and he might be seen as a kind of proconsul in the best traditions of the British Empire. He had to cope with many loose directives from home, the Cabinet did not always have a clear policy, and time and again Collingwood correctly anticipated policy.

Like Nelson, Collingwood had a low view of the British consular service, and the government at home came to value his opinions on a multitude of questions, many of which they might otherwise have secured from civilian representatives. His advice was secured on the question of regulation of trade, and he became the British government's Mediterranean expert par excellence and was de facto their main representative there. It may have been a sense of his own indispensibility that led him to allow the British government to exploit his sense of duty. He stayed in the Mediterranean beyond his time, when his health was failing.

Collingwood was a thoroughbred human being who suffered from the frailties of human nature with sadness but good grace. He had always been like that. Writing to Sir John Orde on May 29, 1793, regarding an inquiry into Orde's conduct in Dominica, Collingwood commented:

> I have seen enough of men to know how closely they are attached to their individual interest— and with what virulence they are capable of acting towards those who oppose Justice to the execution of their schemes. Men of honour and integrity in a high publick station will ever be obnoxious to a certain description of people. . . .[11]

He accepted stoically what he saw. Men were ever thus.

It was, of course, Nelson rather than Collingwood who dominated the imagination of the nineteenth and early twentieth centuries. But it was Collingwood's standards that the orthodox and the disciplined could more realistically emulate. Without histrionics Collingwood performed everything his government wanted him to do. If ever another Collingwood was produced, it was Jellicoe, who had to suffer in his career far greater professional frustration, although no more stress, than Collingwood.

chapter 7

THE AGE OF NELSON—
ALSO TAKING PART—
LESSER MORTALS

Our study of British naval leadership in the Nelson period has concentrated on the most notable leaders: St. Vincent, Nelson, and
Collingwood. The British fleet, however, was so active and its activities so widespread in this era that it would be wrong to to beyond these
years without casting at least a cursory glance at other admirals, some
of whom in a less distinguished period might have made a greater impression on the public mood and memory. All of them illustrate the
challenges, if not always the achievements, of naval leadership. The
figures themselves give a good general idea of the numbers of high-
ranking officers in these years. In 1793 there were 55 officers of flag
rank; by 1804, 123. In 1797 there were 446 post captains; in 1804,
673.[1]

There was in such a large fleet a group of important admirals who
were outside the magic circle of fame and approval, not because of
lack of social position or lack of professional skill, but either because
they never had the full confidence or enthusiasm of their colleagues
and subordinates, or never won the full approval of St. Vincent, or
never managed to seize the imaginative enthusiasm of the British
public. Those who are outside the inner elite are an amorphous group,
but they contain some interesting characters, the most colorful being
Sir Sidney Smith. Their careers generally illustrate the obvious point

Sir Sidney Smith as he might like to be remembered. By J. Eckstein.
(Courtesy National Portrait Gallery)

that an admiral who is at odds with his colleagues or superiors may do his career harm and limit his contribution to the national welfare. James Saumarez is a case in point. He was a notable member of a notable naval family originating in the Channel Islands. As has already been seen, he never found favor with either Nelson or St. Vincent, despite his abilities. In this case, St. Vincent's prejudice against an obvious aristocrat delayed rather than hindered the progress of Saumarez's career, and his main individual achievement was his service as commander-in-chief of the Baltic, 1808–12.

In the case of Sir Sidney Smith, we have a highly talented if unself-disciplined individual and a career full of brilliant and less brilliant achievements and remarkable escapades. *Panache* is the appropriate word for him. Throughout British military and naval history there are awkward yet brilliant figures who infuriated the authorities and their colleagues, yet on occasions illuminated the scene with the excellence of their performance and delighted the public with their achievements. Sir Sidney Smith was one of this breed. He seems at times to be like Nelson carried to excess, without quite having Nelson's greatest gifts of leadership. Smith was a firm believer in new approaches to naval problems.

His escape from a French prison,[2] aided by the infatuated daughter of a jailor and perhaps by just the hint of possible marriage, is a picaresque incident to which only a John Buchan or Rafael Sabatini could have done full justice. Sir Sidney Smith's enthusiasm for combat and his impatience with more cautious minds presages the attitude of Roger Keyes in the twentieth century, and yet his achievement was much more successful than Keyes. Smith was never liked or trusted by his superiors or colleagues. He had the unusual distinction of upsetting both Nelson and Napoleon. Nelson wrote on January 22, 1795, referring to Sir Sidney: "... Great talkers do the least, we see."[3] Napoleon complained that Sir Sidney Smith had marred his destiny at Acre. This was not a mere passing wound to the Napoleonic *amour-propre*. The memory of Smith continued to irk Napoleon, who described him as a deceitful intriguer and instructed historians writing of the period to change what they had written, because they had given too much credit to a man who did not deserve it. In his time Sir Sidney managed to outrage not only Nelson and Napoleon, but St. Vincent; Sir John Moore;[4] the British general of Peninsular War fame, Lord

Strangford;[5] the British minister resident at Buenos Aires; and many lesser men.

Nelson himself had not been conspicuous for his modesty, but Sir Sidney became a byword for his inflated view of himself and his unpredictable ways. In 1789 he volunteered for service with the Swedish government, and then, in 1790, he irritated the authorities at home by posing as the sole intermediary between the Swedish and British governments. In 1793, while on half pay, he persuaded Hood to employ him at Toulon, but, when instructed to destroy some French ships, did not make any great success of the task.

Smith shone brightest when the hand of higher authority was light and remote, as in his greatest coup—the raising of the siege of Acre in 1799.

In 1798 Smith had been appointed, with his brother Charles Spencer Smith, joint plenipotentiary at the porte. His sense of authority knew no bounds and he proceeded to constitute himself a commodore. In 1800, purporting to exercise his powers, he made an agreement with the French general Kléber,[6] the Treaty of El Arish, regarding the French evacuation of Egypt. The treaty was subsequently disowned by Keith, who was, nominally at any rate, Smith's superior in the Mediterranean, and it was disowned by the British government, too. This lack of support was not completely fair to Smith as the man on the spot, who thought he had a special diplomatic authority. But the authorities were never sure what Sir Sidney Smith was about to do next. Sand appears to have an unpredictable effect on British behavior as can be seen in the career of Lawrence of Arabia in the twentieth century. It is not inappropriate to see Smith as a suitably baffling forerunner to Lawrence.

From 1806 Smith was in command in the central Mediterranean under Collingwood. Smith's enthusiasm and individuality must have seemed a mixed blessing to Collingwood, who was disconcerted by Smith's leaning to unorthodox forms of warfare such as rocket boats and shrapnel shells. Collingwood was also harassed by Smith's administrative laxity and negligence in sending information. Smith had a habit of disappearing with his ship, the *Pompée*, so even his own captain and the military commander had no idea where he was or what he intended. In 1808 Smith was in Sicily, and like many adventurers before him, he found it to be fertile terrain. He had himself appointed the viceroy of Calabria. Queen Maria, who had been fascinated by Nelson, now found Smith a new source of interest and attempted to exploit his enthusiasm. Smith organized the relief of Gaeta, showing that he had not lost his flair for attack. As we have seen, in direct contrast to Smith, Collingwood had given the court at Palermo a very wide berth.

How does this miscellany of incident throw a light on the theme of naval leadership? Certainly élan in a leader usually means he is not totally without friends. Smith, despite his ruffling of authority, was never bereft of supporters, whether they were the denizens of London society after some particularly brilliant, dashing episode, or even Nepean himself, who wrote of Smith on September 27, 1798, to St. Vincent, "You will find a little eccentricity about him and will soon discover his weakness, but I am very much mistaken if he will not find the length of your foot, he is certainly an extremely active intelligent man, and unquestioningly brave."[7] But Nepean was not very persuasive, and it might be said that Smith found the length of St. Vincent's boot rather than foot. In remarking about Smith to Nepean on January 16, 1799, St. Vincent referred to ". . . the romantic colouring of Sir Sidney Smith, who has been in a continual maze, of error and importance from the hour of his giving that fatal advice, to the King of Sweden at Wybourg to this present writing."[8] Later, when he was First Lord of the Admiralty, St. Vincent, writing to Keith, commented:

I cannot comprehend what Sir Sidney Smith means. Your Lordship being more conversant with his mysterious manners may, by the aid of the enclosed copy of the only letter I have written to him four months and a half ago that can in the remotest degree be construed into a Secret Instruction, be able to make out his meaning.[9]

Barham was similarly troubled at the Admiralty over the question of Smith, and we can see why Smith's style of leadership led him to high, but not the highest, command. Again it was Keith who received a comment from the First Lord: "There seems to me such a want of judgment in our friend Sir Sidney that it is much safer to employ him under command than in command."[10]

Once a man gets a certain reputation for difficulty among his colleagues, it may dog him throughout his professional career. Sir Sidney Smith was dogged by his reputation for eccentricity, just as Keyes in the twentieth century was to be dogged by a reputation for lack of brain power. Smith remained distrusted and regarded as a maverick, considerable as his achievement was on land even more than on sea. He never rose higher than second-in-command in the Mediterranean in 1810–12. But he remains as the quintessence of the amphibious admiral—adaptability personified.

Sir John Orde's various problems have already been described at length. Keith was a similar figure whose reputation was never as high as the importance of his commands. He was not a famous admiral in popular memory, because he never fought a major action, but he was certainly an industrious officer. His correspondence shows him to be an indefatigable administrator, concerned with every kind of imaginable and unimaginable detail. Like Orde he made a great fortune in prize money, and Hood had a high opinion of him.

For his capture of the Cape of Good Hope in 1795–96 from the United Provinces, Keith was created a baron, which reminds one that in the French revolutionary and Napoleonic wars, there was enough glory for everyone, and some to spare.

Keith was often unhappy in his relations with his military colleagues and he never developed an easy rapport with Nelson. His tidy mind did not appreciate Nelson's unorthodoxy, and Nelson resented that a man with a much less distinguished record of action was his superior.

Whereas Smith had so much trouble with superior officers, Keith had problems with his subordinates, and the Admiralty had to write to them on a number of occasions reproving them for insubordination to Keith.

Yet Keith did show a quality of naval leadership that was so often revealed in the Nelson period among naval leaders—a political and diplomatic sensitivity. In the Mediterranean he acted like a roving ambassador, using high-flown language to the Dey of Algiers and employing a sense of oriental grandiloquence, which Sir Sidney Smith was also wont to employ and which would have been at home in an Errol Flynn movie script. For example, the power and glory of George III were emphasized in an order for food supplies for the British forces when the Dey was reminded of "The great number of

Warriors which His Britannic Majesty has at present to maintain. . . . "[11] Admirals even further afield than the Mediterranean were called to show such sensitivity well into the nineteenth century. Thus Sir George Tryon was to negotiate a colonial naval defense agreement with several Australian colonies between 1886 and 1887.[12]

Keith also, among his duties, tried with the help of Lord Minto at Vienna to make sense of the chaos and corruption at Leghorn.[13] It was this kind of diplomatic and political responsibility that the admirals of the First World War were not called upon to face and that narrowed their role and focus a great deal. In the First World War most of the leading British naval officers served in the North Sea. That sea, unlike the Mediterranean or even the Baltic, has never been a good school for naval diplomats because it is too near the seat of British power for independent judgment to be exercised. In the First World War the Grand Fleet at Scapa Flow in the Orkneys, or later at Rosyth, was never much more than a long train ride from King's Cross, London.

Two other admirals, Sir Hyde Parker and Sir John Duckworth, occupy a relatively humble place in history. They experienced all the moral discomfiture of men whose colleagues did not hold them in the highest opinion. They deserve, however, a brief comment, if only because they put in perspective and highlight the leadership achievements of officers of the highest caliber of the time.

Sir Hyde Parker's acerbity of temper earned him the nickname of "Vinegar." He remains in the memory, if he remains at all, as Nelson's passive superior at the Battle of Copenhagen, who had to be hastened out of the bed of his young bride to attend to the campaign. Nelson had commented on St. Vincent's appointment of Sir Hyde Parker as commander of the Channel Fleet by saying, "I guess that Lord St. Vincent recommended Hyde Parker in the strongest manner because he wanted to get rid of him."[14] Viscount Hood shared this view of Parker. But a man no more lacks fans than critics, and the young William Parker wrote to his mother on March 20, 1800, "I much fear when Lord St. Vincent takes command of the Channel Fleet it will be the means of Sir Hyde Parker's leaving, a circumstance I shall regret exceedingly, as I have experienced so much attention from him."[15]

Duckworth has already been noted as a good captain, but it was his fate as an admiral to be involved in the abortive attack on Constantinople in 1807. Duckworth's greatest success had been in February

1806 when he fell on the French in St. Domingo Bay. For his achievements on that occasion he was honored by the Jamaica Assembly and
with the freedom of the city of London, but not by the king himself.
Duckworth therefore thought he did not get enough recognition, and
comment was made at the time that so many otherwise notable sea
achievements of that period seemed lacking in recognition when
public attention was focused on Trafalgar. It was as if the public's
appetite for glory had been satiated by Nelson's victories.

At Constantinople, Duckworth was in the middle of a difficult
sandwich of authority, with Keith above and Sir Sidney Smith below,
hardly a trio that guaranteed smooth seas. Yet Duckworth had
favorable factors working for him, one was the enthusiasm of Smith,
who anticipated with relish a land and sea action against the Turks,
another, the condition of the Turkish navy, which was in an even more
decayed and moribund state than the Spanish navy.

He had orders to secure the surrender of the Turkish fleet with the
threat of the destruction of Constantinople. But the situation on the
spot was a much more difficult one than Duckworth's superiors contemplated. Duckworth preferred to negotiate with the Turks rather
than issue an ultimatum, and pleading unfavorable tides and the
strength of the Turkish forts (recently strengthened with the assistance of the French), he withdrew without executing his mission.

Inevitably, unfavorable comment was made on his leadership—this
was after all the reverse of the Nelson touch. But Duckworth had used
that necessary element, leadership discretion, as the man on the spot,
which, if used in an offensive action, would otherwise have been ac-
claimed. However, Duckworth's failure and the reasons for it appear
to have been largely forgotten in the planning of the Dardanelles Expedition over a century later.

Duckworth's lack of speed and boldness put him in that lower rung
of naval leaders of this period, largely forgotten except by the naval
history enthusiast. In a less successful era, his deficiencies and lack of
totally positive record would have appeared less disappointing.

The age of Nelson was a great period of battle experience, of unprecedented naval expansion and unrest among the men. All the
challenges to and opportunities for leadership and all its problems
were crowded into a few years. The qualities required for good naval
leadership remained mostly the same as for other great war periods.

That is, the confidence of colleagues and subordinates, clarity of communication, tactical insight, and the offensive spirit—all were needed. The only difference was that the opportunities for renown were that much greater during the Nelson era.

chapter 8

THE LONG VICTORIAN PEACE

As we have already reached the apogee of performance of British naval leadership, we can now pause to reflect on the era between Trafalgar and the First World War. By looking here at trends, rather than personalities, we can see how much naval leadership was a reflection of an age and a society. The so-called Nelson legacy òr tradition hung heavily over the British navy. This legacy was both a help and a hindrance. It was a help in that the British navy had a quantitative and psychological advantage over all other fleets as a result of Nelson's victories, and it was a hindrance in that the lessons of Nelson and his name were increasingly invoked in a spirit of misunderstanding as the nineteenth century progressed. (This aspect of misunderstanding is also discussed in chapter nine in conjunction with the influence of Admiral Fisher immediately before the First World War.)

The period from the end of the Napoleonic wars to the First World War presents no great scenes of naval action, and therefore no great opportunities for reputations to be made. There was unemployment at the highest level, and distinguished names such as Cochrane and Sir Charles Napier[1] found vent for their talents in the Chilean and Portuguese navies, respectively. In 1815 and 1816 manpower in the navy was reduced from 145,000 to 19,000, and in 1818, 94 percent of the commanders were unemployed. Sir William Parker, for example, never commanded a line of battleships until many years after Nelson was dead, and except as a boy under Howe, he never saw two great fleets closing on one another in battle. Thus by the period immediately before the First World War there were admirals without medals. After Trafalgar the British fleet was unquestioningly paramount. The American War of 1812 gave a few frissons, the capacity of American seamanship being surprisingly underestimated, for, after all, the American seaman was very much a child of the British maritime tradition. At the end of the Napoleonic wars, in point of materiel and personnel, the British navy was superior to all the other fleets of the world combined.

Nelson's confreres—James Saumarez, Codrington, Pellew, William Parker, and Collingwood—never had, after Trafalgar, the same opportunity for glory. Nelson had completed his task too well. Nelson was the heir of Hawke, Rodney, and Hood in tactics and the adjutant of St. Vincent as far as discipline was concerned, but the extent of his own influence as exerted through his subordinates never had the opportunity to be tested in subsequent major conflict after his death.

Although Nelson's influence did not have the opportunity of great battle testing, it was his reputation beyond the grave and the drive to emulate it that both benefited and bedeviled British naval leadership for over a century. Even in Nelson's lifetime, the accretions of anecdote and piety made the real nature of his performance difficult to discern. The unusual personal qualities of the man made him difficult to emulate. Hope remained unfulfilled of a new Nelson and of the dream of ultimate great victory—a dream especially pervasive when Nelson's own contemporaries, who might have injected a little realism into the vision, had departed the scene. The Battle of Trafalgar itself became an obsession with the navy, and as late as 1912 an Admiralty Committee was appointed to try to get a definitive version of the victory. Yet despite all the adulation of Nelson, the tactical principles on which the fleet was trained were by the end of the nineteenth century the very antithesis of his methods. It would have been wiser to have cultivated more Collingwoods or Hoods; pocket St. Vincents— in the sense of keen disciplinarians—abounded.

The legacy of Nelson and his era was a mixed blessing in the development of British naval leadership. But the helpful features of leadership established by the end of Nelson's period, such as a sounder form of discipline, greater attention to the men's needs, and an improvement in health and hygiene, were preserved and extended. On the other hand, the qualities necessary for battle leadership—those associated with Nelson, Howe, Rodney, and St. Vincent—were not given opportunities to flourish among their successors, who never faced anything like an equal foreign naval challenge. No one in the nineteenth century, after Collingwood, had the experience or stature to be termed the heir of Nelson. Nelson's legacy was an example of outstanding professionalism and individual gifts. His sources of victory were confident individuality, flexibility, and the offensive spirit.

Yet the lessons that the Victorian and early twentieth-century navy drew from Nelson were different from this. Nelson, the hero, was revered, but the sources of his success were misunderstood. There was an inordinate concentration on the results of Nelson's method, that is, the total victory, but there was less sensitive appreciation of how this victory came about. In the late nineteenth century and in the first decade of the twentieth century, naval success was invariably seen in Nelsonic terms. Naval historians like Mahan and Laughton, by their method of writing, encouraged the cult of the great naval leader, as if that were all that was needed. Find the hero—the victory is then inevitable!

With the Nelsonic focus success was inevitably seen in Trafalgar-like terms, that is, a massive concentration of big fleets leading to total tactical and strategical annihilation of the non-British fleet. Nelson would have seen nothing wrong in that. But he would have been surprised at the notion that such a victory could be anticipated and planned years in advance. Nelson was a great improviser and seizer of the opportunity of the moment. His successors' attachment to rigidity of both tactics and strategy would have amazed him.

As the nineteenth century progressed there grew a distortion in naval thinking on Nelson's role in British naval success. Nelson had been a big naval figure in an age of big naval figures like Howe, Hood, St. Vincent, and Barham, to recite the litany. The late nineteenth and early twentieth centuries tended to single Nelson out and envisage a second Nelson, for whom they searched, as having supreme authority not only in discipline but in tactics and strategy. The second Nelson would be, according to their view, the inspiration, the unchallenged authority. In fact, the first Nelson had never had this amount of authority or influence. Besides this figure of the second Nelson leading the fleet into Armageddon, the Admiralty, his colleagues, and the rest would merely be little more than providers of the *mise-en-scène*. This concept was misleading. For neither the fleet of Nelson's day, nor Nelson's place in it, had ever been like that. Those projecting this vision of a second Nelson had missed the point that Nelson had had in his era a much more limited role in the naval scheme of things. The advocates of the second Nelson seemed to be generalizing and projecting from a past that never was.

Nelson's individualism was never forgotten by admirers such as Sir John Fisher, but the obsession with the selection and cultivation of the great leader meant that the heresy grew: with one great individual at the helm no other cultivation of individualities was needed. Indeed, there was a denial of the individual initiative of subordinates. This again was not how Nelson would have envisaged either the preparation for or conduct of a battle. The result was that the Victorian navy tended to see its ideal fleet as being one of a hero leading automata. Doubters of this concept like Spenser Wilkinson or Sir Herbert Richmond were less influential than Fisher or Jellicoe.

At the end of the Napoleonic wars, Britain was the world's policeman—on the sea, at any rate. The British navy had perforce to settle down to a diet of suppression of piracy and of minor Mediterranean disorders in general, the ending of the slave trade, and the making of Admiralty charts—all worthy humanitarian activities, but not presenting the highest test of action. Very few opportunities existed for the exercise of leadership in war with maritime powers. Pellew's attack on Algiers in 1816, for which he was made a viscount, was a model of this genre of minor naval activity. A later example of this form of limited action, in modern parlance, was the bombardment of Alexandria in 1882—a debt-collecting expedition it might be called.

The lack of battle experience meant that each war or conflict revealed long-hidden fundamental defects. The Crimean War was a case in point. Sir Charles Napier, the commander-in-chief of the British fleet in the Baltic, said that his fleet was not fit for action. Later Britain was to successfully confront Russia, in 1878, with, in A. J. P. Taylor's words, "a navy of museum pieces."[2] The Royal Navy was not the only one in such a state. The United States Navy was in similar plight in 1875.[3]

The enormous naval reputation of Britain, so richly earned up to 1815, remained seriously unchallenged. Although there was no major action to develop and test great leaders in war, there was much concern over the education and training of officers, the career structure, and the materiel of the fleet. If there was no excitement at sea and no outstanding naval leader produced, there was solid progress at home. It was a time for administrative reform at the Admiralty. The Navy Board, which had been the semiautonomous manager of materiel and dockyards, and which, incidentally, had been the *bête noire* of St. Vincent, was amalgamated with the Admiralty in 1832. The office of First Lord of the Admiralty became the perquisite of politicians, and the post of First Sea Lord arose as the highest professional appointment. Sir James Graham[4] was the most important architect of these administrative changes. Finally, in the ten years of 1857–1867, the modern concept of retirement from the navy evolved. The naval profession could then be said to have become fully modern, that is, a career service.

In true nineteenth-century reforming style there were commissions and committees, for example, the committee of Sir Charles Shadwell[5] in 1870, which investigated officer education. All of them reveal inadequacies of naval education and all of them recommend an increase in the age of going to sea. A naval college, at Greenwich, was proposed but nothing was said about leadership in practice. The right kind of entrant, it was assumed, would automatically produce the right kind of leader. As a result of these inquiries there was more formal academic education for naval entrants. Naval training aped that of the public schools. Critics remained, however. For example, Julian Corbett in the *Monthly Review* of March 1902, in an article entitled "Education in the Navy," referred in scathing terms to the prodigious increase in Latin and compulsory games. The quality of education was probably no higher than in the eighteenth century. The education provided to new naval entrants in the late nineteenth century appears to have been less stimulating than that of the Nelson or pre-Nelson era. Certainly the naval leaders at the end of the nineteenth century lacked the intellectual curiosity and quality of mind of a Nelson, Collingwood, or St. Vincent, whose bedtime reading was seventeenth-century philosophy. Surprisingly, therefore, in view of the attempts at reform, the academic educational standards of naval officers may have fallen in the nineteenth century and not risen again until the reforms of naval education at the beginning of the twentieth century.

But is a formal academic education necessarily related to the effectiveness of leadership? The pragmatic answer is no, not necessarily. Yet academic education can help if it opens up minds and imagination. Much of the nineteenth-century naval education did not.

The nineteenth-century navy saw progress on many fronts, but not on the battlefield or tactical front. In this respect, that is, the production of combatant leaders, the clock had stopped at 1805 or had even gone into reverse. The nineteenth-century navy, indeed the navy up to the First World War, neglected fundamental professional exercises such as strategy and tactics—the study of history, even though there were conspicuous exceptions to this as in the work of Philip Howard Colomb and that of his brother John.[6] The navy developed no staff work. It thus very much lived off the reputation of battles of long ago. The world appeared to take it at its own inflated self-assessment.

There was a fundamental complacency that, despite particular and short-term failings, the great tradition would see the navy through. Sir James Graham was quoted in 1869 (after his death) as having said, in commenting on naval officers and their training:

I cannot express in adequate terms my admiration of the naval character. I think it decidedly the very flower of British society. I think that a naval officer trained from his youth in his profession and master of his profession is one of the noblest and finest characters that the history of the country can produce.[7]

Starved of great action, the Royal Navy concentrated on detailed appearance. Neatness and automatic response were cultivated—show in general with a good deal of "spit and polish" in army terminology. For lack of battles to sift the extraordinary from the mediocre, the emphasis was more than ever on unquestioning respect for seniority, and in a culture of seniority deference was the key trait. Sir George Tryon is generally seen by his critics as a personification of the system of unquestioning obedience. He liked to employ the system of follow my lead without signals. His teasing system of making his subordinates guess his command intentions could and did have dangerous

The face that launched a disaster, Vice-Admiral Sir George Tryon
(Courtesy Radio Times Hulton Picture Library)

repercussions. His personality and principles contributed to his death. Ironically enough, signals were used on that occasion and his fatal signal was not questioned by his subordinates.[8] The result was the disaster of the *Camperdown* in 1893, at which Jellicoe himself, who was in the other ship that collided, the *Victoria*, had to swim for his life. The attitude of Tryon's officers speaks for itself. At the court-martial after the disaster, the three most senior officers said they realized that Sir George's ordered maneuver would be impossible, yet they obeyed it. There were few on the staff who would give candid advice. This veneration of senior officers was bad for British naval leadership in two ways. It deprived the senior officer of critical testing of his ideas by subordinates. It also developed junior officers in an autocratic mold and dulled, slowed, or limited their own development as creative and imaginative leaders.

Even before the middle of the nineteenth century there would be reason to speak of a lack of ingenuity and adaptability on the part of local commanders and the Admiralty. One pronounced act of disobedience and unorthodoxy occurred in 1840, when Napier disobeyed his commander-in-chief, Sir Robert Stopford,[9] off the coast of Syria. His insubordination produced success and he was forgiven, but this incident was very much an echo of an earlier era, and it would be fair to remind ourselves, remembering Mathews and Lestock, that quarreling admirals do not always produce favorable battle results.

Unquestioning obedience did not, however, vanish with Sir George Tryon. Admirals were fierce or remote or both. Many had an aura of arrogance about them. Their quarters were more comfortable and the ships bigger. In August 1909 a midshipman under Sir Berkeley Milne[10] wrote that that Milne was a hell of a snob and would not talk to a midshipman. Well, to a midshipman an admiral might inevitably appear somewhat aloof, yet the remark was representative. Being a snob is a superficial characteristic compared with demanding, unquestioning obedience, but snobbery was a barrier that mitigated against the continuance of the kind of ease of communications with all ranks that Nelson had enjoyed.

In looking fairly at this Victorian and early twentieth-century attitude, it would be wrong to see the navy as nothing but monolithic. Unquestioning obedience in act did not necessarily mean unquestioning obedience of mind in the pre-First World War navy.[11] Moreover, is it fair to praise St. Vincent for being a disciplinarian, yet to blame Tryon for the same attribute? There is a difference, however, between the situations of St. Vincent and Tryon. St. Vincent was dealing with a crisis situation during a major war. Tryon was not. St. Vincent did not, whether he wanted to do it or not, submerge individualism. Tryon's methods did. Also, St. Vincent's contemporaries had an independent source of stature from a fund of actual fighting experience, whereas Tryon's subordinates did not, nor could Tryon himself, claim a similar illustrious record.

Why did the Royal Navy develop this ethos of the silent service—gentlemen all, obedience? As has already been pointed out, the officers of the Nelson and pre-Nelson period were especially noteworthy neither for their good order nor for their obedience. Why, then, did uniformity and orthodoxy so prevail in the late nineteenth-century navy?

The issue of orthodoxy is a crucial one in relation to the question of leadership, as so often a part of the role of leader is to walk a tightrope between obedience to superior instructions and policy on one side, and his own instincts on the other. If he attains a pinnacle of leadership without the habit of questioning, his pattern of leadership may not be enterprising. As has been said in the case of Field Marshal Montgomery, a good leader is often a bad subordinate.

The reasons for this rising orthodoxy and uniformity are diverse, but not necessarily unrelated. They have their sources in the regional origins of the officer class, the change in the ethos of social behavior (rather than any change in the officer class structure), the impact of Victorian cultural orthodoxy, as well as in the nature of naval training and practice. As an accretion to these tendencies of orthodoxy and uniformity, there was a political conservatism, a generally defensive attitude to change.

Just after the end of the Napoleonic wars there had been some slight but significant shift or reactionary trend in the social composition of the navy. Because of the demands of wartime emergency, men had actually risen from the lower deck to become officers. This hint of social mobility disappeared with the end of the wars. The postwar navy was considerably more class-bound than the wartime navy. Its officers and men were principally recruited from the most socially conservative areas, the south and southwest west of England, from counties such as Hampshire and Devon. The thrusting and more radical areas of the country, such as Lancashire and the Midlands, provided relatively few men and officers to the Royal as opposed to the Merchant Navy. No doubt fewer commercial employment opportunities in the South and West made men gravitate into the Royal Navy. However, the industrial areas of England and Scotland did provide one class of serviceman, the engineering class, with the coming of steam, and not surprisingly they were looked upon with unreasonable suspicion by more traditional type of officer. It was one of Sir John Fisher's missions to gain all-round acceptance and recognition of engineers in the Royal Navy even though the Royal Navy managed to avoid the integration of line and engineering officers until after the Second World War.

A sense of professionalism, already present at the beginning of the period, continued to develop in the nineteenth-century navy. Robust characters remained in the service, but personality was exercised within more confined limits. It is not that (the Napoleonic wars apart) the officers entering the nineteenth- and twentieth-century navies necessarily came from a social and financial background different from those of the eighteenth century. The navy of the late nineteenth and early twentieth centuries had every bit of the aristocratic veneer of that of the century before—perhaps even more so. Those who have adorned the service include: Alfred, duke of Edinburgh;[12] Charles Beresford;[13] Louis Battenberg;[14] George V;[15] his elder brother, the duke of Clarence;[16] in later years, Mountbatten;[17] Prince Philip;[18] and now the present prince of Wales[19] himself. Mrs. Worthington[20] may have been warned against putting her daughter on the stage, but never against putting her son in the navy.

Nor was there lack of moneyed men or men who married money. Jellicoe married well when he married Gwendoline Cayzer,[21] and Beatty did even better when he married the only daughter of Marshall Field[22] of Chicago. The story goes that Beatty's wife once offered a replacement from her own pocket for a ship he accidentally damaged, so his career would not be harmed! Not all the admirals of the late nineteenth and the twentieth centuries had private fortunes, but not all had them in the eighteenth century either. However, they all certainly had one other thing in common—social pretension. This emphasis on social homogeneity was not exclusive to the British navy. In Germany the engineering officers struggled at the same time for social and military parity with the executive officers and in 1912 Admiral Ludwig Schröder could say, "The Military Leader does not need intelligence but character."[23]

The navy in the late nineteenth and early twentieth centuries did not witness a new class of professional leaders solely dependent on the navy as their only mode of existence, men who owed all their station in life to the navy.

What had changed the ethos of social behavior? Victorian society wanted order in public behavior as well as order in society. Just as the jobbing and the parasitic element in the Civil Service declined with the Northcote[24]-Trevelyan[25] reforms of 1853 onwards, so did the navy become a more dedicated and ordered service with its own administrative reforms. But the admirals did not cease to quarrel. Beresford and Fisher were every bit as quarrelsome as St. Vincent and Sir John Orde, but the growing qualities of public self-restraint, of superficial harmony and unquestioning order, must have stifled initiative where there was lacking the outside stimulus of war.

In the naval training of the period, the rigors and inadequacies of the training ship *Britannia*,[26] followed by the naval colleges Dartmouth[27] and Osborne,[28] were substituted for the paternal if unpredictable instruction and emulation of the captain.

Outside the navy, and reflecting a similar social and cultural trend, there was a similar ordering of academic education. Under headmasters such as Thomas Arnold, Edward Thring,[29] and Samuel Butler,[30] the public schools became much more ordered places than they were in the eighteenth century, and the emphasis was on the unquestioning acceptance of the instructions of superiors, whether they were masters or prefects. The public schools of the nineteenth century tamed not only the aristocracy but the wealthy upper middle class as well, and they brought both segments of the population together in a more formal mold. The prime ministers Peel and Gladstone were the sons of Lancashire businessmen, but they themselves went to Harrow and Eton, respectively, and then on to Oxford, and never touched commerce.

The aim in Thomas Arnold's concept was to produce Christians and gentlemen instructed by Christians and gentlemen. It was no shibboleth, but a deeply felt concept—not merely a way of regulating surface appearances. It would have been difficult to have fitted a Nelson or even a St. Vincent into this kind of mold, although perhaps Collingwood might be said to have anticipated it. Naval training and books of instruction closely followed, even imitated, the development of the public schools, and prominent headmasters were invited to give their opinions on naval education. These stated ideals prevailed until the end of the First World War. For example, Captain J. W. L. McClintock on October 6, 1918, stated the ideal of a naval officer: "We don't want just superior warrant officers. The Naval Officer has often to represent his Country, to deal in diplomacy, confer with a cannibal king and perhaps entertain Royalty. Hence we need a broad education as well as technical and we do want Gentlemen."[31]

Unfortunately, the qualities of a Christian and a gentleman, when overaccentuated, may stifle initiative, restrict imagination, and create a fear of the trial-and-error approach. The taking of risk might lead to disaster. But although a perpetual evasion of risk might avoid the possibility of anarchy, distress, or disaster, it might also miss the joy of experiment and victory. It would be unfair to single out the Royal Navy as being the only institution that tended to play safe. British industry, and not surprisingly the British Civil Service, indeed the British Empire itself, showed signs of being on the retreat—even if up to 1914 the signals were mixed and the signs of decline were more latent than overt.

The late Victorian and Edwardian generation of young officers, who were senior at the start of the First World War, were active and at times hyperactive; to the point of absurdity in their yearning for action. Egypt, the Sudan, and China were godsends in this respect. Successes at an early age assisted in the rapid rise of Jellicoe and Beatty. Yet the nature of naval training and practice, with its emphasis on order, routine, and hierarchy, stifled individuality and delayed maturity, so the Royal Navy became a mutual self-congratulation society, like a kind of superior Old Boys' Association. It had its jargon, its buffoons, its bores, and its heroes. Views of a man and expectations of a man gained by his fellow cadets at the age of fourteen tended to remain attributed to him for the rest of his life. Often a blinkering of social outlook meant a lack of sensitivity to a changing world. A letter of Admiral Sir Thomas Troubridge[32] to Admiral Henderson reveals this rather narrow cast of mind:

We English are fools. We got on very well by ourselves but since every sort of half caste or foreigner was admitted among our rulers we have always been let down. . . . And now we are in the hands of Welshmen, Irishmen, Scotchmen and all the tribes of Palestine, after beginning the war under Anglo-American and German auspices.[33]

This is indeed a far cry from Admiral Rodney's cosmopolitanism, and Troubridge was venting his professional frustrations on Lloyd George, Louis Battenberg, Winston Churchill, and others—anyone, indeed, who appeared to be different from the norm.

The rising radicalism and socialism and subsequent anticolonialism were generally closed worlds for naval personnel of this class. Fisher and Mountbatten were unusual in their sensitivity to or awareness of the twentieth-century trends. The eighteenth-century admirals, although of the same aristocratic class, thought at least in terms of rival if nonideological parties, whereas the late nineteenth- and twentieth-century naval hierarchy settled into a conventional conservatism. In comparison with the eighteenth-century naval leaders, who often became First Lords of the Admiralty, their Victorian and Edwardian successors seemed to have less responsive political antennae, and their dealings with the world of Westminister or Whitehall seemed more self-conscious and assertively belligerent, as if they had set themselves apart, for fear of contamination from civilian life. In all, the concept of naval leadership had become more restricted in its horizons by the end of the nineteenth century.

chapter **9**

ENTERING THE WAR

When the First World War began, the Royal Navy leadership was steeped in tradition, although not necessarily with a good insight into the past, but it was young—dangerously young—in its lack of battle experience. By the end of the nineteenth century not one naval officer in a hundred had heard a shot fired in action. Typical of this lack of battle experience was Sir Thomas Hornby (1825–95), who rose to be Admiral of the Fleet and was from 1881 to 1882 president of the Royal Naval College.[1] He was recognized as a high authority in naval tactics and strategy but had never seen a shot fired in actual war except as a boy in Acre in 1840. Almost the whole of his service had been in flagships. However, the Royal Navy was not alone in this paucity of action. Its main opponent, the German navy, was similarly untested in battle as well as being similarly subject to social elitism. As one officer said of the Royal Navy at the start of the war, "Not having had a war for a hundred years, we didn't know how to behave in wartime."[2] All were willing, but some like Admirals Carden[3] and De Robeck[4] were just not up to it. Roger Keyes observed that at the unsuccessful attempt on the Dardanelles in 1915, Carden, the admiral commanding the Mediterranean squadron, read a novel or dozed in the evening. Keyes also commented that "Carden was very cold hearted and without an ounce of ambition and he never gave—it never seemed to occur to him to do so—credit to anyone for anything. . . ."[5] This is a very long way indeed from Nelson's warmth and generosity of spirit. De Robeck was praised for his tact and ability to work with the army, but Keyes also said, "He won't realise his limitations." The longer Keyes was with him, the more his estimation of De Robeck declined. There was much deadwood in the higher ranks of the navy at the start of the war.

If subsequent commentators have in the light of the First World War focused on the lack of progress, even retreat, in some naval attitudes in the century from 1805 to 1914, there is no doubt that whatever was the case elsewhere, the navy had progressed in a revolutionary fashion in the field of materiel. Especially in the period 1890–1914 there was gigantic development. The greatest figure in this advance was Sir John (afterwards first Baron) Fisher.

Fisher was never himself a participant in a major fleet action. He was the materiel and administrative admiral par excellence, but he deserves attention in this study because he played a key role in the promotion and advancement of Admiral Jellicoe and the appointment of Jellicoe as Commander-in-Chief of the British Grand Fleet at the onset of the First World War. He is also important in this study of leadership because his concentration on materiel improvements inevitably meant there was less encouragement of imaginative leadership in strategical and tactical terms. A situation had developed where the very success of naval technology tended to reduce overall thinking about the purpose of the ships designed. Also it was felt that new machines made obsolete the old way of waging war.[6] Fisher, like St. Vincent, did not always measure his words. He employed a Carlylean strain of expression. He was a connoisseur of heroes and had a steel engraving of George Washington in his cabin. In any event, the British and the American navies had on the whole common heroes.[7] He was typical of his generation in seeing the expected war with Germany as an all-out war to the death. In this struggle Britain, led by a second Nelson selected by Fisher, would destroy the German fleet in an early and definitive big fleet action. Fisher called this action "The Big Thing."

What recent evidence there had been of great naval fighting seemed to bear out this view. The ravaging of the Russian fleet by the Japanese at Tsushima[8] in 1905 was a political and naval *coup de foudre*. The last great European land war, the Franco-German war, also seemed to point to rapid solutions. Curiously enough, the only naval engagement of that war was between two small ships off the coast of Cuba.

Fisher was both a product and critic in the materiel sense. He was not the last to gather around him men of similar interest and outlook in his work for the development of a new navy. He also had supporters from a wider world, for example, Julian Corbett, the naval historian.[9] Favoritism is the secret of efficiency, Fisher once declared. He elevated what many would consider to be a human frailty into a virtue.

Fisher's personal manner was energetic, even aggressive. Yet his views on the timing and occasion of naval action could be more cautious in practice, as was proved in the First World War. He had negotiated his rise up the greasy pole of the late Victorian navy with dexterity—tenacity might be the more appropriate word. Fisher may have been one who reads men well in a cold light on the way to the top but then sees the men from the top as he wants to see them. Once he attained the highest echelons, he showed neither harmony with his colleagues nor sound judgment of his juniors. Even taking into account the deliberately extravagant style of his language, many of his conclusions seem incredible in the light of subsequent events.

He must have delighted in his own image making. Of Winston Churchill,[10] on parting from him as a colleague in 1915, he said, "He is a bigger danger than the Germans."[11] This occurred on May 17, 1915, as Fisher went into the wilderness, only consoled by the friendship of the duchess of Hamilton.[12] Of Beresford (his Orde), he said, "*Never throw a stone at a yelping cur! He only yelps the more!*"[13] His praise was as lavish as his criticism. Lord Hankey,[14] for example, the bureaucrat par excellence, he saw as having both the genius of Napoleon and the thoroughness of Oliver Cromwell. Hankey in a typically less than generous fashion, in return, saw Fisher as a crank, although he never denied his abilities and thought him the most remarkable man of his day.[15]

Fisher believed it was his responsibility to single out the naval commander-in-chief for the forthcoming German war. He himself was too old for the role, or believed himself to be, but he did know that he was the one who must and would discern another Nelson. His judgment alighted as early as 1905 on Jellicoe. He had known Jellicoe since

1884, and in 1889 Jellicoe had been assistant to Fisher when Fisher had been director of Naval Ordnance. In his choice of Jellicoe as another Nelson, he appears to have revealed a great error of judgment and misunderstanding of history and of the factors that make for the exercise of genius. In Fisher's own words, Jellicoe was to become second-in-command of the Home Fleet, ready to emerge as the future Nelson. In Jellicoe, anyone less like Nelson it would be difficult to imagine.

Fisher saw in Jellicoe a materiel man like himself—a man who understood weapons and promoted them, and that was what war was all about. Fisher thought of himself as a man of action and he also saw Jellicoe in this light. This vision of Jellicoe as a man of action remained long with Fisher, for he wrote to Lord Northcliffe on November 28, 1916, "Jellicoe is unable to talk—he can act!"[16]

After all, Jellicoe in the fleet exercises of 1913 appeared to show that combination of aggressiveness and judgment that was needed. Churchill, impressed by Jellicoe's performance on that occasion, wrote to him: "Only a line to congratulate you on the brilliant and daring manner in which you executed the difficult task entrusted to you in the manoeuvres."[17]

Fisher's obsessive puffing of Jellicoe appears again and again in his correspondence. Fisher believed that he, Fisher, had the key to naval leadership. His understanding was based on much consideration of the past, but in applying the standards of the past to the present, there seems to have been in him an element of self-deception—even hallucination.

There were doubters about Jellicoe, and a letter from Admiral Sir Francis Bridgeman[18] to Fisher on December 4, 1911, points out the limitations in Jellicoe's outlook:

He has had no experience of fleet work on a big scale, and is so extremely anxious about the work in it that he really does too much. He must learn to work his captains and his staff more, and himself less! At present he puts himself in the position of, say, a glorified gunnery lieutenant. This will not do when he gets with a big fleet. He must trust his staff and captains, and if they don't fit, he must kick them out![19]

These limitations were exposed when Jellicoe was in command of the Grand Fleet.

Sir Francis's comments do not seem to have made much impact on Fisher. A few comments from his letters illustrate Fisher's belief in Jellicoe. In a letter to Spender[20] in 1911, he wrote, "SIR JOHN JELLICOE IS THE FUTURE NELSON—he is *incomparably* the ablest Sea Admiral we have—perhaps better than Battenberg—yet I should say he is so—so it's important to get him Second-in-Command of our main Fleet."[21] On December 14, 1911, he said: "All I cared for and wished for was that Jellicoe should be Commander-in-Chief of the Home Fleet on December 19, 1913 and THAT now is automatically fixed."[22] The Nelson theme continues on December 26, 1911: "Jellicoe about the same age as Nelson at Trafalgar and possesses all Nelson's attributes except Lady Hamilton, and there I sympathise with him!"[23]

In the following year Fisher returned to the Nelson parallel on April 2: "If war comes before 1914, then Jellicoe will be Nelson at the Battle of St. Vincent, if it comes in 1914 then he will be Nelson at Trafalgar."[24]

In the light of our afterknowledge, Fisher's comments seem then, even for him, wild in nature. Yet Fisher had some justification for his enthusiasm for Jellicoe. Jellicoe in his performance at the Admiralty, and especially with respect to the development of the dreadnought, had done a first-class job. Jellicoe had been a gunnery expert at a time when gunnery was in vogue. Fisher appreciated Jellicoe's mental ability used in employing cogent and convincing arguments in support of Fisher. Above all, Jellicoe had been loyal to Fisher!

Whether Jellicoe would make his mark in action was a matter of speculation. It is really in the incorrect assessment of future potential that Fisher should be faulted, for he claimed to be a prophet and some of his predictions were indeed fulfilled. Fisher therefore must be judged at his own face value. He had a great failure of imagination and saw Jellicoe as the great Nelsonic leader of a great fleet in action—a flight of fancy in that Jellicoe's record was based on performance as a highly competent developer of naval armaments. Fisher is also open to criticism for the strength of conviction of his misplaced judgment and for the retention of this long after events would seem to have suggested otherwise. I return to this question in the next chapter after concentrating on Jellicoe himself, for the whole issue brings into question the standards and performance of naval leadership at the highest level of this period.

The main action of the war, when it came, was in the North Sea with the Battle of Jutland in 1916. There was after the war, indeed during it, an inordinate amount of hand wringing and inquest work about why Jutland had not been another Trafalgar, since its conclusion seemed so indecisive. Jutland, depending on one's view of it, became an indictment of, or justification of, the outlook and methods of the prewar navy. The concentration of comment on this battle was so great because there were no other naval engagements of similar scale during the war. It was the set piece of the naval war. The army had far more action—perpetual action, in fact—and far more disasters on which to meditate. The Somme in 1916 and Passchendaele in 1917 were more inept displays of leadership than Jutland, but they never attracted the same amount of professional calumny. The navy had, however, before the war heightened expectations. Great was the expectation from a naval engagement, and great was the disillusion after it. Perhaps the sheer horror of the Western Front put it beyond the realm of normal criticism, although, between the wars, Liddell Hart,[25] Fuller,[26] and many others pondered on how it could have been avoided.

The navy expected that the German High Command would seek an early engagement with the Grand Fleet in any future war and that there would be a grand British victory. This simplistic view of a future naval war between Germany and Britain prevailed at the highest levels of the Admiralty. It was based on the British superiority in size of fleet, on a confidence going back to Nelson's day, and on an underestimation of the caution of the German High Seas Fleet. As it turned out, the German Fleet only infrequently put to sea, as it did not want to risk the chance of defeat by a superior enemy. For the British fleet the alternative concept of the close blockade of the type of the Nelson-St. Vincent era was impossible in the age of submarines and mines. Jellicoe and Beatty reciprocated with the same caution and were unwilling to gamble with their larger fleet.

There was, too, a misunderstanding by the British of the role of the navy in the German scheme of things. The German navy did contemplate before the war a grand naval engagement with the British when war came, but the German navy was not in the forefront of German strategic and tactical thinking. The German army was the pride of the German Empire, both its spearhead and hammer. The German High Command was satisfied with the German navy, of necessity, playing a much more subordinate, defensive and negative role.

Looking at the critics of the British performance at Jutland, we see that the views of A. C. Dewar and K. G. B. Dewar and those of Commander W. G. Tennant, who exhaustively examined the battle, amounted to the same. Said the Dewars: "Centralised and mechanical command became the vogue and officers were moulded to a system which had been responsible for most of the errors and failures of the eighteenth century."[27] Tennant agreed: "Perhaps one of our greatest errors was the accepting everything we found it and just carrying on—shells, armour, tactics. . . . We had got back to the rigidity of the line of battle to much the same extent as it existed in the 17th and 18th centuries."[28] The sense of flexible aggressiveness developed in the period 1783–1805 had been completely lost. Nelson is mentioned, too, by the Dewars, and in a footnote they say, "Nelson introduced the perfect system based on offensive action, decentralisation of command and co-operation as opposed to mechanical obedience."[29] However, in his appreciation of the battle, Tennant said that of those who fought at Jutland and made the fewest mistakes, Jellicoe and Beatty were at the top of the list.

chapter 10

JELLICOE AND JUTLAND

Jellicoe was the Uncle Arthur of admirals—a Christian, a gentleman, and a good cricketer to boot.[1] He was a man of whom it could be difficult to make a hostile and unfriendly comment. In the orthodox sense of the word, he was very much a Victorian. He was a man of the prewar armament era, the age of the dreadnought. He was a manager rather than a heroic leader—the rising star of the managerial revolution. He was the personification of the naval dogma of his time. Professionally, in his lack of fighting experience, he could be described as one of the victims of the long Victorian peace.

Yet it might be argued that major fighting experience, if not reflected upon in an intelligent and farseeing way, is little better than no fighting experience at all. Certainly experience may mean a general or admiral fighting yesterday's wars in today's situation. In Jellicoe's case we have to ask ourselves if earlier experience of prior command in action would have assisted his leadership in the First World War. It is a moot point. Perhaps not, for he lacked flexibility and he lacked an inquiring mind. The experience of the Boer War did not necessarily prepare British generals for the Western Front. A lot depends on the type of earlier fighting experience. In contrast, the admirals of Nelson's day had been fighting round after round against the same enemy, the French. But certainly earlier fighting experience of a major war

Admiral Jellicoe and Admiral De Bon of the French Navy, 1917
(Courtesy Radio Times Hulton Picture Library)

against a major power can be of psychological importance, giving some sense of anticipated demands, even if it might not give strategical or tactical insight.

At the age of fifty-four, Jellicoe was precipitated into the leadership of the Grand Fleet in place of Sir George Callaghan[2]—not without protest from himself and many other senior officers—for there was a case for the retention of Callaghan, and not merely on sentimental grounds. Callaghan knew best his fleet and had long experience at sea with it, but Jellicoe was due to succeed Callaghan in December of 1914, so the date was brought forward. The ostensible reason was the medical condition of Callaghan; the real reason, as we have seen, was Fisher. Two months later, in October 1914, Fisher was to become First Sea Lord in place of Louis Battenberg, who had fallen a victim of Teutophobia and his professional critics.

Jellicoe had no prior experience of leadership in major battle. Yet he was in charge of the greatest fleet in history and the great victory of the war was expected from him, at least as far as the British Empire was concerned. Although he had to prove his power of battle leadership, he had, at least, no need to prove his own personal bravery. He had a heroic record during the Boxer Rebellion, which had left a bullet in his lung in 1900, not discovered by X-ray until 1934.

Jellicoe must, because of his position, be judged by the very highest criterion of naval leadership. He was responsible for a much bigger proportion of the British fleet and a much bigger fleet than Nelson ever was. If Nelson had been defeated at Trafalgar, a stronger fleet in being could have taken its place—not so in the case of Jellicoe at Jutland. In the whole British scheme of things, Jellicoe was of far greater importance relative to the military than was his counterpart in Germany.

The first quality to consider is the question of Jellicoe's confidence in his officers and men and theirs in him. As far as the men were concerned, Jellicoe had the same ability to attract loyalty, even affection, as Nelson possessed. Survivors of Jutland still speak warmly of Jellicoe over half a century later. The cries of distress that went up from ordinary seamen on his leaving the Grand Fleet at the end of 1916 were deeply felt.

One could hardly see the army in France beckoning to Sir John French, Sir William Robertson,[3] and Field Marshal Haig in such terms! Jellicoe received, years after his period as commander-in-chief, correspondence from former men of the Grand Fleet. For example:

November 25th, 1918   FROM H. L. HOWES 30 MALLISON ROAD
                         CLAPHAM JUNCTION SW 11.
. . . I speak for many discharged soldiers and sailors and assure you that the general feeling is strongly of opinion that it should have been you standing on the bridge of the "Iron Duke" to receive the enemy's surrender. . . .[4]

The men of the lower deck did indeed like Jellicoe. More than the other admirals he seemed to have rapport with them. Jellicoe was not a poseur, not an image maker; ordinary men could relate to his very lack of the extraordinary and yet respect him for his professionalism. Thus H. K. Oram wrote:

. . . though Admiral Jellicoe had not the presence of Beatty. . . he nevertheless gave an immediate impression of knowledge, judgement and, above all human understanding. . . . I shall never forget the small figure of the Admiral springing up the accommodation ladder with the agility of a robin to stand, alert and smiling, to acknowledge our salute. A short visit, unrehearsed and informal, but it made a striking impact on the ship's company.[5]

The men always thought it was Jellicoe's fleet, never Beatty's, even after Jellicoe had left it.

Even in making discount for the effusive style of the time and the conventional praise for a very senior admiral, there was obviously a deeply felt trust in Jellicoe as a leader of quality. Indeed, at his most effective, Jellicoe could give a good impression to his most important subordinates. Thus Beatty wrote to his wife on May 21, 1915, "I saw several friends at Scapa, gloomy most of them. The most cheerful man there is the C-in-C who thank God is well, very well, and as bright and as far seeing as one could wish but I do wish he were not so *simple* and charitable."[6]

Jellicoe's secret was firmness with kindness, but not mildness. Sir Charles Dreyer,[7] writing in two letters to Chatfield, sums up the picture. On December 30, 1933: "I wrote an Essay on 'Discipline.' That can be read to contain 'I told you so,' and I quoted Lord Jellicoe to show I relied on modern practice and of [*sic*] a great man when I ventured to advise how Discipline could be maintained with kindness in a modern Navy."[8] On October 15, 1936, Dreyer returned to the theme of whether Jellicoe was a mild man: "That is precisely what he was not—but he had the most *enormous* self-control. When angry he became silent—whenever that was with me—I wilted on the stalk and would have preferred a couple of dozen!"[9] This self-control took a toll, no doubt, on Jellicoe's nervous system. But whatever the ravages of the war Jellicoe remained a very trusted and popular commander whose personal appearance was received by acclamation when the men gathered together whether for a boxing show at Scapa or more serious purposes. Sailors living in a closely knit community tend to be suspicious of new authority and loyal to the memory of the old, but when he replaced Callaghan, Jellicoe quickly established a moral authority over the Grand Fleet, and his memory was revered.

We have established that Jellicoe possessed one very useful attribute of leadership, a good relationship with the ordinary seaman. We shall examine his relationship with his immediate subordinates. Here the picture is not such a cloudless one.

The Grand Fleet was not of his making, and for the most part he had to take his senior officers as he found them. He considered his vice-admirals as "always a little shaky,"[10] to use his own words, and he later wrote, "Burney[11] [is] very safe, though possibly over-cautious. Bayly[12] is I fear occasionally a little mad. Sturdee[13] is full of fads. Warrender[14] is too deaf."[15] History shows that Sir Frederic Sturdee and Jellicoe detested each other.

Sir Charles Madden,[16] his brother-in-law, Jellicoe trusted, but there is no impression that anything Jellicoe saw in his period with the Grand Fleet, 1914–1916, increased his confidence in his subordinates. The main complaint against him was that he did not rely enough on them. He had his own good reasons not to. As the war went on, the materiel of the fleet improved and the experience of senior officers inevitably improved, but their level of excellence remained thinly spread, and the general level of command did not rise.

Jellicoe's reluctance to delegate meant that he worked inordinate hours. His remark to Beatty in a letter of June 4, 1915, tells its own story: "Please forgive a typed letter, but my hand is worn out with writing."[17]

Jellicoe did not have the good digestion and sleeping powers of an optimist, qualities that Brigadier General Sir John Smyth says are needed in war.[18] All of these trials, all of this overwork with the concomitant ill health and frustration, increased Jellicoe's innate caution until it became a very distinct and pervasive pessimism. Even Jellicoe's advocate Admiral Bacon recognized this trait in him. However, in fairness to Jellicoe, in assessing him as a war leader, it should be said that his pessimism reached a culmination at the Admiralty in 1917, rather than earlier with the fleet.

Jellicoe failed to sort out the big from the little: the Nelsonic and Napoleonic simplicity eluded him. Hence at Jutland there was a plethora of signals and instructions and a failure of communication in which Jellicoe himself, Beatty (who was in command of the battle cruiser squadron at the time), and the Admiralty were all at fault. Beatty pointed out this fussiness of Jellicoe some months after Jutland: "... messing about finicky things and consequently the big questions got slurred over or overlooked altogether."[19]

This lack of understanding between Jellicoe and Beatty cannot be completely unrelated to their rarity of meeting before Jutland. Again and again Beatty asked for a meeting. In replying on one occasion to Beatty's request for more contact, Jellicoe commented, "I should indeed like to have an opportunity to have a yarn but I assume that is impossible."[20] On April 14, 1916, Beatty wrote:

I am afraid I have given you a terrifically long letter to consider but I do not write you to burden you with unnecessary detail. And the points I have dwelt upon appear to me to be of very great importance. More especially ... the desirability of my being acquainted ... with all your views and those of the 1st Sea Lord on the subjects which are of paramount importance.[21]

This theme of the need for community of thought was a frequent strain in Beatty's letters, even when Beatty became commander-in-chief of the Grand Fleet and Jellicoe was at the Admiralty. Beatty wrote on June 27, 1917, "What we want is closer Communion between you and I and between us we can knock at [out?] any hare brained schemes. I will come down and see you if necessary but we must collaborate. There can be no question of any difference of opinion between us."[22]

The impression from their correspondence is that there was an eagerness by Beatty to be of the same mind and outlook as Jellicoe, but that they were never naturally in communion, despite good intentions on both sides. Jellicoe was always so busy. Beatty never felt himself to be a devotee of Jellicoe, and, being of a more exuberant nature than Jellicoe, must have found the latter's relative remoteness irritating. Jellicoe could not infect his senior subordinates with enthusiasm in the way that Nelson so readily did.

In the end, Beatty without publicly showing his distress, privately lost patience and came to the conclusion that Jellicoe did not want men of talent too close to him. Beatty, no doubt reflecting on his past experience of Jellicoe at sea, as well as at the Admiralty, wrote to Lady Beatty on May 13, 1917: ". . . Jellicoe is absolutely incapable of selecting good men because he dislikes men of character who have independent views of their own. . . ."[23]

This criticism by Beatty of Jellicoe may have had a sense of the extreme, a reflection of Beatty's frustration in other directions—the kind of explosion a man in wartime makes in writing to his wife. But with Jellicoe at the Grand Fleet, and later at the Admiralty, there is a sense of mental isolation, not only from the politicians with whom he never was at home, but from his own senior officers. Moreover, Jellicoe never went out of his way to seek mental stimulus from others or from history itself. On May 15, 1917, Sir Herbert Richmond wrote that Beatty had told him that ". . . Jellicoe's ignorance of war was astonishing. He had never read a book in his life before the war."[24]

On the scores of decisive clarity of exposition, confidence in subordinates and communication with them, Jellicoe can therefore be faulted. But it is by his performance at Jutland that he has so often stood or fallen. The battle reflects his ingrained caution or even fundamental pessimism, although he exhibited his normal high standard of professionalism, especially in his forty five-degree effective turn away from the German fleet at the crucial moment, when torpedoes were coming in his direction.

Jellicoe remained convinced before and after Jutland that the only possible decisive action was one of big fleet gunnery, in daylight, and that no risks should be taken to ensure that it would be a success. That is, care should be taken to ensure that it was not a failure, and that the fleet was substantially preserved. Jellicoe was rigidly attached, indeed dedicated, to the single line-ahead battle formation. In this he had powerful supporters, including Sir Arthur Wilson,[25] the foremost

fleet tactician of the day, Fisher, and Beatty. Jellicoe attempted to
control in every tactical detail a great fleet. He thought in terms of a
cut-and-dried plan applicable only to one set of circumstances. The
contrast with Nelson's concept of the pell-mell battle is obvious.
Jellicoe worried about anything that threatened the status quo,
especially mine fields and submarines. On October 30, 1914, he
wrote: "If for instance the enemy battle fleet were to turn away from
an advancing Fleet, . . . I should assume that the intention was to lead
us over mines and submarines, and should decline to be so drawn."[26]
It is not, however, surprising that Jellicoe had such anxiety, especially at the onset of the war, as he was leading a fleet full of new
materiel whose performance powers had still to be battle tested.

On Feburary 5, 1915, Sir Alexander Duff[27] wrote in his private
journal, at a time when Burney was acting commander-in-chief, as
Jellicoe was having a minor operation in a nursing home:

Burney is a much more tactful C-in-C. By that I mean he is not subject to the
excursions and alarums that take possession of our C-in-C. With J, the faint-
est rumour of a submarine sets the whole fleet in motion and he gives one the
impression that it is Jellicoe's reputation that is being constantly safe-
guarded.[28]

The predominant mood at Scapa Flow and Rosyth was one of worry.
It was a contrast to the joyful enthusiasm for battle that had been so
widespread in the more innocent early days of the war, especially
among the junior officers.

There was never a serious search for an alternative to the orthodox
strategy of Jellicoe and his supporters. Strategy was not his final responsibility in the years 1914–1916, but he and the Admiralty shared
an ossification of view, and the sideshows against Constantinople or
the purported schemes against Pomerania were never taken all that
seriously while Jellicoe was in charge of the Grand Fleet. Everything
was focused on Fisher's "Big Thing," and that Big Thing was to be in
the North Sea.

Jellicoe's pessimism does not make for exciting reading. His com-
ment on Lloyd George on April 17, 1917, when Jellicoe was First Sea
Lord and Lloyd George was prime minister, reveals the bleakness of
Jellicoe's outlook, an outlook no doubt aggravated by the nervous

strains of the war. "He is a hopeless optimist. . . ."[29] he remarked of the prime minister. Well, certainly someone had to be that in one of the most depressing years in the twentieth-century experience of the British people. Jellicoe had a storekeeper's approach to the naval war. He seems to have reversed Napoleon's dictum that in war the moral is to the materiel as three to one. For Jellicoe it seems to have been at least one to three. In recent times there was a similar flaw in the American approach to Vietnam, when there was too great of a reliance on the efficacy of technology and fire power.

On January 25, 1916, Jellicoe wrote to Balfour, then first lord of the Admiralty, ". . . in my opinion, the only possible naval offensive that can be contemplated does not now appear to be one which offers the prospect of much success if carried out."[30] While commander-in-chief, Jellicoe could not suggest anything particularly useful in dealing with the submarine menace. His lack of success had a part to play in the fall of the Asquith ministry at the end of 1916.

One has the impression that, at least for a few months at the end of the year 1914 and in the early months of 1915, Whitehall had more fire in its belly than had Scapa Flow. Fisher made aggressive noises as First Sea Lord, and Churchill, as ever, was restlessly searching for new directions in strategy, but the commander-in-chief was already displaying an ingrained caution. After Fisher and Churchill had departed, there was no one of similar authority or temperament to spur Jellicoe on.

So in action and command Fisher's putative Nelson turned out to be one of the most cautious naval leaders in British history. His caution was based on the whole strategy of the big confrontation. This big confrontation was to be so big it had to be successful. Thus, in preparation, the fleet must not be diminished. Jellicoe and his professional superiors and the British public believed the British fleet was the strongest card in the Allied pack. Jellicoe was determined not to throw it away on minor engagements where there was any risk of his superiority being destroyed. As the war went on, the fleet became the biggest British instrument in a war of attrition rather than the spearhead of decisive victory. It took time for Jellicoe's generation, if not Jellicoe himself, to realize the implications of this change of role.

Jellicoe's friends rallied to his cause, and after Jutland there were conventional sentiments of praise, but the greater the period elapsed after the battle, the more expressions of disappointment and criticism were vented, until in the hands of harsher critics like Richmond, the Jutland episode became a focal point of criticism not only of Jellicoe but of the whole policy of the post-Victorian navy up to that time. Unfortunately, personalities became involved, and a rather arid dispute about Jellicoe's and Beatty's respective responsibility for the lack of success and a comparison between the two admirals, made commentators take sides not only for purely professional reasons.

Keyes and Chatfield, who were not basically hostile to Jellicoe, came to a reasonable conclusion after the war on the question of Jellicoe's reputation. They agreed that Jellicoe had failed to seize the great opportunity before him on May 31, 1916, and that he had failed to make any dispositions or give any instructions that would bring the enemy to action at dawn on June 1 (1916).[31]

This is not meant to be a study of Jellicoe in his political attitudes, but a man who was commander-in-chief of the largest fleet in the world inevitably had to have some kind of public presence. In this field, Jellicoe, so popular with the men, seemed gauche in his dealings with the world beyond Scapa Flow and unwilling to expose himself to new notions. Jellicoe's inability to conceive solutions to new war situations rapidly and his rigid pattern of leadership were aspects of an attitude that was generally conservative. He was also unwilling for his views to be exposed to criticism and comment, indeed to evaluation. The cut and thrust of the political world was particularly abhorrent to him. An office above controversy was another matter, and he eagerly grasped at the opportunity of being governor-general of New Zealand after the war. In New Zealand, Victorian England was preserved well into the twentieth century and Jellicoe was very much of a Victorian.

Jellicoe's public persona was unsatisfactory. He was typical of his naval generation of officers in being anti-Liberal and anti-Socialist. He was also extremely suspicious of the press—of whatever political label. Journalists and lawyers he held in contempt. No doubt he had suffered enough from Northcliffe[32] the press lord, from Asquith the barrister, and from Lloyd George the solicitor. Even the pro-Conservative and pro-big-navy journalists like Arnold White[33] found in Jellicoe no friendliness and spirit of cooperation. In this he was a contrast to Fisher, who loved to feed the press. It has been said that Jellicoe and Wilson were high priests of the tight-lipped school of admirals. Jellicoe was carried away by a passion for secrecy and wanted censorship of naval news. He rejected the idea of a newspaper correspondent with the Grand Fleet. Balfour wrote to Jellicoe on July 4, 1915, "I have stopped (at your suggestion) all idea of sending up a correspondent."[34] He even deplored professional criticism continuing during the war and wanted the *Naval Review*, a possible source of new or dangerous ideas and criticism, censored or stopped for the duration of the war. For this he earned the inveterate hostility of naval intellectuals such as Richmond. Richmond did not think that Jellicoe had the will to victory and that he was always thinking of what would happen if he was beaten.[35] Jellicoe seems to have confused the very laudable desire to keep naval secrets from the enemy with a stifling of naval debate, which might have vented new political and strategical ideas. Perhaps he was alarmed by the lack of security and political circumspection of the time, for there were hardly any secrets in Asquith's cabinet or, if there were, they did not remain secrets for long.

The preservation of the Grand Fleet had become an obsession with Jellicoe, and a largely static and uneventful war plus his lack of sensitivity to public feeling meant that he became boxed in, in a rather narrow focus.

There was a large, although not as yet quite fully democratic electorate. They deserved much more information about the fleet. They were after all giving much in service and flesh and blood, as well as money. If Jellicoe had had more egotism, more sense of showmanship, he might have wanted the world to know more about what he wanted to do or not do, and his reasons for it. The British public sorely wanted and needed a great victory in June 1916, just as they needed one in 1797 or 1941. But unlike St. Vincent in 1797, or Cunningham in 1941, Jellicoe was not able to provide one. Jellicoe's less spectacular qualities or attention to detail and care of his men diminished under a pall of disappointment. There was much promise rather than performance.

In Fisher's mistaken assessment of Jellicoe, we can learn more about both men. Fisher continued for a large part of the war to see Jellicoe and the fleet in Nelsonic terms. When he expressed disappointment, it was with reference to the Nelsonic example. Writing to Jellicoe on February 7, 1915, Fisher complained, "You must admit that neither on the Scarborough cruise nor on January 24 was there any manifestation of any Nelsonic instinct."[36] Here, Fisher was referring to the way in which the Germans had managed to slip through and bombard Scarborough in December 1914, and to the disappointing performance of the navy in the Dogger Bank action of the following month.

Churchill at an early date became restless with Jellicoe, who kept clamoring for more materiel against a background of disappointing results. Yet Fisher and Jellicoe seemed to be generally at one in their outlook and understanding. Fisher was essentially cautious in his view of the deployment of the Grand Fleet. He could not bear the idea of risking ships in battle. Jellicoe's role, in Fisher's view, was to be with the Grand Fleet, not at the War Council or anywhere else and certainly not at the Admiralty.

Fisher reverted to the Nelsonic theme in an early reaction to Jutland on June 18, 1916: "I hear from an onlooker that your deployment into Battle was Nelsonic and inspired as you could see nothing and that in consequence you saved Beatty from destruction and in one hour (*given vision*) you would have ensured Trafalgar."[37] Fisher's lingering attachment to the theme of Nelson and Jellicoe was shown on March 28, 1917, when he wrote to his good friend the duchess of Hamilton, "I 'went' for Jellicoe and he took it beautifully. I said even Nelson would have made a mess of the German submarine menace— not his line any more than Jellicoe's. Jellicoe's place the Fleet!"[38] Fisher had his vision of Jellicoe with the fleet and he was upset and felt betrayed when Jellicoe went to the Admiralty at the end of 1916. He thought that Jellicoe was never an administrator, anyway. Beatty, as Fisher once told him, was better at that kind of thing. In Fisher's view in March 1917, Jellicoe was incomparably the best admiral for command at sea.[39] One senses that Fisher's continued ring of praise for Jellicoe by this time had a diminishing and increasingly incredulous audience. Jellicoe's reign at the Admiralty seemed to bear out Fisher's lowly view of him as an administrator, but by then Jellicoe was an exhausted man.

Why did Fisher misjudge Jellicoe so much? In defense of Fisher, one need only look at the other admirals in 1914 to see that Jellicoe virtually selected himself as the obvious and inevitable man. If the naval crop of 1914 was not of the Nelsonian vintage, one has only to look at the generals to find equivalent mediocrity. The caliber of generals on the Western Front was not particularly high and they were equally lacking in imagination. Fisher liked a technical man. He thought it was a new age and he was both its Moses and John the Baptist. Jellicoe could go out as Fisher's protégé and test the faith—the faith in the big gun, that is. He believed that a man who performed well in the materiel field would inevitably perform well in battle—would show expertise in the Big Thing—a transferability of leadership qualities, as it were. In selecting a man for a major fleet action, Fisher was inevitably making a decision beyond his own experience. He could only rely on his reading of history and he seems to have got that reading wrong. Yet Jellicoe in many respects was not all that dissimilar from Fisher himself, although very dissimilar in his style of life. Jellicoe was cautious, with little tactical and strategic insight and no sense of staff planning. So was Fisher, despite his aggressive style of communication. Jellicoe shared with his patron Fisher an outlook that belittled the importance of staff work. For Fisher, it was said, a naval war staff was merely an excellent organization for cutting out and arranging foreign newspaper clippings. The commander-in-chief once appointed, in Fisher's view, could carry the ideas, the war plan, around in his head. But if Fisher really wanted a new variety of Nelson, a cautious variety if that were at all possible, he never implied it. There is an unresolved conflict in Fisher's attitude. For although he, as much as Jellicoe, feared the loss of the fleet and had no real heart for unorthodox measures, he always emphasized the value of Nelson's unorthodoxy. He wrote to Beatty on January 31, 1915, "In war the first principle is to disobey orders, Any fool can obey orders!"[40]

Ultimately, Fisher admitted that Jellicoe had no sense of the unorthodox. Jellicoe was certainly not the one to disobey orders. On December 27, 1916, Fisher wrote, "I told the Dardanelles Commission (why they asked me I don't know) that Jellicoe had all the Nelsonic attributes except *one*—he is totally wanting in the great gift of insubordination. Nelson's greatest achievements were all solely due to his disobeying orders."[41] The truth of Jellicoe's fundamental limitations dawned slowly on Fisher, who had staked the latter part of his career on Jellicoe's reputation. Fisher's prophecy in the case of Jellicoe fell far short. He was trapped in his own slogans and had a vision of Jellicoe that did not correspond to reality.

It is at this point, just before we look at the other main naval figures of the war, Beatty and Keyes, that we must consider the question of whether, in putting Jellicoe to the Nelsonic test of leadership, we are being grossly unfair. Were the tactics of breaking the line, surprise, and agile deployment now obsolete in the age of the great range of the big gun—in the age of the greater distance at which battles could take place between fleets? Certainly, the close range of Nelson at the Battle of St. Vincent in 1797 could hardly be repeated in 1914, and the German fleet was a far more efficient mechanism than the fast decaying French and Spanish fleets that Nelson had to contend with. Also, Nelson and his generation (and we must again emphasize this point), like the admirals of the Second World War, had the great experience of major battle which Jellicoe and his generation lacked. Yet despite these circumstances, which must be taken into consideration, a comparison can be validly made.

Nelson had an aggressive and optimistic spirit and a tactical imagination. He had confidence in, and the total confidence of, his subordinates. Nelson had outstanding clarity of perception, the power of decision, and a mastery of the art of communication. Jellicoe in the supreme leadership had none of these qualities. That is the measure of his failing by the highest standards.

chapter 11

AFTER THE GREAT WAR: BEATTY AND KEYES

In pitting Jellicoe against Nelson we have inevitably concluded that the all-round caliber of First World War leadership never reached the height of the Nelson era.

Nothing we can say about Keyes and Beatty, our other selected admirals of that war, can change the direction of this opinion, but it is useful to look at Beatty and Keyes, since they both put Jellicoe into perspective and present interesting variations in styles of leadership compared to Jellicoe's style. Jellicoe, Beatty, and Keyes are a balancing trio to the greater trinity of the Napoleonic wars of Nelson, St. Vincent, and Collingwood. A study of Beatty and Keyes also completes the picture of the challenge that First World War naval leadership faced. Beatty is a figure second only to Jellicoe—his most enthusiastic admirers might say an equal to Jellicoe—whereas Keyes was never in the same highest position of command.

Beatty never commanded a major fleet in major action, but his name is irrevocably linked with the Grand Fleet from the end of 1916 onward. Jellicoe and Beatty were at one time household names, as well known to the British public of the 1920s as another pair of heroes of the culture of that decade, the cricketers Hobbs and Sutcliffe. Jellicoe and Beatty are not well known in Britain now, and in this fading away, time has been fair to their reputations. After the Great War,

A composite picture of World War I naval officers with Admiral Beatty standing in foreground. By A. S. Cope (Courtesy of the National Portrait Gallery.)

they became associated in a controversy in which the enthusiasm of the pro-Beatty and pro-Jellicoe advocates for making comparisons exceeded the enthusiasm for and interest in the issue by the principals. The controversy was over the responsibility for the incomplete victory at Jutland and a comparison of their respective stewardships of the Grand Fleet.

When better days came and the German fleet came steaming into Scapa Flow in November 1918, the man in command at that time, Beatty, was bound to benefit in the public memory, if not in the purely professional judgment. In the distribution of honors in 1919, Beatty gained his earldom before Jellicoe, who did not win his until 1925. Indeed, Beatty was also awarded £100,000 on the principle, no doubt, that unto him that hath shall more be given. He was in command at the naval harvest home and reaped the benefit thereof. His monetary award added to his considerable fortune made him in more ways than one a child of good fortune. Jellicoe had to be content with a viscountcy and £50,000, and Keyes was awarded a baronetcy and £40,000. The relative size of the award to Keyes was presumably because he was still fresh in the public memory after Zeebrugge. This was, after all, a crude marketplace-type assessment of reputation, but these things mattered in a navy highly conscious of formal recognition of service and public honors, which no longer had prize money to assuage the cuts of professional slight. As it was, Beatty's earldom in 1919 was to put the navy on a par with Field Marshal Haig's earldom. Beatty, who was not without vanity, thought it was solely due to his own personal reputation. Jellicoe was not even invited to witness the surrender of the German High Seas Fleet on November 21, 1918.

Richmond was an advocate of Beatty, Madden of Jellicoe, in the debate about their respective merits. Duff, who was sour about both Jellicoe and Beatty, wrote on November 8, 1916, "B or J are equally unthinkable as C-in-C."[1] But it really was family supporters who so aggravated the situation. Just as Lloyd George and Asquith's relationship suffered from the acerbities of their womenfolk, so did Beatty's and Jellicoe's. David Beatty's son, the second earl, commenting on this in a letter to Professor A. Temple Patterson on July 6, 1967, said, "I am afraid a lot of the blame of the controversy which arose after the War can be laid at the door of the ladies."[2]

In many respects there was no great contrast between Jellicoe and

Beatty. Beatty was every bit as much a single-line formation man as Jellicoe and just as cautious and aware of his awesome responsibilities when he commanded the Grand Fleet. Beatty had all the conventional yearning for action and frustration at lack of it. Yet he had an inability to think beyond the set-piece confrontation. He was acutely conscious of the sense of disappointment at the performance of the fleet, but he was not sure how to put it right. His words at Jutland have become immortalized: "There seems to be something wrong with our ships. . . . And something wrong with our system."[3]

Beatty seems to have had no sense of false optimism and did not magnify what little achievement there was. Like Jellicoe his outlook was limited in not being able to see what could be done to correct the situation radically, at least in the field of action as opposed to improvement of materiel.

Beatty's performance at Jutland has been controversial. He failed to give the most effective support to Jellicoe. He failed to cooperate effectively when cooperation was essential. Admiral Harper, a Jellicoe partisan, in his assessment of Beatty's performance at Jutland, faulted him for a lack of precise information to his commander, incorrect disposition of his ships, and faulty signaling. Harper also criticized the shooting of Beatty's battle cruisers as below the standard expected. When Beatty came to command the Grand Fleet, then, it was not with a completely uniform record of previous success.

Beatty, when he assumed his command of the Grand Fleet, had the problem both of keeping up morale after a long period of frustration and of coming as he did in the footsteps of a much beloved predecessor, beloved especially among the men. Madden in the *Marlborough*, in command of the First Battle Squadron as second-in-command of the fleet, reported back to Jellicoe in December 1916, on Beatty's taking over of the fleet. The verdict was that Beatty had acted diplomatically and emphasized continuity:

Beatty had a meeting of the Flag Officers this morning and impressed on them the necessity of reading and re-reading *your* Battle orders, which would be the guide to all his tactics[?] and embodied the experience of 2 years war; he has lost no opportunity so far of impressing on the newcomers the necessity for a close study of your methods which pleases both the old and new Flags.[4]

Madden and Jellicoe had married sisters and they had close ties, so Madden kept a watching brief on Beatty, but the tenor of Madden's correspondence was quite favorable for a man who would be expected to seize on any comparisons unfavorable to Beatty. Madden considered Beatty as essentially sound. This word, sound, may appear to a later and more critical generation to be a description of Beatty's limitations rather than his attributes. But Madden found Beatty very approachable and ready and willing to accept criticism.

Madden continued to be reasonably contented with Beatty; writing on December 27, 1917, at the time of Jellicoe's dismissal from the Admiralty, he remarked, ". . . the Grand Fleet is all right as Beatty is strong enough to refuse to throw it away on wildcat schemes, but the wider field of operations are not in such able hands."[5]

Thus, fundamentally, Beatty had a respect for continuity, and he was very much in the nineteenth-century tradition of naval orthodoxies.

Wherein, then, are Beatty's distinguishing features as a leader? He was a golden boy of the navy, marked out for a rapid rise, just as Jellicoe had been. He had just the right mixture of self-confidence and good manners. He had been a commander at age twenty-seven and a rear-admiral when just under twenty-nine—the youngest flag officer since Nelson's day. He suffered during the war from every bit as much frustration as Jellicoe did. But unlike Jellicoe he was something of a showman. The three-button monkey jacket, the jaunty angle of his cap, gave an impression of confidence and individuality—of a more positive outlook which was not always borne out in his professional attitudes and performance. To the authorities, hoping for a breakthrough in the impasse into which the war had settled, Beatty seemed to symbolize good luck. As the war dragged on, there was an increasing tendency to make the most of any gleam of talent and turn geese into swans.

Beatty's private mood was much more depressed, as can be seen in the correspondence with his wife. His mood tended to be uxorious, and, troubled by his wife's psychosomatic ailments and sexual adventures (not mentioned by his biographer), and his own sense of unfulfilled achievement, with long periods of uncertainty about the intentions of the Admiralty and the Germans, he may have found some solace in soothsayers.[6] Certainly he had the type of personality that is called magnetic, and he was aware himself that he possessed magnetism, but it is doubtful whether he had much depth of vision and insight.

Beatty as commander-in-chief showed greater confidence in his subordinates than Jellicoe did and believed more in staff work. He also delegated more work. Under him the paperwork was just as great, but he did not allow it to so nervously exhaust him as it it did Jellicoe. His personality excited interest and loyalty, although he never aroused the kind of affection among the junior officers and men that Jellicoe did. A junior officer in the Grand Fleet during the change-over from Jellicoe's to Beatty's leadership reflected, in later years, that they did not like Beatty too much after he succeeded Jellicoe. They thought that although Beatty was a fine admiral in many ways, he was not particularly intelligent. But no one likes a new headmaster as much as the old one, at least at the beginning of his reign.

Leadership is very much concerned with the relationship of leaders and led, and Beatty was conscious of the different physical situation of the men as opposed to the officers. He wrote to his wife on July 30, 1915, "You judge everybody in the Fleet by me. I am having a perfectly easy and comfortable time. Not so the men. They haven't their wives and families here."[7]

The Grand Fleet was too near home and its fighting actions too few and far between for the men and officers to be actively welded together by prolonged fighting experience. The geographical situation of the Grand Fleet, acting from a home base, meant that the social gap between officers and men was accentuated by the wives of the officers being nearby, whereas the families of the men were relatively and mostly far off.

The officers' wives lived near Scapa Flow or Rosyth in homes of varying and appropriate comfort and grandeur. There was established a kind of naval court in exile. The boredom of the situation made for acrimony or at least acerbity and this scarcely helped the relationship of Beatty and his senior colleagues. The wives of Beatty, Jellicoe, and Keyes criticized one another, as, for example, in this letter from Lady Beatty to her husband: "[As to Mrs. Roger Keyes] She is anxious to get settled. She is very *dull* I think and talks about servants and all the difficulties of a *household*. However she may improve. She is longing to see Roger poor thing."[8] Lady Beatty, of course, possessed the key that in the twentieth century opens all doors: very great wealth. Beatty himself sharply commented to his wife on August 9, 1916, ". . . Lady Jellicoe who it appears is the joke of the Fleet."[9] These are titillating social trivia or little better, but the men below deck and their wives had sterner things to worry about.

The social situation of officers and men had a significant light to bear on the question of the style of naval leadership in the First World War. In distant campaigns the officers and men are thrown together much more. The officers, remote from their wives and families, could develop among one another and with their men a much closer association, as in Nelson's day in the Mediterranean or later in Cunningham's command in the Second World War. In the First World War the relative proximity of the Grand Fleet to home meant that the officers, especially the senior ones, never quite attained that professional and social intimacy and unity they might have achieved had operations been farther afield. Moreover, this closeness to home in a wartime situation was unsettling, especially for the senior officers who could afford to see their womenfolk more frequently than the rest of the fleet. There were too many farewells, too many leave-takings, which could be emotionally draining to all concerned. One wonders if Nelson or Montgomery could have had the same impact if Nelson's flag had been in the Thames, or Montgomery's Eighth Army in Ireland. The correspondence of Beatty and Keyes, in particular, shows the impact of domestic and family pressures upon them throughout the war.

Beatty, then, had a sense of this gap between leading and led without necessarily seeing or realizing how it might be diminished. On July 1, 1918, he referred to his lack of awareness of what the men really thought, in commenting on a visit to the fleet by an American bishop: "American Bishop Blunt [?] visited—given address to a lot of men which seemed to please him immensely. Whether it pleased the men I cannot say, but what he said has been said before a thousand times and I think they were slightly bored with it but who knows?"[10] The men remained a mass, generally obedient and loyal, but inscrutable and unfathomable because of class and professional barriers.

One essential attribute of modern leadership, as Montgomery was to show, is a sense of—indeed, at best, a flair for—public relations. Beatty had this much more than Jellicoe. The Grand Fleet was so relatively static that it became a prey to or sitting target for visiting potentates. The archbishop of York[11] was never far away. American and colonial statesmen and the king himself sojourned there. Thus, added to the frustration of a lack of naval action was a lot of time spent on what would now be called "VIPs." The longer the war went on, the more the Allies were involved, the more the trains brought these visitors. The Grand Fleet was very much of a showpiece, a special jewel in the Allied crown, something that not even the Germans could claim to have in superior form. Beatty had the patience of Jellicoe, but a greater appetite and stamina for social life and a more active sense of humor. As he commented to his wife on April 13, 1917, "Thank God I've got a sense of humour and can still laugh."[12] After trying to explain a joke to George V, Beatty wrote on July 9, 1917, "He is not very quick."[13]

Beatty was as preoccupied with the woes of the present as Jellicoe had been, but found time to take an interest in history. For this he received praise, indeed fulsome praise, from Richmond. Beatty certainly had more sense of the past than Jellicoe. Before the war he had always read history when naval business was slack. He wrote to the First Lord, Reginald McKenna, on July 21, 1911, that a sea officer with few duties would have "nothing to occupy himself with except study of naval history."[14] On June 12, 1918, he wrote to his wife, "Will you go to my friends Hatchards in Piccadilly and ask them to send me a Tucker's life of St. Vincent. I have lost mine and the sayings and doings of that wise old man I find of considerable help. There is a parallel in his life for every conundrum I am faced with. . . ."[15] Beatty certainly read more than Jellicoe, but whether he knew more is a moot point.

Writers on leadership, especially those of an academic vein, have always praised leaders who have read widely, especially in the history of their profession. But besides being a sign of some culture, does the reading of history actually assist the practice of leadership? One can only say there is no general rule. One person may find in reading history an intellectual stimulus, another may merely find it a pastime. One has the impression from Beatty that history reading gave him a form of psychological relaxation or comfort (for history presents a form of certainty) rather than an intellectual stimulus to rethink strategy or tactics. Beatty's personal letters contain little intellectualizing on war.

In Beatty's style of command of the Grand Fleet there is a less obsessive concentration on its perils—a little more fresh air; a wider world could be contemplated if not necessarily understood at Scapa Flow and at Rosyth whence the Grand Fleet was finally transferred in April 1918.

Certainly Beatty had a much better press than Jellicoe, and his charm, confidence, persuasive powers, and more outgoing disposition made better copy.

The Great War seemed to test, strain, and ultimately diminish Jellicoe's powers, whereas with Beatty, it brought out the best in him and ultimately gave him a background of leadership at the highest level to enable him to go to the Admiralty and give an unusually lengthy and competent performance as First Sea Lord, 1919–1927. If a sense of public relations is necessary in the leadership of a modern navy, it is even more necessary in political and administrative leadership. Beatty seemed even more at home at Whitehall than at Scapa Flow. His wide range of social and political contacts made him an excellent mover in the political world. His wife's position in London society paid dividends for him. The reports of what she heard at dinner tables in London had been useful to him at Scapa Flow. Hankey recognized Beatty's political skills when he wrote to him on the occasion of the admiral's retirement. As the years went on, Hankey more and more tended to take a trip down memory lane, so now he reminisced, "Still you will be very missed. You are the only First Sea Lord I have known in my 26 years experience who could really talk on even terms to the highest Cabinet Ministers and stand up to them in argument. Fisher is an exception, but Fisher was a crank, and even he didn't really state a case clearly."[16]

In one respect, at least, Fisher was to be proved right. Beatty performed much more effectively as First Sea Lord than Jellicoe did. One has to bear in mind, however, that Beatty, unlike Jellicoe, occupied the office in peacetime and under much less critical conditions than Jellicoe experienced. Beatty always professed that being commander-in-chief of the Grand Fleet during the war was a greater job, but his approachability and sense of effective public posture fitted him well both with the fleet and in Whitehall.

Beatty had, unlike Jellicoe, more than his fair mete of praise, especially in the immediate postwar euphoria. In both America and

Britain he was hailed by more reckless spirits as greater than Nelson. In his obituary notices (which for some are a fate worse than death and for others—the majority—a fate a little better), Beatty was greeted as the Nelson of the Great War. Fortunately, Fisher was not around to read this. Beatty was never, in fact, a Nelson. In Beatty there was great promise, greater self-awareness, and more perception of the possibilities and the limitations than in Jellicoe. In war Beatty had a greater temperamental inclination and flexibility to new ideas than did Jellicoe. He drew up new battle orders in 1917–1918 in which there seemed a more aggressive note, but there was no revolution in tactics.[17] He was no more offensively minded in strategy than Jellicoe.

In Beatty, as in Jellicoe, there remains a yawning gap between promise and performance. Beatty saw that things needed to be done, but he was not sure how to do them. There are questions, but few answers, few illuminating answers, that is. He was in this respect reflecting the trained response of his generation. Creative strategic and tactical thinking had been discouraged in the navy of his time.

It was not easy to develop new directions after an upbringing in the Victorian navy. Richmond believed that Beatty should have commanded the Grand Fleet throughout the war, and Beatty favored a naval thinker like Richmond, but the conclusion must be that it would have made little difference. Both Jellicoe and Beatty were trapped by the thinking of their generation, they had no previous background of battle experience, and no habit of creative thinking to help them out in the impasses of the war at sea.

The third great naval figure of the First World War, Keyes, is a study in professional and personal frustration. Keyes always felt he never was granted quite the recognition and position he deserved, and his time of frustration spanned two world wars. He was either too soon or too late for his own professional good. He was never quite senior enough for the highest position in the First World War. He almost became an anachronism in the Second World War. His career shows an intense search for glory and the heroic, at times almost to the point of desperation, as if he wanted to be a real-life Henty figure.

All officers in times of peace or in war search to distinguish themselves in what rare moments are afforded to them, but Keyes's search was almost demonic in its intensity. In China during the Boxer Rebel-

If you had to do it all over again would you do it any differently? Sir Roger Keyes and Sir Ian Hamilton at Gallipoli Day ceremonies April 25, 1929 (Courtesy Radio Times Hulton Picture Library)

lion he had sought renown with some success. When the Great War started, he, like so many of his contemporaries, expected rapid and decisive action but experienced a similar frustration. However, he certainly had his opportunities as a senior officer close to the center of things at the Dardanelles in 1915, and then, as the chief factotum of the famed Zeebrugge raid in April 1918, came his chief personal contribution to the war effort.

There was a well developed element of showmanship in Keyes's life, and he embraced his causes as if they were crusades—whether he was fighting in action, or fighting Trenchard[18] over Royal Air Force control of the Fleet Air Arm after the war, or fighting Chamberlain's ministry in 1940,[19] where he appeared dressed in his uniform of Admiral of the Fleet for the debate that led to the fall of the government—but the show was not always convincing. His ambition seemed greater than his ability.

Despite his qualities of enthusiasm and aggressiveness, he never managed to secure the total confidence of his professional superiors or subordinates. It was Sir Sidney Smith all over again. But Keyes was at the same time less talented and more serious than Smith. One gets the impression that Smith enjoyed it all much more than Keyes.

Keyes had impeccable social connections, which for him were very important. He had a great enthusiasm for the princely sport of polo. It was said that when he was commander-in-chief of the Mediterranean Fleet in 1925–1928, a sure way to gain promotion was to play that game. As a lieutenant commander once said in the lounge bar of the Union Club at Malta, "I have cashed in on all my savings and bought a string of ponies; this will get me promoted to commander."[20] (And it did.) The preferences of senior officers in making promotions may be natural, but Keyes was not good at disguising his favoritism.

Keyes met Winston Churchill before the First World War and impressed him with his enthusiasm and zest for action—a zest Churchill shared. In 1911 Keyes took Churchill to sea in one of his submarines, and on December 21, 1914, Churchill described Keyes as "a brilliant officer with more knowledge of and feeling for war than almost any naval officer I have met. I think the work and efficiency of our submarines are wonderful.[21] Churchill was always readily available to Keyes, both in the First and Second World Wars; an availability that others resented.

Keyes was widely thought of as a snob. An officer, Commander R. Travers Young, who served under him in the Mediterranean, found him aloof. Young said that he had served under Keyes for six months in the Dover Patrol without seeing him, and that when he served under him in the Mediterranean, he thought Keyes was completely out of touch with his fleet—other than his staff and his flagship—as well as being prone to favoritism.[22]

Although the factors of favoritism and snobbery told against him among his subordinates, the career of Keyes depended on the views of higher men, and he never managed to live down the impression that he was limited in his abilities and limited, particularly, in his intelligence. He did not appear to be perceptive enough to make the most of his limitations. There is a virtue, indeed an attraction, in appearing to be uncomplicated and a repository of the popular average virtues. Stanley Baldwin and Clement Attlee, both pipe smoking and cricket loving, were, in the political sphere, past masters at this technique. They could easily appear to relate to the man in the street. But Keyes always wanted to be the man on the white horse or, more appropriately, the knight in shining armor. This desire to be at the center of the stage in any action, combined with merely average ability, often had an unfavorable effect.

Keyes's leadership always seemed affected by a sense of insecurity, as if he was ever conscious that his detractors were vigilant in the wings, waiting to pounce and remove him from the center of the stage. One explanation of this trait may have been in his early struggle to get professional recognition. He never had Jellicoe's or Beatty's silver spoon. But the key to many of his generation was, of course, the approval of Fisher.

He had great difficulty in getting this approval, and he felt that Fisher was one of the many mysterious and harmful forces at the Admiralty working against his career, thwarting him and obstructing his rise to greatness. On November 1, 1914, Keyes wrote to his wife, "I would so very much rather fight the Germans than the people I am about to be up against at the Admiralty!"[23] On December 7 of the same year, he continued, "he [Fisher] is determined to knock me out."[24] The performance of Keyes in the early part of the war was not impressive, and Fisher wrote to Jellicoe on February 3, 1915, "What I really cared about is getting rid of Keyes *who is no good at all for submarines* but he is a special pet of the First Lord—why I don't know. He has made a mess of the submarines in the last 3 years but of course he knew nothing about it."[25] Fisher was at the time preoccupied with much bigger targets than Keyes, none less than Churchill himself.

Others had none too high an opinion of Keyes. On November 9, 1915, Jellicoe wrote, ". . . Keyes is a fine fellow but is not blessed with much brains."[26] Jellicoe never thought Keyes was fitted for staff work at the Admiralty, and Beatty almost repeated Jellicoe's earlier sentiments in a letter of May 7, 1916: "Keyes is a good fellow, but he has had no experience of big ship command, has not too many brains. . . ."[27]

Keyes not only anxiously watched Fisher in the early stages of the war, but also the career of Sir Reginald Tyrwhitt,[28] whom he thought of as a competitor himself for promotion. His feelings about Tyrwhitt, in his correspondence with his wife, verge on the paranoic.

But the Dardanelles had beckoned, and in the expedition there in 1915 he was chief of staff under Admiral Carden and then Admiral De Robeck in HMS *Queen Elizabeth*. Here at last seemed the path to glory. Unfortunately, the Dardanelles became a symbol of ill luck and mismanagement to his generation. Keyes's optimism and instinct for the offensive failed to energize his superiors. By March 17, 1915, Keyes realized that the Turkish defeat might take a little longer than expected, and he wrote to his wife, ". . . the glorious success I am confident is before us. . . . But it will succeed—tho' it is unfortunately harder than anyone thought."[29] On March 27 he wrote of De Robeck, who had succeeded Carden, "I always knew my Admiral was a gallant stout hearted gentlemen, now I know he is a great man and his name will go down in history as such and one 'qui sait attendre.' "[30] But his enthusiasm was premature and his judgment unsound. He opposed for a long time the concept of military withdrawal from the Dardanelles and he favored a renewed naval attack. As the months went on, this view seemed increasingly out of touch. Here we have one particular defect that limited Keyes's capacity for leadership. He let his enthusiasm for people and projects blind him to the realities of a situation. The Dardanelles, in the end, was no source of glory, only frustration and a source of sober reflection.

Keyes wrote a long letter to his wife on July 2, 1915, summarizing the situation and showing that he was aware of his limitations. "I believe, perhaps it is my conceit, that I know my limitations very well—that I have good judgment, at any rate about things that matter in my profession, and that I know how to make good use of other people to carry out what I want."[31] On September 23, 1915, referring to his problems in writing out and preparing things, he commented in a letter to his wife: "As you know darling I am horribly slow—"[32] Keyes sorely needed the confidence derived from success in a big action to make him less conscious of his own inadequacies and to still the persistent voice of his critics.

At Zeebrugge in April 1918, with the battle cry of "St. George for England," he had his chance. He had aimed to deny passage through the Straits of Dover to German submarines. The attack on Zeebrugge and Ostend was an attempt to block the exits of the Germans for their advanced submarine and destroyer base at Bruges. As a result of the raid, Zeebrugge was only blocked for a few days, and the attack on Ostend was a failure. Keyes himself exaggerated its success and was reluctant to see the limited nature of its results. His family continued to assert the success of Zeebrugge to the point of influencing, against his own better judgment, Aspinall Oglander, the biographer of Keyes.

However, the raid, with its action and daring had both psychological and political value, but no strategical value. It seemed to illuminate a static war. Lloyd George, grateful for good news, any good news, described it as an example of the irresistible Nelson touch. This reminds us the the phrase "the Nelson touch" can, dependent on the mood of the time when it is employed, become infinitely elastic, being applied to any naval success that catches the public eye.

The Zeebrugge raid was both daring and carefully planned. It was the greatest achievement of Keyes's life, and he showed qualities so often associated with occasions of successful leadership: thoroughness, patience, and good judgment, coupled with that necessity of war—good luck. Above all, the men sensed in Keyes a unifying spirit for the whole operation. He inspired the operation with enthusiasm and purpose. His physical presence was also a source of inspiration. At last something was being done to take the war into the enemy camp, even if the ultimate significance of the material damage inflicted on the Germans was insignificant. Keyes had had his moment in history. Yet the action was not a big enough achievement to seal his reputation. The doubters remained, and so did his appetite for glory.

The substitution of Keyes for Admiral Bacon as vice-admiral of the

Dover Patrol in January 1918 was a controversial decision which led to a good deal of acrimony. Bacon was a protégé of Jellicoe, and Jellicoe's defense of Bacon had hastened his own end at the Admiralty. R. Travers Young has further written:

The Dover Patrol under Roger Keyes was a very different affair from what it had been under Reginald Bacon who was the Vice Admiral when I was first there in the *Lochinvar*. Keyes's tactical dispositions were much better, but despite the fact that he was bathed in the glory of the Zeebrugge raid, I don't think he had the confidence of his Command to the same extent that Bacon had had.[33]

It was that full confidence of superiors and immediate subordinates that so often eluded Keyes. One may speculate that, despite his aura of self-confidence, there was a basic uncertainty in Keyes, perhaps due to a sense of mental inferiority. The uncertainty must have had its effect on his relations with others in the profession and limited his effectiveness as a leader.

If Keyes's career had ended just after Zeebrugge, his reputation would have remained higher. He remained a notable figure and at times a sensational one in his political interventions. The fighting quality, the enthusiasm and aggressiveness, were as high as ever. But his limitations were never forgotten by his detractors, and his deficiencies became even more apparent as the years went on. His disappointments continued, as he was passed over in 1930 for the position of First Sea Lord. Sir Frederick Field[34] got the position instead, since Madden, the outgoing First Sea Lord, was against Keyes, as was George V, who, like his predecessor William IV, was no mean judge of admirals.

The intervention of Keyes in the Second World War was quixotic. If he had restricted his gallantry to a more personal, more limited, and less ambitious role, as Walter Cowan[35] did, he would not have aroused such professional criticism. As it was, his friendship with Churchill secured for him in July 1940 the first directorship of the new combined operations command. By October 19, 1940, Keyes was bombarding A. V. Alexander[36] at the Admiralty, with comment and plans for action, reminding him, if he needed to be reminded, that three of Keyes's close relatives were in the war.[37] Dudley Pound, the

First Sea Lord, was furious, writing on December 1, 1940, to Sir Andrew Cunningham regarding Keyes, "Roger Keyes intrigued himself into the position of Director of Combined Operations in spite of protests of the C.O.S."[38] On December 12 Pound, repeating his earlier remarks, wrote to Cunningham, "He only did this [get the appointment] in order to take charge of an operation as soon as it suited him. . . . R. K. is not capable of making out a plan."[39] Pound had served under Keyes in the Mediterranean and obviously had no high opinion of him.

As director of combined operations in these circumstances, Keyes wrote to Cunningham regarding his appointment on December 3 1940: "I have had it for four months but owing to lack of landing craft, vessels to carry them, aeroplanes to drop parachutists and the objections raised by certain brass bound soldiers in the War Office who hate the very thought of my irregular troops, I found it exceedingly hard to make any progress."[40] Always the office-bound administrators, either of the Admiralty or the War Office, were diverting him from the path of glory.

Keyes's tenure of this command was neither long nor fruitful, and he was removed from it in October 1941. Our last unfriendly comment is from Pound to Cunningham on November 25, 1941: "Roger Keyes is making himself very unpleasant because he has been removed from being the Director of Combined Operations. . . . He has never had much brain but what he has got left is quite addled."[41]

Keyes's wish to be of use was patriotic and laudable, but like Bottom in *A Midsummer Night's Dream*, Keyes always wanted to have a very big part, one where he could set the scene for a role of glory. Sir Philip Vian's[42] heroics in Norway and then the Mediterranean were considered strictly relevant and necessary, and thrilled Cunningham himself, and at the age of sixty-nine, Cowan, a real-life Evelyn Waugh character, was regarded as a source of admiration. But Keyes's posturing and search for a fitting scenario for himself became a source of ridicule.

Keyes's career is an excellent example of one aspect of leadership failure, the failure to secure the confidence of superiors and colleagues. He had too overt an ambition, and his continual suspicion that his enemies at home were always trying to exploit his limitations made him all the more aggressive and abrasive in trying to get his way.

Yet by any ordinary standard his career was a great success. He fell just short of being First Sea Lord, and he was commander-in-chief of the Mediterranean Fleet, a historic post and, at the time he held it, the largest fleet in the world. For a man so criticized by many of the influential he went far. But, like Beatty and Jellicoe, his relative success and eminence is a criticism itself of the caliber of First World War naval leadership. This leadership showed great enthusiasm and competence, even awareness of the need for improvement, but sorely lacked the inspiration of genius, and, as Captain Roskill has pointed out, it showed a failure of intellectual capacity.

chapter 12

INTERLUDE BETWEEN THE WARS

The pre-First World War navy was a repository of confidence, even at times arrogance. The navy between the wars, in contrast, experienced much soul searching and uncertainty. Before going on to the Second World War it is useful to cast a brief glance at the trauma of the interwar navy, especially as it affected the issue of leadership.

The disputes about Jutland and the whole performance of the Royal Navy during the First World War continued into the 1930s. The British public before the First World War had never anticipated Britain becoming a great military power, fighting a prolonged continental war on an unprecedented scale, but it had expected an ultimately decisive sea victory against the German fleet. As was said by the director[1] of the Royal Naval Staff College in 1927 in a summing up of the Jutland lectures, "As regards public opinion on the battle there was a sort of national misconception that whenever the German Fleet and the Grand Fleet met, the former would instantaneously disappear to the bottom."[2]

Well, all went well in the end and the German fleet did disappear, although scuttled by its own men in 1919 at Scapa Flow rather than by British efforts, and the total British performance during the war seemed well below expectations. Most Jutland inquests, whether by book or lecture for professional purposes, attempted to seek lessons for the future. The quantity of introspection seems, however, to have been more a source of self-mortification than future enlightenment. Indeed, the navy between the wars was disturbed on several levels: first, by its diminishing power relative to the Japanese and the Americans, second, by its sense of competition from the new arm, the RAF, and third, at a disciplinary level by the unusual if grave incident, the Invergordon Mutiny. The first two factors of disturbance do not concern the main theme of this study, but they contributed to a sense of worry for a navy which thought it was in for a time of challenge and uncertainty.

In the background, society itself was changing, if slowly, with the Admiralty slowly responding to this change. In 1929–1931 A. V. Alexander, the First Lord of the Admiralty in the second Labour government began efforts to widen the social background of the Dartmouth intake, but selection remained, at least to the start of the Second World War, on a narrow although slowly widening basis. Accents and social background of applicants were widely discussed. Alexander also attempted to increase opportunities for promotion from the lower deck and to reduce corporal punishment, but he was not successful in the case of junior officers or ratings.[3]

The Invergordon Mutiny in September 1931, when part of the Atlantic Fleet refused to muster—about fifteen thousand men all told—revealed British naval leadership at its most unresponsive and intensive. As in 1797 the quarrel was fundamentally about pay, but in 1931 there was an announced pay cut in time of deflation, whereas the 1797 mutinies were about a pay claim in a time of inflation. Another contrast between the two mutinies was that in 1797 the men thought the Admiralty Board might in the end listen to them, but in 1931 the board appeared at its most insensitive by ineptly announcing severe pay cuts. In that respect its critics from different points of view such as Roskill and Leonard Wincott the naval mutineer agree.[4] In 1931 the lines of communication between men and senior officers had become very formal and were not working effectively. Captain A. R. Henderson, secretary to Admiral Tomkinson,[5] senior acting officer of the Atlantic Fleet, noted the conclusion, which rapidly became prevalent among the men, that the ordinary service channels for complaint were valueless in this case and that the men had no other course than the one they took.[6]

Leonard Wincott has mentioned the attitude of the officers, who seemed during the mutiny to be quite out of touch with the ethos and problems of the men. Thus Captain Prickett at Invergordon tried to rebuke the men by saying that many millions of pounds had been lost by British interests in Argentina alone, because of their action, and Wincott recollects Rear-Admiral Astley-Rushton[7] calling the men to their faces, "Bledy fools, bledy hooligans." The spirit of Captain Bligh seemed to be still abroad. Wincott points out that the officers had behaved to one another as if the men did not exist, and he refers to public sexual misbehavior by the officers with civilian women.[8] Obviously, Admiral Jervis's admonition of 1797 had not been taken to heart. He had written to Nelson in that year: "I dread not the men, it is the indiscreet licentious conversation of the officers which produces all our ills."[9] Certainly Wincott does not purport to be an impartial observer and he does not refine his case. Forty-five years after the event Wincott's words still arouse much ire in naval circles. For example, Commander H. Pursey in the *Naval Review*, April 1976, has described Wincott's book on the mutiny as a literary hoax—the hallucinations of eleven years in a Soviet labor camp! At any rate Wincott had been, according to himself, a leading agitator in the dispute and had urged his fellow seamen on by evoking the example of the miners, the bogey group of the British establishment then and now.[10] The mutineers succeeded in extracting concessions from the government and the cuts were modified.

The whole affair shook the Admiralty, which made Tomkinson, at the senior end, a scapegoat by suspending him from duty in February 1932.[11] The Admiralty also hunted down with administrative vindictiveness after the event any men who seemed to have played a significant part in the incident. Sir Frederick Field stated the line to be taken in writing to Beatty:

I am however getting a list of those who have agitated since our order that any more trouble would be treated in accordance with the Naval Discipline Act, and we shall find a way of getting rid of them. This and other measures are to be considered by the Board as soon as we can get the pay settled and published.[12]

A mutiny in the Royal Navy was tantamount to the veil of the temple being rent in twain. It was an occasion as traumatic as would have been a run on the Bank of England. Sir Austen Chamberlain,[13] speaking in the Commons, put a brave face on the incident when he stated, "As for the action of the men, if technically inexcusable, it had been marked neither by rowdyism nor disrespect. The movement had never been general and many had not deserted their duty at all."[14] In the reports of the time the euphemism unrest was employed, the word mutiny being too fearful to be contemplated. But the Invergordon Incident, or mutiny, was a significant factor in the abandonment of the Gold Standard on September 21, 1931. In practical terms of national security, it endangered the integrity of the British Empire probably even less than the cricket bodyline[15] bowling controversy between England and Australia a year later! However, as with the famous King and Country resolution at the Oxford Union in February 1933,[16] the Invergordon Mutiny led to an exaggerated foreign view of the reluctance of Britain to defend herself.

The mutiny did make the Admiralty more aware of the needs and outlook for the lower deck and more sensitive to public or press criticism; yet pay and conditions were not radically improved. Nor did the mutiny really lead to any fundamental change of heart in the service or any reduction of social and professional elitism. Even another war did not radically change matters and Hannen Swaffer,[17] in the role of a latter-day Arnold White, had to take up the cudgels on behalf of the ordinary seamen in 1946 in his *What Would Nelson Do?*[18] The Royal Navy continued to see Reds under every bunk, if not bed, for many years, and as late as 1945, the year of Labour's great electoral victory, Swaffer could say, "There is one man on the lower deck today on whose service papers I have seen written 'I do not recommend the man for advancement. He has socialist tendencies.' "[19]

In all, the Royal Navy between the wars had little chance to redeem itself in the public eye after the disappointments of the First World War. As Captain Roskill has pointed out, fundamental weaknesses remained. Senior officers were anti-intellectual and the training of British specialist officers remained inadequate. Officers such as Sir Roger Backhouse[20] had never learned to use their staff properly.

Yet it was by no means a completely dark scene. Although the interwar period did not give clear signs of better times in the future, some of the leadership lessons of the First World War had been taken to heart by the rising generation of leading officers who were to be prominent in the Second World War. This generation was more psychologically attuned to face uncertainty and the new technological era with the advent of air power. It realized that the rigidity and orthodoxy that restricted the vision of the First World War naval leaders would be a serious if not fatal disadvantage in any future war where Britain could no longer count on an overwhelming lead in naval strength. Of that naval generation, Sir Andrew Cunningham was the most distinguished fighting Admiral.

chapter **13**

CUNNINGHAM: THE LESSONS OF THE GREAT WAR LEARNED AND THE SEARCH FOR ANOTHER NELSON CONCLUDED

In considering Sir Andrew Cunningham as a naval leader, we see that it is in him that the Nelson tradition comes to rest and the ghost of Nelson is laid to rest as well. The last admiral whose career was considered in detail in this study was Roger Keyes. Cunningham's career is a great contrast to Keyes's. Cunningham was the right man at the right age at the right time in the right place. The implications of his great victory at Matapan on March 28 and 29, 1941, were significant for British morale. It was the equivalent, in psychological impact, to St. Vincent's victory in 1797 and came at a very important moment. Cunningham showed by his power of improvisation, his self-reliance, his close contact with the men, his recourse to new tactics commensurate with new weapons such as radar, and his appreciation of the use of aircraft that he and officers like him had liberated themselves from the orthodoxies and rigidities of the pre-and First World War navy in which they had been trained and become junior officers.

Cunningham's first period as commander-in-chief in the Mediterranean in 1939–1942 was a time of major losses, especially at the hands of Italian torpedo boats and German aircraft. Air cover for the British fleet was insufficient. Indeed, in the end there were such great losses that for a time Cunningham was a commander-in-chief without any battleships capable of action. As was admitted in March 1942 by

Undaunted! Sir Andrew Cunningham broadcasting his "all's well" message April 6, 1942 (Courtesy Imperial War Museum)

Dudley Pound, the First Sea Lord, "As you say, there is no fleet to go to sea in. . . ."[1] But whereas in 1796–1798 the British left the Mediterranean in very difficult circumstances, in 1941–1942 they hung on. Cunningham exhibited all the Nelsonic qualities for which the navy had so long yearned. He was the embodiment of the offensive spirit, an exponent of the tradition of close action and ardor in pursuit. He was an officer who was against any precautionary measures when they applied to himself and yet was full of the authoritarian approach toward anyone who omitted such precautions.

S. W. C. Pack, Cunningham's most recent biographer,[2] has described him as a second Nelson, and Admiral Ernest King, USN[3] (no great friend of Britain incidentally), saw him as the spiritual successor to St. Vincent. Even if allowance is made for pious hyperbole, Cunningham had numerous formidable qualities that deserve detailed assessment for his place in the British naval tradition. He was the last fully independent British commander-in-chief in the Mediterranean, before the British naval effort became part of the Allied effort and before British naval power ceased to be a major world stategic factor.

Like so many senior British officers in the Second World War, Cunningham had an advantage over the senior officers in the First World War; that is, he had had battle experience in a major and relatively recent war. He had been in the Dardanelles in 1915 and had made intelligent reflections on the leadership shortcomings exposed there and also elsewhere in the Great War, such as poor security, poor army and navy cooperation, and the time wasted by indecision. He made good use of these lessons and had an agile if not brilliant mind. Cunningham was never thought of as the intellectual equal of, say, Alanbrooke[4] or Portal[5] on the chiefs of staff committee, but in his subsequent work in Washington and later in the Mediterranean, in alliance and harmony with the Americans, he showed that he had great powers of adaptability and could tread warily where need be. Moreover, Cunningham adapted far more quickly than Jellicoe had done to new naval factors and indeed to changing social values. He was a conservative, yet recognized the changes in values and the loss of political and spiritual certainties in the twentieth century.

Two examples illustrate Cunningham's flexibility. Writing on October 23, 1939, to his aunts Helen and Constance Browne, he remarked that one young woman he met in Egypt had been very much against all war for whatever cause. He continued, "I must say she had some right on her side as I don't think the Great War led to anything better and now it's to do all over again."[6] In another very different situation he commented in August 1942 on sending his English valet home from Washington. "He is a stupid little cockney and only partially trained, as insular as possible and doesn't know how to behave to coloured people. . . ."[7] Thus Cunningham's adaptability is evident.

In his relations with the British government, Cunningham was very fortunate in having the constant backing of A. V. Alexander, the First Lord, and Sir Dudley Pound, the First Sea Lord. Not the least part of Pound's assistance to Cunningham was that he handed over to him a fine instrument, the Mediterranean Fleet. Cunningham did not get on with Churchill particularly well, as was seen when he became First Sea Lord. Pound, fortunately, had won and retained Churchill's complete confidence and even affection and was able to act as a useful lightning conductor in the uneven relationship between Cunningham, when in the Mediterranean, and Churchill. Cunningham often needed advocates, as, for example, when sniping at his efforts came from the direction of the wings in the person of the Marquess of Salisbury,[8] who wrote to Churchill on April 23, 1941, casting some doubt on the optimism expressed over Matapan and referring to the Admiralty obsession with saving its ships.[9] Cunningham was well aware that he was not a favorite at Winston's court. He was not a "Whitehall warrior" by nature. Pound's mediacy was invaluable; otherwise there might have developed the kind of unfortunate relationship that existed between Churchill and General Wavell. Ultimately, Churchill indeed preferred Fraser[10] to succeed Pound as First Sea Lord rather than Cunningham. Churchill somewhat surprisingly labeled Cunningham as an officer of the old school and the preair age when Cunningham came to be considered for First Sea Lord. But Tovey[11] and Alexander praised Cunningham, and Alexander pointed out in a memorandum of September 25, 1943 to Churchill, that no admiral in the whole of the Royal Navy had more experience of air operations over the sea in that war.[12] Cunningham was indeed appointed First Sea Lord, but although he had no great liking for Churchill, he did consider him to be a great leader. Opinion was to be mixed regarding the performance of Cunningham as First Sea Lord.

Relatively secure, then, in his position with regard to Whitehall, what was Cunningham like with regard to those who worked under him? Admirals like Nelson and Jellicoe were loved, but Cunningham was not. He was a keen disciplinarian and a parsimonious man. He was a martinet down to the smallest details. He could quickly rage in an immoderate way and find faults. Yet these explosions were an ideal channel of release, especially during the tensions of wartime Mediterranean command. He was a man who hated to be bested in argument and would take refuge in emotion. His fellow officers thought he had the dogma of a cruiser man, but his mental powers had never been extended by specialization. He never minced words about naval officers who failed to please him. Yet service under him could be a great stimulus. Even before the war he had been an excellent example of the offensive spirit to his subordinate officers. Thus Admiral Sir Geoffrey Oliver[13] wrote of him, "Service in Destroyers under him was an eye opener. I believe his unrelenting drive and brinkmanship to have done much to make the quality of so many 2nd World War Captains."[14]

Cunningham was a prolific letter writer and must have found relaxation in his correspondence. His laconic comments to his aunts hint at a good deal of the stress of the time as on Feburary 7, 1940, from HMS *Birmingham*: "Rather a sad week last week. My captain of the Fleet shot himself death with his own shot gun on Tuesday. Poor man too long abroad I think."[15]

His incisive comment revealed a confidence and rapidity in making up his own mind. These qualities revealed themselves not only in his letter writing but in his leadership in the field of naval operations. Once his mind was made up it was difficult to change it. In this he was like St. Vincent and he enjoyed throwing the verbal dart every bit as much as St. Vincent or Sir John Fisher had done. His private comments on nonnaval personnel were incisive and barbed. Anthony Eden was ". . . a nice man, perhaps a little full of Anthony Eden. . . ."[16] King Farouk was a "damned young ruffian."[17] Churchill was ". . . a rascal but he's a great leader."[18] Churchill's son Randolph[19] was described as "A proper unlicked cub but clever in a way."[20] Leslie Hore-Belisha[21] he described in mixed terms:

I wonder what Alan thinks of Hore-Belisha's disappearence from the War Office. I called on the general here that morning to offer him my congratulations but one mustn't be blind to the fact that he did a lot for the Army.

He managed to get a lot of money spent on the Army and woke them up well but he was a dirty dishonest little brute to work with.[22]

Cunningham had the common Anglo-Saxon distaste for General de Gaulle and appreciated Eisenhower's description of him looking like a shark that had been hauled up out of the water and left to die.[23] Cunningham's verbal judgment like his leadership was no-nonsense stuff—a little rough at times—not given to temporizing, but exuding confidence.

Cunningham could be difficult to serve under, as Sir Algernon Willis,[24] his second-in-command and chief of staff in the Mediterranean, pointed out.[25] But he had no use for "yes men" and he had a sense of humor, juvenile as it might tend to be at times. One had to stand up to him to make one's point. In fact, like Nelson, he turned a blind eye to any superior order that he knew to be wrong, and he expected his officers to do the same and frankly state their opinions.

He was always aware of the needs of the men. He realized the anxiety that poor mail service caused the officers and men, and he appreciated the need for sending reassuring telegrams to next of kin in England. He attempted, not always successfully, to ensure that his men in the Mediterranean got a better airmail service.

Cunningham was inevitably profoundly moved by the waste of war, whether in sending his ships to almost inevitable destruction in the evacuation of Crete or at the very personal tragedy of the sight of a youngster in the hospital at Tobruk who had just lost both his legs by a bomb in the *Ladybird* at Tobruk. Cunningham wrote to the lad after he had seen him in the hospital, and had the brave reply regarding his Navy service from L. Atkinson, "It has taught me, among other things, the true meaning of comradeship."[26]

Cunningham's most useful asset for dealing with the stress of high command, in comparison with Jellicoe, was a greater sense of balance. Cunningham could stand back and look at the war, however appalling the situation, and he could realize that not all wisdom resided in him or, what is more, was expected to reside in him. Writing to Pound on August 19, 1940, he commented, "Personally I think that as one rises in the Service one is apt to underestimate the abilities of the officers junior to us, quite naturally as we know that at certain stages of their careers they certainly did not know as much as we did and were lacking in the experience we had."[27]

Cunningham was naturally aggressive and he was an optimist. Sometimes, in the difficulties of the Mediterranean in 1940–1941, being like this was like whistling in the dark. Appreciating optimism in others, he wrote on August 23, 1942, of President Roosevelt, "He is a most delightful man but rather inclined to sweep difficulties away with a wave of the hand. A very good trait in wartime, however. You'll never do anything if you let the difficulties overawe you."[28] On July 13, 1940, he had written to Pound at a most difficult time in the war, "Don't think I'm discouraged. I am not a bit."[29] He said this even though in that particular letter he had to list the problems of the Mediterranean Fleet.

Cunningham showed an imaginative use of his scanty resources, making the most of them. This was inevitably a prevalent and ubiquitous feature of the British war effort in the early months of the war, before the full advent of American help. For example, he tried to make it appear that the fleet at Alexandria had not been devastated by Italian midget submarines. When materiel was in short supply, he supplemented it with psychology. He delighted in deception of the enemy and their sympathizers, even if it was merely by publicly playing golf at Alexandria to deceive the Japanese Consul about the fleet's movements. This puckish, almost boyish, zest for war helped to lighten the load of responsibility and kept him from assuming the weight of worry that had aged Jellicoe so quickly. Two conspicuous successful expressions of his robust confidence in his own judgment are seen in his handling of the French fleet at Alexandria after the fall of France and in his conduct of the Battle of Matapan in 1941.

The question of the disposition of the French fleet at the fall of France was a vexing one. Britain did not want the fleet to fall under German control; yet a French government remained that could demand first loyalty of the French fleet, which might then ultimately be at the mercy of the Germans. The British government was prepared if necessary to use force to prevent any possibility of it being used against them, or as a possible threat against Britain, and indeed force was used against that portion of the French fleet that was at Oran.[30]

Despite intense and impatient pressure from his government at home, Cunningham was determined to do things his own way. He had no intention of obeying orders to attack the French fleet if he could avoid it. Thus he signaled to the Admiralty, "I would emphasise frank and cordial relations exist here and feel more can be done by friendly negotiation than by threatening forcible measures. In any case the ships will not go to sea."[31] In his French counterpart in Alexandria, Admiral Godfroy,[32] Cunningham had a sympathetic person to deal with, since Godfroy was equally unwilling to obey Vichy. By a mixture of tact and confidence Cunningham succeeded in gaining and preserving the cooperation of Godfroy and thereby succeeded in neutralizing the French fleet without bloodshed. His message to Godfroy on July 3, 1940, is a masterpiece of tact and creative diplomacy:

My Dear Admiral,
   I have been casting round in my mind for some solution to this terrible impasse.
   ... If you can make a gesture, which indeed you have already offered to do, which will allow our Government to realise that your ships will not proceed to sea, perhaps even now we may prevent a disaster as painful to me as to you.[33]

Cunningham had developed an effective rapport with Godfroy and there was a peaceful and satisfactory solution for Britain. Churchill thought Cunningham was being too "pussyfoot"[34] with Godfroy, but he came around to Tovey's view that Cunningham had had the best policy—to leave the French ships afloat but demilitarized, still a potential reserve, and soon a possible ally. Pound congratulated Cunningham on July 20, 1940: "I am very glad you were able to square things up so successfully with the French ships at Alexandria. It must have been a very difficult business and required great patience and determination."[35]

Cunningham gave Godfroy room for a dignified withdrawal, or at least to climb down, without too much loss of face. Under a different leader, one less confident or more alarmed by the pressure from Whitehall for a speedy solution, there might have been a less satisfactory dénouement and a more explosive situation in Alexandria. Here Cunningham very consciously carried out his own independent judgment, as the man on the spot.

The Battle of Matapan between the Italian and British fleets was the first major naval action in the world since 1916. It took place on March 28 and 29, 1941, off the coast of Western Greece. As a link with the past, all three British battleships had been at Jutland. Cunningham himself was in the *Warspite*, which was built in 1913 and had no radar, although some of the other British ships did have this relatively new feature. The engagement showed Cunningham at his tactical best. He reacted effectively to new conditions. It was the first use of airplanes on a large scale in a sea battle. The conflict emphasized the invaluable quality of the new radar. Above all, it was a night action, the kind of action that Jellicoe, and indeed the whole of the Royal Navy in the First World War, had decided was not a feasible proposition. This was because pre-First World War night exercises had been confused. Night action had not, of course, been unprecedented in British naval history, for St. Vincent had captured the *Pégase* in 1782 at 1 A.M. off the coast of France near Brest. Cunningham had an advantage in the night conflict as the Italians had no radar at all and had no training in night fighting. For the first time in modern action, in peace or war, a British battle fleet turned toward an unknown force of enemy ships and defeated it soundly. The Italian battleship *Vittorio Veneto* was torpedoed and damaged and three Italian cruisers were destroyed. It was a great boost for British morale, although not in any way a decisive strategic encounter.

Cunningham's resolute manner and good humor throughout the battle made it very evident, despite the appearance of consulting his colleagues, that the decision to engage the enemy in a night action was his and his alone. Once the action was decided upon, Cunningham realistically gave scope for individual initiative to his subordinates. Neither he nor they had accurate information of the whereabouts of the enemy fleet and its composition. Indeed, his order to disengage the action at 11:12 P.M. on March 28 led to part of his fleet, which might have chased and sunk the battleship *Vittorio Veneto*, abandoning the pursuit. Cunningham had thought in the confusion that his fleet might have sunk one of its own ships and was fearful of possible accidental losses when he had so little in reserve.

The action showed the correct mixture of calculation of risk and aggression of the kind Nelson had so brilliantly displayed. Writing to Churchill on May 6, 1941, after the event, A. V. Alexander commented:

The real facts are, of course, that the absence of casualties are due, firstly to good fortune and, secondly to great efficiency at night fighting displayed by the Mediterranean Fleet. Knowing the efficiency of his Fleet, the Commander-in-Chief had no qualms about a Fleet action at night.[36]

The battle did indeed show Cunningham at his best, with a flexibility of response to new conditions of warfare and a trust in the discretion and initiative of his subordinates.

However, Cunningham was prepared to admit his errors, for example, the premature disengagement order referred to earlier and the underestimation of the effectiveness of Italian torpedo boats. On another occasion, July 13, 1940, he wrote to Pound about an earlier failure: "The brush with the Italian Fleet was most irritating and disappointing, but there is no doubt that it was a carefully set trap. . . . I walked into the trap with my eyes open."[37]

Above all, Cunningham was a great believer in backing the other service arms, even at great peril to his own service, as he did in the evacuation of Crete in 1941. The navy would not and must not let the army down. He would defend his own force against criticism, but would give credit where credit was due to the other arms. As he wrote again, to Pound on August 3, 1940, "I don't wish to appear pessimistic but I hope you are aware of the Army and Air position out here. If we have to withdraw from Egypt, it will not be for naval reasons but because the Army and Air Force have not been given sufficient reinforcements."[38] Cunningham had learned the lesson well from the First World War, it was imperative to have interservice cooperation and harmony.

Cunningham's combination of realism and his offensive spirit make him an eminently suitable final figure in his study of leadership in the Royal Navy. He demonstrated a Nelsonian quality in his recognition that nothing could be gained from a defensive posture, if there was a reasonable possibility of an offensive one. It is typical of the man that in calculating the risks of taking to sea against the Italians if war broke out, he favored the more positive approach. For example, he wrote on July 26, 1939:

I think a policy of holding back the Battlefleet would be a mistaken one. Wherever they go in the Mediterranean they are within range of air attack and liable to damage. I feel that in spite of the submarine danger, they are safer at sea than in being in such a poorly defended harbour at Alexandria.[39]

It is satisfying that with Cunningham we end on a note of optimism. The hitherto seemingly endless search for another Nelson ended with Cunningham, who, if not of quite the same historic stature, nor quite the same decisive figure as Nelson, showed that the Nelsonic virtures were still relevant in the twentieth century. It is an irony of history that when the Royal Navy got as near to a Nelsonian figure as it could muster in the twentieth century, the conditions in which Nelsonic qualities could be freely exercised, or a Nelson type of admiral could flourish, were passing away; that is, the independent naval power of Britain was coming to an end.

chapter 14

RECESSIONAL: ADMIRALS ALL FOR ENGLAND'S SAKE!

The approach in this study of leadership has been chronological, with an emphasis on the details of personality and conduct set in a period perspective. I have not attempted to establish a model of leadership to judge everyone, but inevitably Nelson has stood out as the all-round yardstick of excellence.

The first chapter took issue with others who have generalized about leadership by listing certain general or universal qualities of mind and conduct as essential for its successful performance. However, the purpose of this study has not been to say that general terms cannot be used at all. The purpose has been to emphasize that, when general terms such as patience and orthodoxy are employed, what must be borne in mind is the particular function for which leadership is being exercised and the period during which it is exercised—call it, perhaps, the "time factor." Sir John Fisher's six principles of leadership or Geoffrey Bennett's fifteen qualities, for example, mean nothing unless applied to a particular situation. We must always ask: are the particular qualities of a particular naval leader appropriate for that particular situation? To look at a specific example, Sir Sidney Smith's élan and powers of improvisation were invaluable at Acre, but would have been much less useful in the long blockades that St. Vincent and Collingwood had to conduct and endure. In the right situation Smith was the best man for the job; in other less appropriate situations such as Toulon in 1793 he was well nigh a disaster. In considering successful leadership, then, two factors in particular should be borne in mind: the type of situation in which leaders exercise their role and the historical time factor.

Successful leadership is very much the exercise of the qualities of the right man performing at the right time in the right situation. The previous chapter gave an excellent example of this in Sir Andrew Cunningham at Matapan and Alexandria. Leadership is not an exercise of intrinsic qualities that can be applied to every situation. Moreover, it is much more than a display of individual qualities *in vacuo*. It is by definition very much of a societal activity. I have, therefore, emphasized the importance of the relations of the naval leader with his fellow officers and of his rapport, good or otherwise, with his men.

The time factor is also important. Leading the British fleet at Trafalgar was in some ways a kind of operation similar to leading at Jutland. For example, unity of purpose was essential in both cases. Yet in many ways it was obviously a very different kind of operation, because of the long range of gunnery and the much greater speed of the ships used at Jutland compared to Trafalgar. To return to the similarities, both Nelson and Jellicoe had to have an element of confidence of their seamen in themselves. Thus, because of certain similarities in demands of the highest leadership in different periods, especially as they relate to the management of men, we can use words like tradition and phrases like continuing excellence in relation to naval leadership, without being misleading or uninformative.

The second chapter discussed the issues that have concerned writers on leadership since leadership was first written about: Is the power of leadership an innate quality or can it be instilled by education or training? How significant is the contribution of an individual leader to the attainment of success in war?

From the evidence of British naval leadership, the most successful individual acts of leadership have arisen from the individual spark of unusual ability exercising itself in a suitably favorable situation. There seems no way yet known of artificially producing such a spark. One cannot produce genius; one can only produce, at the most, good professionals. One can train a whole generation of so-called leadership material to have an officerlike outlook, but one cannot produce or raise like a hothouse plant a Rodney, Nelson, or Cunningham. It seems quite possible that one can produce good second-raters by contrived means, and no derogatory sense is necessarily meant to be implied by the term *good second-rater*. A navy full of Nelsons or even Cunninghams might be as out of control as a prepartition Polish parliament! Indeed, in a certain perverse sense, unorthodoxy and genius can so often only flourish in orthodox soil. A solid backup of good administration and subordinate loyalty is generally needed for even the most talented and idiosyncratic supreme commander. But in the end the most talented form of leadership, just like the highest form of creative art, can only be encouraged not instructed.

Concerning the significance of the individual leader or great man— an issue that incidentally concerned Tolstoy—we can only give a temporizing verdict. Is the leader really all that significant in the success of a nation? Tolstoy, for example, cast doubt on the role of the leader and saw accident and the chance performance of the masses as the determining features making for the success or failure of a nation in war.

Individual genius can certainly be an important factor in the success of warlike operations. Playing the pleasant, if not necessarily edifying, game of "ifs" in history, we can try to think of a Trafalgar not led by Nelson (remembering, of course, that he only led the British fleet for the crucial opening of the battle). It is safe to say that a leader like Nelson can ensure total annihilation whereas a less gifted leader might not fully exploit favorable opportunities. Yet in the issue of national victory or defeat in the long term, much depends on the wealth of a nation, its commitment to a struggle, and the morale of the men. The morale of the men brings us back, of course, to the impact of the leader. Besides these factors, the factor of individual genius is much less significant. One might safely speculate that without a Nelson, a St. Vincent, or a Collingwood, Britain would still have defeated France on the sea even if the attainment of victory might have been more prolonged and exhausting. Again and again in history, as in the Napoleonic wars, so in the Second World War we see that personification—the will of a nation—is crucial. To take a leading example of the question of the contribution of an individual to a nation's effort, we have Churchill's role in Britain's determination in 1940. Here we have an exaggeration of his contribution, although more by overseas opinion than by British comment. The British had their tails up in 1940. Churchill was the right man but not the only man who could have successfully expressed defiance of Hitler, for the British were aroused and would have responded to any leadership of vigor.

When we descend to less resounding figures, the significance of a change of face would seem to have even less importance in the final result. Substitute David Beatty or Sir George Callaghan for Jellicoe at Jutland, and one cannot imagine much difference in the result. Substitute all the top echelons of the Admiralty in the First World War by other products of the same background, and the result would have been much the same, for the navy in the First World War was making the trained response of a generation.

It is indeed important to be cautious about the impact of individual leaders, especially since a redress is needed of the balance of writing on leadership, writing that hitherto has placed such emphasis on the great man. This is a quite natural phenomenon. A writer on any subject tends to magnify the significance of that subject. So writers on leadership tend to exaggerate the role of the leader. Moreover, writers on leadership, whether of military, naval, or academic background, have tended to have elitist assumptions and have often held positions among the elite. Rarely have they been toilers down below or born losers. Six months as a private in an infantry regiment, or in what used to be called a ship's boiler room, might have made them a little more cautious in their assessment of the impact of leadership and their attachment to the dogma of the crucial role of the leader.

Good leadership may delay but cannot prevent disaster. Similarly, good leadership may speed but not produce a national victory. When the will to fight collapses among the lower echelons, as it did in Russia in 1917–18 or most recently in Vietnam, no amount of prodding from above or from outside allies, can save the day. So the reader should pay tribute to the leaders but above all remember the led!

Earlier in this this study I described the three main aspects of British naval leadership as the *variable*, having to do with changing times; the *particular*, having to do with a national tradition particular to the Royal Navy; and the *universal*, having to do with the qualities of personality or of personality working within an institution that seem relevant to any age or any country.

The *variable* factor is the background condition to the exercise of leadership at different historical periods. It encompasses changing social conditions and values, the changing assumptions about the behavior of leaders and led, and the varying qualities of education and training. It also encompasses the world of manpower, including discipline and the general welfare, physical or otherwise, of the men. It also includes the change in materiel.

In the aspect of social conditions, we see both change and continuity. The aristocratic tradition of leadership gave way to, although was not completely superseded by, professional elitism. It was a relatively slow process in the period under study. In changing times, continuity was preserved in the Royal Navy by families such as the Fremantles, who sent at least one son in each generation into the navy, and the same family names crop up generation after generation in the navy lists of admiralty and captains. In a way not all that unique in English history, a naval family tree could be started by the son of a Westminster barber,[1] for example, Admiral Sir Thomas Troubridge. Nor untypical in English history was the way in which improverished gentry might see the sea as a way to fortune. In its social and political attitudes the naval hierarchy in this period revealed a slowness of response—indeed, an ingrained suspicion regarding the advent of democracy, perhaps reflecting a nation that has still never had a social revolution. The deferential element in English society declined only slowly and in the services only at a snail's pace. As an American commentator said, "In Europe the proper relationship between officer and men exists automatically."[2]

Although changes in social outlook have often been slow, too slow from the progressive point of view, there has been a strong and distinctive element of change in the command assumptions of the leaders and the led. At the upper end of the service, orders were not necessarily carried out unchallenged or even obeyed at all in the eighteenth-century navy, and the courts-martial of that period represent at times political debating exercises rather than disciplinary tribunals or investigative processes. Despite this, British naval leadership rose to the occasion in a series of major wars with a high and adaptable standard of leadership and then entered into calmer seas in the nineteenth century with a much clearer and firmer code of obedience and chain of command. This was largely due to the work of St. Vincent.

At the lower end of the naval scale, men who in the eighteenth century were pressganged or misled into the navy from any part of the world where able or less than able-bodied men could be found were clearly different from the professional, literate, and more technically advanced seamen of the twentieth century. Even a St. Vincent would not have had quite the same effect or been able to employ the same brutality of authority in an age such as the Second World War, when socially the seamen were more conscious of their rights, more progressive, and had greater political consciousness, as they showed in the 1945 election.[3]

In education and training the standards of the men were obviously a world apart in the twentieth century in comparison with the eighteenth century. On the other hand, attempts to improve officer education were not always successful in the light of subsequent performance, but through the trial and error of the nineteenth century effective improvement was ultimately made, at least by the start of the First World War, and, of course, had to be made for the sake of national survival.

In the physical condition and health of the seamen and the change in materiel we see the most striking changes. The improvement in health and living conditions of the men was due to deliberate policy, due to pressures from both within and without the navy. The calculation of turnover of men in the mideighteenth and twentieth centuries is like making calculations in two different worlds. A twentieth-century admiral leads fitter men with greater stamina, who are provided with all the facilities of modern medical science. Also the men have a much greater expectation of medical and welfare services and consideration from the navy for the well being of their families. Both officers and men marry younger. Certainly, the waste of men from which the eighteenth century suffered had been largely eradicated.

In the materiel world there has been a series of revolutions. We saw changes from sail to steam and then to oil in the period of this study, to be followed after the end of it by the onset of nuclear power. Not only was there change but a speeding up of change. Nelson's flagship the *Victory*, although constructed in 1759, was still up to date in 1805. In contrast, many of Cunningham's ships at Matapan, built for the First World War, were already virtually rendered obsolescent by the advent of air striking power, just as before the First World War the building of the dreadnoughts rendered obsolete all earlier ships. The rapidity of materiel change has had an effect on the demands made on leadership. Materiel factors indeed cannot be completely disassociated from manpower factors. The adaptations necessitated by materiel changes caused resentment in the nineteenth-century navy and continued to cause stress in the twentieth-century navy. Many of Jellicoe's worries were caused by the question of the ability of the dreadnoughts to perform according to strategic and tactical demands. They had not, of course, been tested in a real battle. As it turned out, the problems caused by flash and insufficient armor plating of the magazine confirmed that Jellicoe's worries were not without foundation. The old certainties of sail had gone.

The question of which service should control the air arm of the fleet seemed to raise a question in the 1920s and 1930s of the fundamental role of the navy. The bedrock of the navy for so many years was sail, but in the twentieth century there have been fewer fixed points in a materiel sense, and this has made for psychological uncertainty.

Those preoccupied with materiel changes tended to discount the value of tradition and experience. The nineteenth century was above all a great age of engineering that seemed to provide the key to the future in every walk of life. All is new, the age seemed to suggest; comparison with past naval lessons is at best not too helpful, at worst irrelevant. A constant, if concerned awareness existed that new wars might not be quite like old wars, and old preoccupations required new examination, if not replacement. But the greatest exponent of the materiel school, Sir John Fisher, was also a man imbued with historic tradition. He may have missed the point on occasions in his prediction of the future from his knowledge of the past, but he always paid attention to the past.

Thus we have seen the many different features that make up what we have called the variable aspect of British naval leadership, and we are reminded that in talking in the same breath about Nelson at Trafalgar, Jellicoe at Jutland, or Cunningham at Matapan, we must not forget the very different social and materiel backgrounds of these engagements.

The second main aspect of this study, the *particular*, is used in this analysis to mean the particular nature of the British navy, special to itself. It is a very historic quality, a tradition. It is especially concerned with an offensive mentality of leadership in action and an encouragement during much of the period of individual officer initiative. This tradition of the offensive developed in the eighteenth century. It became such a significant feature of the British navy that as a result it limited the confidence of the French navy. Pierre Villeneuve and his immediate predecessors made a habit of the defensive. Aggressive action against British shipping in European waters was left to the French or American privateers. Hawke, Rodney, Hood, St. Vincent, and Nelson—their success bred success. They built up a capital of prestige that was to sustain the navy into the twentieth century. How this success had come about tended to be forgotten or misunderstood, but their memories were an example, a stimulus, and a source of moral support. This tradition of the offensive gave a moral advantage to the British over all the navies of the world for several generations. But this element of self-confidence in the British naval tradition decayed into complacency in the nineteenth century and was followed by the anxiety of the twentieth century as the British naval superiority evaporated and ultimately disappeared. However, the British naval assumption of the offensive, and of superiority, was an obvious psychological advantage for the British navy for the greater part of the two hundred years, which is the period of this study.

The second feature of the *particular* aspect of British naval leadership, especially significant in the Royal Navy tradition, was the combination of a very general overall control by the Admiralty with backing for the particular initiative of the man on the spot. It is true that the man on the spot like Admiral Rodney or Sir Sidney Smith might, indeed, and often did run the risk of hostile repercussions at home. But the general assumption that fostered initiative was that in far away places, whether it be the China coast or the Caribbean, a man had to take his opportunities as they came without waiting for further orders to tell him what to do.

Two examples, widely separated in time, illustrate this point. Hawke at Spithead on May 5, 1762, wrote to John Cleveland,[4] secretary of the navy, regarding Hawke's interpretation of his commission: "From the tenor of my commission I did conclude, that the destination of the King's ships within the limits of my command rested with me & among others for this good reason, that otherwise, in pressing exigencies of service, too much time would be lost in apprizing their Lordships of the destination of ships, and receiving their answers."[5] Later in the same month, on the 23rd, he wrote to Commodore Moore: "I leave you at liberty to make what alterations you shall think proper in the disposition of the ships, only carefully attending to the principal point, the guarding against the enemys coming out, or escaping if they should. . . . But be that as it will risques must be run."[6] Nearly two centuries later, on May 10, 1941, Admiral Sir Sidney Fremantle,[7] approved the following comment in Alfred Von Tirpitz's[8] *My Memoirs* (1919): "How differently has England dealt with similar questions of sea power! For centuries the principle has held good there that any action on the part of a British officer, so long as it is energetic, will be protected against outside consequences."[9] Fremantle himself wrote, in approving the comment of Tirpitz, "My view was that the Admiralty would not have placed me in a position of responsibility if they had not confidence in my judgment in unforeseen circumstances."

This reliance on individual initiative became discounted toward the end of the nineteenth century with the unparalleled focus on the destiny and responsibility of the "Big Leader" of the "Big Fleet" ordering all and being the repository of all professional wisdom. With its reverence of Nelson, the late Victorian navy forgot that Nelson, with all his authoritative planning, never ruled out the independent initiative of subordinates. The weakening of this tradition had a stultifying effect on the late Victorian navy and among senior officers in the Great War, but the tradition was recaptured in the Second World War. This lesson of the First World War had been well learned.

These two elements, then, a continuing recourse to the offensive and a convention of independent action, contribute especially to the formation of the second main aspect, the *particular*, that is, the British naval tradition.

The *universal* factor includes those elements that contribute to successful leadership in very different situations over a long period. These elements are not particular to or restricted to the history of British naval leadership.

Here we see three features that are especially valuable: past battle experience, the harmonious working together of key leaders, and breadth of vision. Of course, many other features could also be considered, such as the age-old recourse to surprise, as relevant to the Arab-Israeli War of 1973 as to Nelson's sudden onslaught during the Battle of St. Vincent in 1797.

Undoubtedly, the intelligent consideration of past major battle experience is a key aspect in the success or failure of British naval leadership. It was the misfortune of Jellicoe, Beatty, and Keyes that they did not have great battle experience in modern conditions to reflect upon before they held the highest command. But it was the good fortune of Rodney, Hood, St. Vincent, and Nelson that they had had years of fighting their major enemies, France and Spain, before they held the highest command. Sir Andrew Cunningham and his generation shared this professional luck of Nelson and the officers of his time. Earlier experience as combatants stood them in good stead. Yet experience is not enough in itself. There must be intelligent appreciation of the experience of the past. After all, to take an example from the military sphere, the French Marshal Bazaine had far more battle experience than Count von Moltke had at the onset of the Franco-Prussian War, and yet Bazaine became a byword for ineptitude. It is here that a mixture of percipience and intelligence, and a sense of history added to experience, can be so decisive in the exercise of successful leadership in action.

A second important universal factor is the harmonious working together of a partnership of leaders, whether it is paternal and filial or patron and protégé in style. Senior command in the Royal Navy is never exercised in a vacuum. There are always the Admiralty, professional colleagues and rivals, and a wider political world to bear in mind. A rising professional officer, especially in the eighteenth century, would expect his fortunes in the navy to depend on individual patronage. But even in the highest command, survival and success so often depend on good backing. We see throughout history the importance of a sailor or soldier administrator backing the sailor or soldier activist in a complementary and sustaining, although not always totally amicable, relationship. From British naval history we have the examples of Anson working with Hawke, St. Vincent with Nelson, and, finally Dudley Pound with Cunningham. It has been one of the purposes of this study to emphasize the significance of this nexus. In the military sphere, in recent times, the pattern has been repeated, with Eisenhower and Patton or Montgomery, Marshall and MacArthur, and Alexander and Montgomery.

These kinds of successful relationships smoothed the nettle path to glory. Where there was less decisive or obvious success, as in the Fisher and Jellicoe relationship, there may have been a misunderstanding of roles or a failure to anticipate or predict performance. The wrong man was in the wrong place. The patron had more élan than the protégé. Both Jellicoe and Fisher were materiel men in a world where brilliant new strategic and tactical insights were desperately required. Thus we see the importance of a good working relationship with key superiors, and its necessary concomitant, the confident exercise of authority over subordinates.

The offensive instinct combined with optimism are ageless qualities that contribute to success when allied with sound judgment. The brilliant exploitation of tactical opportunities, as displayed by Nelson, needs no further explanation as a examplar of successful naval leadership in action. These features added to enemy vulnerability and enemy lack of confidence—above all, lack of confidence—have led to success after success for the British navy. Also, simplicity, clarity, and effective communication are essential, since otherwise we have the confusion of Lestock, Mathews, and Byng, or the disappointment of Jutland.

The final *universal* quality, a continuing breadth of vision, is paramount. We have concentrated on admirals who had participated in major action. None of the more successful naval leaders was narrow in his outlook. They all had a political and strategic sense. They were at home in wider and more turbulent seas than, and as well as, the ocean blue of nature. Only when they seemed determined to exclude all but purely professional considerations, as possibly in the case of Jellicoe, or fail to retain perspective in the pursuit of professional glory, as in the case of Keyes, do we get profound disappointment arising.

We may end as we began with the quality of the particular leader in the particular situation being crucial. St. Vincent could terrorize the officers and men of the Mediterranean and Channel fleets, but not the satraps of the Navy Board or the dockyard contractors. Rodney could sweep the Caribbean, but not without debilitating expense to the hustings of Northampton.[10] Jellicoe could arouse the enthusiasm of the men at Scapa Flow, but not that of the less happy breed at Whitehall. Leadership competence successfully exercised in one situation may transfer a sense of authority and confidence to another sphere of operation. But there is no sure recipe for this. In the end, the unpredictable remains to irritate the social scientist and delight the historian. As has been so often said in the case of Nelson, one cannot legislate for a genius. Nor can one legislate for leadership in general. All that can be said is that in the exercise of a successful response to a changing situation, in the creation and retention of a tradition of excellence, and in the exercise of particular qualities of genius that resound in any age, we have with the history of British naval leadership from 1750 to 1945 an unprecedented record of achievement.

NOTES

INTRODUCTION

1. Horatio Nelson, first Viscount Nelson, 1758-1805; vice-admiral; Britain's greatest admiral; distinguished himself at Cape St. Vincent, 1797; led British fleet at Nile, 1798; under Sir Hyde Parker at Copenhagen, 1801; died in battle of Trafalgar, 1805. His association with Emma, Lady Hamilton, caused a scandal.

2. John Rushworth Jellicoe, first Earl Jellicoe, 1859-1935; Admiral of the Fleet; director of Naval Ordnance, 1905; Third Sea Lord and controller of Navy, 1908; Second Sea Lord, 1912; commander-in-chief, Grand Fleet, 1914-16; First Sea Lord, 1916-17; governor-general of New Zealand, 1920-24.

3. Roger Boyle, Baron Broghill and first Earl of Orrery 1621-79. A royalist who, however, supported Cromwell in Ireland. See his "Treatise of the Art of War," which was dedicated to Charles II.

4. Quincy Wright, *A Study of War* (Chicago: University of Chicago Press, 1965), calculated at p. 650 that England in the period 1480-1941 had headed the war league with seventy-eight wars and that France was second with seventy-one. This is a curious book. Wright believed the best way to abolish war was to write about it.

5. Andrew Bruce, first Viscount Cunningham, 1883-1963; Admiral of the Fleet; deputy chief of Naval Staff, 1938-39; admiral and commander-in-chief, British naval forces in the Mediterranean, 1939-42; Gulf of Taranto success, 1940; Matapan, 1941; head of British naval delegation in Washington, 1942; First Sea Lord and Chief of Naval Staff, 1943-46.

6. Edward Hawke, first Baron Hawke, 1705-81; Admiral of the Fleet; married an heiress, 1744; MP for Portsmouth under patronage of duke of Bedford, 1747; successful action off Finesterre, 1747; failure of Rochefort expedition, 1757; Quiberon Bay Victory, 1759; First Lord of the Admiralty, 1766-71.

7. John Byng, 1704-57; admiral; son of George Byng, Viscount Torrington, who had been successful at Cape Passaro, 1718; First Lord of the Admiralty, 1727-33. Byng was a member of the court-martial of Richard Lestock and Thomas Mathews in 1746; commander-in-chief, Mediterranean, 1747-48; MP for Rochester, 1751-57; unsuccessful expedition to Minorca, 1756; court-martial, 1756-57; shot by firing squad, 1757.

8. Sir George Tryon, 1832-93; vice-admiral; private secretary to Goschen, First Lord of the Admiralty, 1871-74; commander of first British seagoing iron-clad, 1861; gave fatal order sending the *Camperdown* into collision with his flagship *Victoria*, in which he went down along with many officers and men in 1893. He was heard to say just before going down, "It is entirely my fault."

9. John Jervis, Earl of St. Vincent, 1735-1823; Admiral of the Fleet; under Boscawen, 1755-56, then Saunders, 1756; in Mediterranean, 1758; in North America, 1759; at Ushant, 1778; captured *Pégase*, 1782; MP (a Whig), 1783; with Sir Charles Grey captured Martinique and Guadaloupe, 1794; commander-in-chief, Mediterranean, 1795; victory over Spanish fleet at St. Vincent, and created earl, 1797; averted mutiny through strict discipline, 1798; commander-in-chief, Channel Fleet, 1799-1801; First Lord of the Admiralty, 1801-4, during which period attacked corruption; commanded in Channel, 1806-7.

10. Cuthbert Collingwood, Baron Collingwood, 1750-1810; vice-admiral; served in North America, 1774-75; West Indies, 1776-81; in Mediterranean, 1795; blockaded Cadiz, 1797-98, and Brest, 1799-1805; took command on death of Nelson at Trafalgar, 1805; commander-in-chief, Mediterranean, 1805-10.

11. David Beatty, first Earl Beatty, 1871-1936; Admiral of the Fleet; in Kitchener's expedition to the Sudan and gained DSO in 1896; commander, 1898; in China during Boxer Rebellion, 1899; captain, 1900; rear-admiral, 1910; secretary to Churchill, 1912; in charge of battle cruiser squadron, 1914; succeeded Jellicoe as commander-in-chief, Grand Fleet, 1916, and commander of it until 1919; First Sea Lord, 1919-27.

12. Roger John Brownlow Keyes, first Baron Keyes, 1872-1945; Admiral of the Fleet; in China during Boxer Rebellion, 1899; in charge of submarine service, 1912-14; Chief of Staff, Eastern Mediterranean squadron, under Carden then De Robeck 1915; Grand Fleet captain, 1916-17; director of plans at Admiralty, 1917; commander of Dover Patrol, 1918; commanded operations

against Zeebrugge and Ostend, 1918; commander-in-chief, Mediterranean, 1925-28; director of combined operations, 1940-41.
    13. See, for example, Norman F. Dixon, *On the Psychology of Military Incompetence* (London: Cape, 1977).

CHAPTER 1
EARLY WRITINGS ON LEADERSHIP

    1. The word is said to have been used at the start of the nineteenth century. The earliest reference I have noted is the one in the *Oxford English Dictionary Supplement*, 1976, as used by C. W. Wynn in 1821.
    2. St. Louis, Louis IX, 1214-70; king of France, 1226-70; went on Sixth Crusade, 1248-54; one of the greatest of French medieval kings; canonized, 1297. There are many other examples of particularly venerated medieval monarchs: in England, Edward the Confessor, 1002?-66; Henry III, 1207-72; and Henry VI, 1421-71.
    3. The French term *carrière ouverte aux talents*, popular in the nineteenth century, gives a good sense of this trend.
    4. Archibald Percival Wavell, first Earl Wavell, 1883-1950; field marshal; commander-in-chief, India, 1941; field marshal, 1942; viceroy of India, 1943-47; *Generals and Generalship* (London: Times Publishing Co., 1941).
    5. Stephen Wentworth Roskill, born 1903; captain RN; fellow of Churchill College, Cambridge, 1961; *The Art of Leadership* (London: Collins, 1964).
    6. *Naval Review*, 1912-. See bibliography for further comment.
    7. I am grateful to Professor Henry Tosi of the Department of Management, Michigan State University, East Lansing, for introducing me to social science research on the theme of leadership. The best modern survey of work in the field is Ralph M. Stogdill, *Handbook of Leadership. A Survey of Theory and Research* (New York: Free Press, 1974). For examples of theoretical studies of leadership, see Victor H. Vroom and Philip W. Yetton, *Leadership and Decision Making* (Pittsburgh: University of Pittsburgh Press, 1973), and F.E. Fiedler, *A Theory of Leadership Effectiveness* (New York: McGraw-Hill, 1967). Other articles and books, as well as the above, are referred to in the bibliography.
    8. I give my own views on these questions in the final chapter.
    9. For a discussion and description of such testing, see Philip E. Vernon and John B. Parry, *Personnel Selection in the British Forces* (London: University of London Press, 1949).
    10. See, for example, the work of Sir Cyril Burt, 1883-1971, first psychologist to the London County Council. Attacks have been made in recent years on

the validity of his methods and evidence. For example, see, L. S. Hearnshaw, *Cyril Burt: Psychologist* (London: Hodder & Stoughton, 1979).

11. See James MacGregor Burns, *Leadership* (New York: Harper Row, 1978).

12. Arthur Wellesley, first Duke of Wellington, 1769-1852; general and statesman; campaigned in India, 1797-1804; chief secretary for Ireland, 1807-9; in Peninsular War, 1808-14; dukedom, 1814; representative of United Kingdom at Congress of Vienna, 1814-18; command British forces at Waterloo, 1815; commander-in-chief, 1827-28, and 1842-52; prime minister, 1828-30; foreign secretary under Peel, 1834-35.

13. Pierre Charles Jean Baptiste Silvestre de Villeneuve, 1763-1806; French vice-admiral; Commander of the Fleet designed to invade England, 1805; defeated by Nelson at Trafalgar, 1805.

14. Denis Decrès, 1761-1820; French minister of marine, 1801-14, during which time the French navy expanded from 55 ships and 41 frigates to 103 ships and 54 frigates.

15. John Moncreiff. A writer who apparently flourished in the period 1748-67.

16. *The Naval Chronicle*, 1799-1818, was a regular publication with many articles on naval personalities and on other matters of general naval interest. See vol. 5, p. 213.

17. Alfred Thayer Mahan, 1840-1914; American naval officer and historian; president, Naval War College, Newport Rhode Island, 1886-93; *The Influence of Sea Power Upon History 1660-1783* (Boston: Little Brown and Company, 1890); *The Life of Nelson, the Embodiment of the Sea Power of Great Britain* (London: Sampson, Low, Marston & Co. 1897); *Types of Naval Officers* (London: Sampson, Low, Marston & Co., 1901).

18. John Arbuthnot Fisher, first Baron Fisher, 1841-1920; Admiral of the Fleet; entered fleet under Sir William Parker, 1854; Egypt, 1882; Lord of Admiralty, 1892-97; commander-in-chief, North American and West Indies station, 1897-99, and Mediterranean, 1899-1902; First Sea Lord, 1904-10, and 1914-15.

19. Sir William Hannam Henderson, 1845-1930; founder and editor of *The Naval Review*, 1912-30. A collection of his papers is in the Library of the National Maritime Museum in Greenwich (henceforth referred to as Greenwich).

20. Sir Herbert William Richmond, 1871-1946; admiral, member of naval staff, 1912; Grand Fleet, 1917; director of training and staff duties, Admiralty, 1918; master of Downing College, Cambridge, 1933-45; *Command and Discipline* (London: E. Stanford Ltd., 1927).

21. Arthur Marder, born 1910; naval historian. The leadership traits are noted in *From Dreadnought to Scapa Flow. Victory and Aftermath*, vol. 5

(London: Oxford University Press, 1970), p. 327. See also material in *Portrait of An Admiral—The Life and Papers of Sir Herbert Richmond* (London: Cape, 1952); and *Fear God and Dread Nought. The Correspondence of Admiral of the Fleet Lord Fisher of Kilverstone*, 3 vols. (London: Cape, 1952-59); the earlier volumes of *From Dreadnought to Scapa Flow*; and "Nelson, a Case Study," *The Naval Review*, April 1961.

22. Omar Nelson Bradley, born 1893; general; World War II commander, Europe; first chairman of Joint Chiefs of Staff, 1949-53. He listed nine leadership qualities in an address to 12th Army Group Association, Carlisle Barracks, Pennsylvania.

23. Bernard Law Montgomery, first Viscount Montgomery, 1887-1976; field marshal; commander, Eighth Army, 1942-44; Chief of Imperial General Staff, 1946-48. *Military Leadership* (London: Oxford University Press, 1949).

24. John Winthrop Hackett, born 1910; general; commander-in-chief, British army of the Rhine; commander, Northern Army Group, 1966-68; principal of King's College, London University, 1968-75. *The Profession of Arms—The 1962 Lees Knowles Lectures* (London: Times Publishing Co., 1963); *The Third World War: August 1985* (London: MacMillan, 1978).

25. Sir John Smyth, born 1893; brigadier; Victoria Cross, 1915; instructor at Staff College, Camberley, 1931-34; *Leadership in War, 1939-45* (Newton Abbott: David & Charles, 1974); *Leadership in Battle, 1916-18* (Newton Abbott: David & Charles, 1975).

26. Martin Geoffrey Bennett, born 1909; captain RN; naval historian and writer. See *Nelson the Commander* (London: B. T. Batsford, 1972), p. 5.

27. Professional military journals. The Ministry of Defence Library (Central and Army), London, has a large collection of cuttings of articles on leadership from professional military journals throughout the world. The author is grateful to the librarians for their assistance in providing these for him.

28. Edward Pelham Brenton, 1774-1839; captain RN; naval historian; *Life and Correspondence of John Earl of St. Vincent. GCB, Admiral of the Fleet* (London: Henry Colburn, 1838).

29. Thomas Arnold, 1795-1842; headmaster of Rugby, 1828-42.

30. Oliver Cromwell, 1599-1658; successful general in civil wars, 1642-46, and 1648, and subsequently in Scotland and Ireland; protector, 1653-58.

31. Richard Howe, Earl Howe, 1726-99; Admiral of the Fleet; on part of Anson's circumnavigation, 1740; Mediterranean, 1752-54, under Boscawen; MP for Dartmouth, 1757-82; under Hawke at Rochefort, 1757, and at Quiberon Bay, 1759; in America, 1776-77; in relief of Gibraltar, 1782; First Lord of Admiralty, 1783 (January-April), and 1783 (December)-1788; commanded Channel Fleet in great victory over the French on June 1, 1794, "The Glorious First of June"; Admiral of the Fleet and general of marines, 1796.

32. Georgy Konstantinovich Zhukov, born 1896, died 1974. Russian marshal who directed the defense of Stalingrad.

CHAPTER 2
NAVAL LEADERSHIP: SOME DISTINCTIVE FEATURES

1. Prince Rupert, 1619-82; general and admiral; fought in Civil War and in naval wars with the Dutch; First Lord of the Admiralty, 1673-79.

2. Robert Blake, 1599-1657; Commonwealth and Protectorate general and admiral; captured Spanish Treasure Fleet, 1656.

3. George Monk (or Monck), first Duke of Albemarle, 1608-70; one of three generals of the fleet, 1652; key figure in the restoration of Charles II as general-in-chief of land forces and joint commander of navy.

4. Sir William Sidney Smith, 1764-1840; Admiral of the Fleet; under Rodney, 1782; a volunteer in the Swedish fleet, but not permitted by the Admiralty to accept command in that fleet, 1789; persuaded Hood to employ him at Toulon, 1793; joint plenipotentiary at the porte, 1798; raised siege of Acre, 1799; Treaty of El Arish disavowed by British government, 1800; MP for Rochester, 1802; second-in-command, Mediterranean, 1812-14.

5. A sociologist has attempted a study of this. See Norbert Elias, "Studies in the Genesis of the Naval Profession," *The British Journal of Sociology* 6 (1950): 291. More than one article was promised on this subject but apparently only one was published.

6. Oliver Papers, Greenwich, BEL/2A.

7. Rear Admiral H. G. Thursfield, ed., *Five Naval Journals* (London: Navy Records Society, 1951), p. 104. Peter Cullen was a surgeon in the navy from 1789 to 1813. The entry was for June 26, 1800.

8. Sir Nicholas Harris Nicolas, *The Dispatches and Letters of Vice-Admiral Lord Viscount Nelson*, vol. 2, 1795-97 (London: H. Colburn, 1845), p. 397.

9. Jellicoe Papers, British Library (formerly British Museum). Henceforth cited as BL. Additional Manuscripts 49037. Henceforth cited as Add MSS.

10. Edward Vernon, 1684-1757; admiral; MP for Penryn, 1722; stormed Porto Bello, 1739; Vernon's "grog" first consumed, 1740; failed in Cartagena expedition, 1741; cashiered for pamphlets attacking admiralty, 1746.

11. Douglas Haig, first Earl Haig, 1861-1928; field marshal; commander-in-chief of expeditionary forces in France and Flanders, 1915-19.

12. Charles McMoran Wilson, Baron Moran of Manton, 1882-1977; fashionable general practitioner; medical adviser to Winston Churchill among others; an army medical officer, 1914-17; *Winston Churchill: The Struggle*

for Survival (London: Constable, 1966); *The Anatomy of Courage* (London: Constable, 1966).

13. Robert Georges Nivelle, 1856-1924; general, 1914; succeeded Joffre as commander-in-chief of the French armies of the North and Northeast, 1916; relieved of command when his offensive of April 1917 failed.

14. Moran, *Anatomy of Courage*, p. 43.

15. Sir Gilbert Blane, 1749-1834; private physician to Admiral Rodney and physician to fleet, 1779-83; physician at St. Thomas's Hospital, 1783-95; commissioner for sick and wounded seamen, 1795-1802.

16. Christopher Lloyd and Jack L. S. Coulter, *Medicine and the Navy, 1200-1900*, vol. 3, 1714-1815 (Edinburgh: E. & S. Livingstone, 1961), p. 354.

17. George Brydges Rodney, first baron, 1719-92; admiral; under Thomas Mathews in Mediterranean, 1742; governor of Newfoundland, 1748-52; MP, 1751; too ill to sit on Byng's court-martial, 1756; with Boscawen in North America, 1758; rear-admiral, 1759; reduced Martinique, 1762; baronet, 1764; governor of Greenwich Hospital, 1765-70; elected MP for Northampton, 1768; lived in France because of debt, 1775-79; relief of Gibraltar, 1780; St. Eustatius and other settlements seized, 1781; Battle of the Saints, 1782, and raised to the peerage.

18. There are many naval Hoods and they have similar forenames. The most famous were two sets of cousins. The first set is Alexander Hood, 1758-98, captain; and his brother Sir Samuel Hood, baronet, 1762-1814, rear-admiral. The second set is Samuel Hood, Viscount Hood, 1724-1816; and his brother Alexander Hood, Viscount Bridport, 1727-1814. There is a collection of Hood papers at Greenwich, the most interesting of which for the naval historian have to do with Viscount Hood. Samuel Hood, first Viscount Hood, 1724-1816; admiral; commander-in-chief, North American station, 1767-70; outmaneuvered de Grasse off St. Kitts, 1782; under Rodney at Battle of the Saints, 1782; took temporary possession of Toulon, 1793, and Corsica, 1794; governor of Greenwich Hospital, 1796-1816. In this work he will be referred to as Hood.

19. Wynne Papers, Greenwich, WYN/103.

20. William IV, 1765-1837; known as the sailor king; third son of George III; captain of frigate, 1785, and stationed in West Indies; rear-admiral, 1790; duke of Clarence, 1789; king of Great Britain, Ireland, Hanover, 1830-37. William IV's popularity, with the naval community at any rate, is seen in the number of inns named after him. See also comment on Vernon p. 31— another popular inn sign.

21. Sir Benjamin Hallowell Carew, 1760-1834; admiral; commanded ship at Nile, 1798. The coffin was made of the mast of the *Orient*, one of Nelson's prizes. Captain Hallowell gave it to Nelson with these words, ". . . that when

you are tired of this life, you may be buried in one of your trophies." Nelson's comment in reply is not known. See W. H. Fitchett, *Nelson and His Captains* (London: Smith, Elder & Co., 1902), p. 159.

22. A fact noted in Lloyd and Coulter, *Medicine and the Navy*, vol. 3, p. 142.

23. G. L. Newnham Collingwood, ed., *A Selection from the Public and Private Correspondence of Vice-Admiral Lord Collingwood Interspersed with Memoirs of His Life*, vol. 2 (London, 1828), p. 239.

24. Ruddock F. Mackay, *Admiral Hawke* (Oxford: Clarendon Press, 1965), 154. Letter dated January 14, 1757.

25. Alfred Ernle Montacute Chatfield, first Baron Chatfield, 1873-1967; Admiral of the Fleet; flag captain under David Beatty, 1914; at Jutland, 1916; First Sea Lord and Chief of Naval Staff, 1933-38; minister for coordination of defence, 1939-40.

26. Alfred Dudley Pickman Rogers Pound, Sir Dudley Pound, 1877-1943; Admiral of the Fleet; commanded *Colossus* at Jutland, 1916; commander-in-chief, Mediterranean, 1936-39; First Sea Lord and Chief of Naval Staff, 1939-43.

27. Chatfield Papers, Greenwich, CHT/4/10; Letter, 2 July 1937.

28. William Pitt, earl of Chatham, 1708-78; MP, 1735; paymaster general and privy councillor, 1746; secretary of state and leader of House of Commons, 1756-57, 1757-61, final period of office, 1766-68. Conducted a vigorous prosecution of Seven Years War against France. He was a highly successful grand strategist.

29. Major-General Mundy, *The Life and Correspondence of the Late Admiral-Lord Rodney*, vol. 1 (London: J. Murray, 1830), p. 160.

30. Charles Middleton, first Baron Barham, 1726-1813; admiral; comptroller of the navy, 1778-90; MP, 1784; First Lord of the Admiralty, 1805-6. A very successful administrator who organized the Trafalgar campaign.

31. Hood Correspondence, Greenwich (HOO/1); George III to Hood, July 12, 1778.

32. Sir John Knox Laughton, ed., *Letters of Charles Lord Barham Admiral of the Red Squadron, 1758-1813*, vol. 3 (London: Navy Records Society, 1909), pp. 37-38.

33. Especially between 1760 and 1860 the rate of fertility among ducal families was remarkably high. See T. H. Hollingsworth "A Demographic Study of the British Ducal Families," *Population Studies* 11 (1957).

34. Richard Kempenfelt, 1718-82; rear-admiral; British naval commander of Swedish descent; interested in improvement of signaling; died in loss of the *Royal George*.

35. See article in that work entitled "Admiral," vol. 1.

36. Hermann Maurice Comte de Saxe, 1696-1750; Marshal of France,

1744; *Les Rêveries* (The Hague: P. Gosse junior, 1756).

37. Quoted by Sir Herbert Richmond, *Command and Discipline* (London: E. Stanford, Ltd., 1927), p. 257.

38. Sir Evan Nepean, first baronet 1751-1822; entered navy as a clerk; purser in *Foudroyant* under St. Vincent; a commissioner of privy seal, 1784; under secretary of war, 1794; secretary of the admiralty, 1795-1804; a commissioner of the Admiralty, 1804-6; governor of Bombay, 1812-19.

39. St. Vincent Papers, Greenwich, NEP/4, 31 April 1797.

40. Sir John Thomas Duckworth, first baronet 1748-1817; admiral, in *Orion*, June 1794, and awarded gold medal; West Indies, 1801; defeated French fleet off Santo Domingo, 1806; governor and commander-in-chief, Newfoundland, 1810-13.

41. Henderson Papers, Greenwich, HEN/8/5. In *Remarks on the Training Promotion and Retirement of Executive Officers.*

CHAPTER 3
THE EIGHTEENTH CENTURY: THE MAKING
OF A TRADITION

1. A good general introduction to the period is J. Steven Watson, *The Reign of George III* (Oxford: Oxford University Press, 1960). See also G. J. Marcus, *Heart of Oak. A Survey of British Sea Power in the Georgian Era* (London: Oxford University Press, 1975).

2. George Anson, Baron Anson, 1697-1762; Admiral of the Fleet; was in Carolina from 1723-24 to 1730, where there is an Anson County; circumnavigated the world, 1740-44, and captured the Acapulco ship off Manila with 500,000 pounds worth of treasure, 1743; on Board of Admiralty, 1744; success against the French off Finesterre, 1747; First Lord of the Admiralty, 1751-56, and 1757-62.

3. James Cook, known as Captain Cook, 1728-79; charted coasts of New Zealand, Australia, and New Guinea; in important expeditions in these areas and off the coast of North America. Enforced strict hygienic and dietary rules for his crews.

4. Matthew Flinders, 1774-1814; mariner and hydrographer; with George Bass explored and surveyed coast of New South Wales, 1795-1800; first to correct for deflection of compass caused by iron in ship.

5. George Bass, explorer off coast of New South Wales; discoverer of Bass Strait, 1798; last authenticated report of him being alive made in 1803.

6. Sir Charles Douglas, died 1798; rear-admiral; fleet captain to Rodney at the Battle of the Saints, 1782; commander-in-chief, Halifax station, 1783-86; invented improvements in naval gunnery.

7. Nelson Papers, BL, Add MSS 37076; Nelson to Dr. Moreley, March 11, 1804.

8. *Annual Register*, 1763 (London, 1796), p. 50. It employs the term *missing* for desertion and gives no further breakdown of figures.

9. Dr. Thomas Trotter, 1760-1832; surgeon's mate, 1779; for lack of employment later worked on a slave ship, which made him an ardent abolitionist; appointed physician of the fleet by Howe; *Medicina Nautica*, 3 vols. (London: T. Cadell jun. and W. Davies, 1797-1803); in later life in private practice in Newcastle-upon-Tyne. He was also a tragic playwright in the Romantic style.

10. Dr. James Lind, 1716-94; surgeon of the *Salisbury* in the Channel Fleet, where he experimented regarding treatment for scurvy, 1746; *A Treatise of the Scurvy* (Edinburgh: A. M. Millar, 1753). Dr. Gilbert Blane and Dr. Thomas Trotter were his disciples.

11. In the shortage of manpower in the 1790s there was a frequent, even desperate, resort of the authorities to scavenge manpower by pressing from any possible source—hence the term a *hot* press.

12. Daniel A. Baugh, *British Naval Administration in the Age of Walpole* (Princeton: Princeton University Press, 1965), p. 476.

13. There is a vast amount of critical literature that touches on the social and political significance of the Romantic movement. One worthwhile example is M H. Abrams, *Natural Supernaturalism Tradition and Revolution in Romantic Literature* (New York: Norton, 1971).

14. For a general study of the utilitarians, see Ernest Albee, *A History of English Utilitarianism* (New York: Macmillan, 1957).

15. Jeremy Bentham, 1748-1832; English jurist and philosopher; one of chief expounders of utilitarianism; influenced by Adam Smith in his economic views and wrote on prison and poor law reform.

16. Sir Samuel Bentham, 1757-1831; naval architect and engineer; worked for Russian government, 1780-95; subsequently worked for British naval improvements; a commissioner of navy, 1807; his office subsequently abolished, 1812.

17. Christopher Lloyd and Jack L. S. Coulter, *Medicine and the Navy, 1200-1900*, vol. 3, 1714-1815 (Edinburgh: E. & S. Livingstone, 1961).

18. George John Spencer, second Earl Spencer, 1758-1834; First Lord of the Admiralty, 1794-1801; home secretary, 1806-7.

19. Thomas Corbett, died 1751; secretary to Admiral George Byng in the Sicilian expedition, 1718-20; secretary of the Admiralty, 1741-51.

20. Thomas Mathews, 1776-1851; admiral; at Cape Passaro, 1718; in virtual retirement, 1724-41; Toulon expedition, 1743-44; court-martial, 1746, acquitted.

21. Richard Lestock, 1679?-1746; admiral; at Cape Passaro; passed over

for promotion, 1733-39; under Admiral Vernon at Cartagena, 1741; under Thomas Mathews at Toulon, 1743-44; unanimously acquitted by court-martial, 1746.

22. David Hannay, ed., *Letters of Sir Samuel Hood* (Viscount Hood) in 1781, 1782, 1783 (London: Navy Records Society, 1895), p. xxxix.

23. Frederick William I, 1688-1740; king of Prussia, 1713-40. Lieutenant Hans Hermann von Katte helped the king's son Frederick (king from 1740-86), excape from confinement. Frederick William forced his son to watch the execution of Katte in 1730 and there were rumors, which caused widespread protest, that the king was also contemplating the execution of his son Frederick.

24. *The Trial of the Honourable Admiral John Byng at a Court Martial as Taken by Mr. Charles Fearne Judge-Advocate of His Majesty's Fleet* (London: R. Marby, 1757), p. 101.

25. Sir John Mordaunt, 1697-1780; at Culloden, 1745; in broken health in 1757 expedition. A general court-martial unanimously found him not guilty regarding charges arising from the 1757 expedition.

26. Baugh, *British Naval Administration*, p. 66.

27. John Russell, fourth Duke of Bedford, 1710-71; Whig statesman; First Lord of the Admiralty, 1744-48; a lord justice of Britain, 1745, 1748, and 1750.

28. Thomas Pelham-Holles, first Duke of Newcastle-upon-Tyne and Newcastle-under-Lyne, 1693-1768; Whig statesman; secretary of state for the Southern Department, 1742; prime minister, 1754-56, and 1756-62.

29. Vernon Papers, Greenwich, VER/1/2J.

30. Sir Charles Hanbury Williams, 1708-59; satirical writer and diplomatist. The statement has been attributed to his father, John Hanbury, but this does not seem possible as John Hanbury died in 1734.

31. Philip Yorke, first Earl of Hardwicke, 1690-1764; lord chief justice, 1733; lord chancellor, 1737-56.

32. Thomas Parker, first Earl of Macclesfield, 1666?-1732; lord chancellor, 1718-25; ultimately impeached for taking bribes, but a favorite of George I.

33. Augustus Keppel, first Viscount Keppel, 1725-86; admiral; served under Admiral Hawke, 1757; second in naval command at capture of Havana, 1762; commander-in-chief of Grand Fleet at Ushant, 1778; indecisive engagement but acquitted by court-martial, 1779; First Lord of the Admiralty, 1782.

34. Sir Charles Saunders, 1713?-75; admiral; with Anson around the world; with Hawke, 1747; MP for Plymouth, 1750; commander-in-chief of fleet for St. Lawrence, 1759; First Lord of the Admiralty, 1766.

35. Philip Saumarez, 1710-47; captain in the navy; with Hawke at action of

October 14, 1747, where killed.

36. Edward Boscawen, 1711-61; admiral; won distinction at Porto Bello, 1739 and Cartagena, 1741; a Lord of the Admiralty, 1751-61; victory at Finesterre, 1747; defeated French at Lagos Bay, 1759.

37. James Wolfe, 1727-59; under Mordaunt at Rochefort; commanded Quebec expedition, with rank of major-general, at which killed, 1759.

38. Alfred T. Mahan, *Types of Naval Officers* (London: Sampson Low, Marston, & Co., 1902), p. 100.

39. Ruddock F. Mackay, *Admiral Hawke* (Oxford: Clarendon Press, 1965).

40. Mackay, *Admiral Hawke*, p. 181.

41. Hood Correspondence, Greenwich, HOO/1.

42. Louis Antoine de Gontaut, duc de Biron, 1700-88; marshal who commanded the French Guard in Paris.

43. Major-General Mundy, *The Life and Correspondence of the Late Admiral-Lord Rodney*, vol. 2 (London: J. Murray, 1830), p. 291.

44. Of the many Grenvilles this was apparently James Grenville, 1742-1825; privy councillor, 1782.

45. HOO/1.

46. Sir Howard Douglas; general 1776-1861; member of Parliament for Liverpool, 1842-46. He made these remarks in his *Naval Evolutions* (London: T. & W. Boone, 1832).

47. John Clerk, 1728-1812; naval writer and successful merchant in Edinburgh; originally privately printed an *Essay on Naval Tactics* (London: T. Cadell, 1790; enlarged, 1797). The second edition of Clerk's work is referred to in the bibliography.

48. St. Vincent thought that Admiral Rodney's success was accidental. See Jebediah Stephens Tucker, *Memoirs of Admiral the Right Hon. Earl of St. Vincent*, 2 vols. (London: R. Bentley, 1844).

49. Thomas Graves, first Baron Graves, 1725?-1802; admiral; commanded in indecisive action with De Grasse off Chesapeake, 1781; second-in-command to Howe at the Battle of the First of June 1794, where badly wounded; for his services in that action he was awarded an Irish peerage.

50. Mackay, *Admiral Hawke*, p. 353.

51. Isaac Coffin, 1759-1839; admiral; convicted of signing false muster roll, 1788; conviction suppressed, 1789; commissioner of the navy in Corsica, 1795-96.

52. HOO/1.

53. Sir John Barrow, *The Life of Richard Earl Howe KG* (London: John Murray, 1838), p. 402. There are other examples in history of misleading or ambiguous sobriquets. Thus John Poyntz, Earl Spencer, 1835-1910, First

Lord of the Admiralty, 1892-94, was known as the "Red Earl," for his beard, not his political views.

54. Barrow, *The Life of Richard Howe KG*, p. 117.

55. Alexander Hood, first Viscount Bridport, 1727-1814; admiral; at Ushant, 1778; under Howe at Gibraltar, 1782; at Battle of First of June 1794; second-in-command to Howe; commander-in-chief, Channel Fleet, 1797-1800, succeeding Howe in this command.

56. *Suaviter in modo*—here meaning pleasant in manner and *fortiter in re* meaning formidable in action. I am grateful to Professor Richard Frank at the University of California, Irvine, for this appropriate translation. See Barrow, *The Life of Richard Howe KG*, p. 427.

57. G. J. Marcus, *A Naval History of England: The Formative Centuries* (Boston: Little, Brown & Co., 1961), p. 391.

58. Sir Thomas Pakenham, 1757-1836; admiral; commanded *Invincible* at Battle of First of June 1794; his conduct at the battle highly approved by Howe.

59. William Montagu, 1720-57; captain; stories of his eccentricity abounded.

60. Augustus John Hervey, third earl of Bristol, 1724-79; admiral; entered navy, 1736; at Havana, 1762; Lord of the Admiralty, 1771-75.

61. These and other escapades during this period of service are detailed in David Erskine, ed., *Augustus Hervey's Journal* (London: William Kimber, 1953).

62. A. Lane Poole, *From Domesday Book to Magna Carta* (Oxford: Clarendon Press, 1951), p. 441.

63. HOO/1.

64. Sir Edward Codrington, 1770-1851; admiral; commanded a ship at Trafalgar; commander-in-chief, Mediterranean, 1826 and at Navarino, 1827; retired from active service, 1842.

65. Lady Bourchier, *Memoir of Life of Admiral Sir Edward Codrington*, vol. 1 (London: Longmans, Green & Co., 1869), p. 27.

66. Thomas Cochrane, tenth earl of Dundonald, 1775-1860; admiral; accused of connivance in speculative fraud, fined, imprisoned, and expelled from navy, 1814; with Chilean navy, 1817-22; Brazilian navy, 1823-25; Greek navy, 1827-28; commanded each one of these navies; received free pardon and promoted rear-admiral, 1832; commander-in-chief, North American station, 1848-52; fertile with new technical ideas.

67. Bourchier, *Memoir*, vol. 1, p. 1.

68. Henry Addington, first Viscount Sidmouth, 1757-1844; Speaker of House of Commons, 1789-1801; prime minister, 1801-4; home secretary, 1812-21.

69. Sir Hugh Palliser, baronet, 1723-96; admiral; governor and commander-in-chief, Newfoundland, 1762-66; under Keppel, 1778.

70. William Anne Keppel, second earl of Albemarle, 1702-1754.

71. George Keith Elphinstone, Viscount Keith, 1746-1823; admiral; at reduction of Charleston, 1780; rear-admiral, 1794; successful at Cape Town against Dutch, 1796; commander in Mediterranean, 1799, having been second-in-command to St. Vincent in 1798; commander-in-chief, North Sea, 1803-7, and in Channel, 1812; a very important commander who never took part in a major fleet action. The family name is also Elphinstone.

72. Hon. and Revd. Thomas Keppel, *Life of Augustus Viscount Keppel*, vol. 1 (London: H. Colburn, 1842), p. 348. This quotation is from an earlier work by Charles Johnson and may well be apocryphal.

73. George Keppel, third earl of Albemarle, 1724-72; elder brother of Augustus; at Culloden and Fontenoy; commanded land forces in capture of Havana, 1762-63.

74. Sir George Pocock, 1706-92; admiral; commander-in-chief of the expedition naval forces of which Augustus Keppel was second-in-command.

75. For further details of the distribution of the spoils, see David Syritt, ed., *The Siege and Capture of Havana 1762* (London: Navy Records Society, 1970), p. 305 *et seq.*

76. Etienne François, duc de Choiseul, 1719-85; minister of foreign affairs, 1758-61; of war and marine, 1761-66; of war and foreign affairs, 1766-70.

77. Pierre André de Suffren de Saint-Tropez, 1726-88; prisoner at Battle of Finesterre, 1747; fought engagements with Britain in Indian waters, 1782-83.

78. Luc Urbain du Bouexic, comte de Guichen, 1712-90; an adversary of Rodney in the West Indies.

79. François Joseph Paul, Comte de Grasse-Tilly, 1723-88; at Battle of Dominica, 1780; Chesapeake Bay, 1781; captured at the Battle of the Saints.

CHAPTER 4
ST. VINCENT: THE SAILOR WHO DID *NOT* FALL FROM GRACE WITH THE SEA

1. Admiral Sir William James, *Old Oak Life of John Jervis* (London: Longmans, Green & Co., 1950), p. 64.

2. Sir Edward Berry, baronet, 1768-1831; rear-admiral; lieutenant under Nelson at Porto Ferrajo 1796; Trafalgar, 1805; created baronet, 1806.

3. Captain E. Jurien de la Gravière, *Sketches of the Last Naval War* (London: Longman, Brown, Green & Longmans, 1848), p. 110.

4. Sir Peter Parker, first baronet, 1721-1811; Admiral of the Fleet; took

part in reduction of Long Island, 1775; rear-admiral and commander-in-chief of Jamaica, 1777.

5. Sir Thomas Fremantle, 1765-1819; vice-admiral; served with Hood and Nelson in the Mediterranean, 1793-97; wounded at Santa Cruz, 1797; at Copenhagen, 1801; Trafalgar, 1805; commander-in-chief, Mediterranean, 1818.

6. See Ann Parry, ed., *The Admirals Fremantle* (London: Chatto and Windus, 1971), pp. 43-46.

7. Sir Thomas Troubridge, first baronet, 1758?-1807; vice-admiral; at St. Vincent and Santa Cruz; a commissioner of the Admiralty, 1801-4; lost at sea.

8. Edward Pellew, first Baronet and first Viscount Exmouth, 1757-1833; MP, 1802; commander-in-chief, East Indies, 1804; commander-in-chief, Mediterranean, 1811; commander-in-chief, Plymouth, 1817-21.

9. Sir John Orde, first baronet, 1751-1824; admiral; governor of Dominica, 1783; baronet, 1790; joined St. Vincent, 1797, and was third-in-command in Mediterranean; privately circulated correspondence with St. Vincent, 1799, published in 1802; MP, 1807-24; a warm admirer of Nelson, but his regard was not reciprocated; a pallbearer at Nelson's funeral.

10. William Pitt, 1759-1806; second son of the first earl of Chatham; Chancellor of the Exchequer, 1782; prime minister, 1783-1801, 1804-5.

11. Rear-Admiral Augustus Phillimore, *The Life of Admiral of the Fleet Sir William Parker Bart GCB*, vol. 1 (London: publisher, 1876), p. 243. It is interesting to note that after 1806 when Barham was First Lord, the only First Lord who was a naval officer was the duke of Northumberland (1852). This was a marked contrast to the practice of the eighteenth century when officers frequently occupied the post.

12. Sir William Parker, 1781-1866; Admiral of the Fleet; China, 1842; commander-in-chief, Mediterranean, 1845-52.

13. Phillimore, *The Life of Admiral Sir William Parker*, vol. 1, p. 163.

14. Colonel Drinkwater Bethune's account is a very good one. See *A Narrative of the Battle of St. Vincent with Anecdotes of Nelson Before and After That Battle* (London: Saunders and Otley, 1840). Also known as John Drinkwater (1762-1844), he was at the siege of Gibraltar, 1779-1783. He was comptroller of Army Accounts from 1811 to 1835.

15. A view put forward by John Creswell, *British Admirals of the Eighteenth Century: Tactics in Battle* (Hamden, Conn.: Archon Books, 1972).

16. David Bonner Smith, ed., *Letters of Admiral of the Fleet the Earl of St. Vincent whilst First Lord of the Admiralty*, vol. 1 (London: Navy Record Society, 1921), p. 101.

17. Collingwood Papers, BL, Add MSS 52780.

18. Garnet Joseph Wolseley, first Viscount Wolseley, 1833-1913; field marshal. "All Sir Garnet" means just so—all correct.

19. Journal of St. Vincent, BL, Add MSS 31188, April 1800-October 1801.

20. Sir William George Tennant, 1890-1963; admiral; flag officer, Levant and Eastern Mediterranean, 1944-46; commander-in-chief, American and West Indies station, 1946-49.

21. See pages 144-46 for comment on the mutiny.

22. G. J. Marcus, *Heart of Oak. A Survey of British Sea Power in the Georgian Era* (London: Oxford University Press, 1975), p. 151.

23. Keppel Papers, Greenwich, KEP/6.6.

24. KEP/8.

25. Hood Correspondence, Greenwich, HOO/2.

26. Sir John Barrow, *The Life of Richard Earl Howe KG* (London: John Murray, 1838), p. 301.

27. Philip Patton, 1739-1815; admiral; a commissioner of the Admiralty, 1804-6. At the time of the letter in 1797 he was in retirement.

28. Wynne Papers, Greenwich, WYN/109/7.

29. Henry Dundas, first Viscount Melville, 1742-1811; home secretary, 1791-94; secretary of war, 1794-1801; First Lord of the Admiralty, 1804-5; impeached 1806 for malversation (the last impeachment in British history, although the process remains); found guilty of negligence, but acquitted as to the impeachment.

30. Alan Gardner, first Baron Gardner, 1742-1809; admiral; with Rodney, 1782; commander in Jamaica, 1786-89; MP, 1792; a Lord of Admiralty, 1790-95.

31. Sir Charles Morice Pole, 1753-1830; Admiral of the Fleet; in command in Newfoundland, 1800; in command in Baltic, 1801.

32. WYN/102.

33. Nepean Papers, Greenwich, NEP/4.

34. Lord Hugh Seymour, 1759-1801; vice-admiral; friend of George, Prince of Wales; at relief of Gibraltar, 1782; a commissioner of the Admiralty; commander-in-chief, Jamaica, 1799-1801.

35. George Cranfield, seventeenth Baron Berkeley, 1753-1818; admiral; at Ushant, 1778; surveyor general of ordnance, 1786; MP for Gloucester, 1781-1812; held chief command on Portuguese Coast and on Tagus, 1808-12; supported Pitt in his attack on St. Vincent, 1804.

36. Sir Robert Calder, 1745-1818; admiral; at St. Vincent, 1797; rear-admiral, 1799; failed to outmaneuver the French, 1805, and censured for lack of judgment.

37. Sir Charles Thompson, baronet, 1740(?)-1799; vice-admiral; at Battle of the Saints, 1782; second-in-command at St. Vincent, 1797. Because of this

protest St. Vincent had him recalled home and he was appointed Commander of the Fleet off Brest.

38. Jebediah Stephens Tucker, *Memoirs of Admiral the Right Hon. Earl of St. Vincent*, vol. 1 (London: R. Bentley, 1844), p. 328.

39. NEP/4.

40. Evelyn Berckman, *Nelson's Dear Lord*. (London: Macmillan, 1962), p. 134.

41. William Bligh, 1754-1817; vice-admiral; *Bounty* mutiny, 1789; governor, New South Wales, 1808-10. Bligh in history and fiction has become a symbol of harsh and tyrannical naval authority. George Mackaness has done his best to rehabilitate him.

42. WYN/101. Undated letter received by Pole October 1797.

43. NEP/4.

44. NEP/4.

45. The United Irishmen was a movement formed in Ireland in 1791 to achieve the complete separation of Ireland from England. It included both Catholics and Protestants. The French tried to assist the movement, but it was defeated at Vinegar Hill, June 21, 1798. Ultimately, on January 1, 1801, Great Britain and Ireland were joined by legislative union.

46. Sir Richard King, the elder, baronet, 1730-1806; vice-admiral; commander-in-chief, at Plymouth, 1794.

47. Oliver Papers, Greenwich, BEL/1.

48. St. Vincent Papers, BL, Add MSS 36708. To Evan Nepean.

49. NEP/6.

50. Robert Man, admiral, died 1813.

51. Sir George Young, 1732-1810; admiral; at Louisburg, 1758; at Quebec, 1759; a colonial developer and promoter.

52. WYN/102. Letter to Admiral C. M. Pole.

53. O. A. Sherrard, *A Life of St. Vincent* (London: G. Allen & Unwin, 1933), p. 132.

54. BL, Add MSS, 52780. Letter to Edward Collingwood, December 14, 1798.

55. Orde Papers, Greenwich, ORD/16.

56. NEP/4.

57. Ibid. NEP/4.

58. ORD/11.

59. Ibid.

60. Ibid.

61. Tucker, *Memoirs*, vol. 1, p. 353.

62. ORD/11, July 11, 1801.

63. NEP/6. Letter to Nepean.

64. NEP/4. Letter of December 20, 1798.

65. *The Naval Chronicle* 11 (January-July 1804): 193-94.

66. James Saumarez, Lord de Saumarez, 1757-1836; admiral; made commander for gallantry off Dogger Bank, 1781; at St. Vincent, 1797; wounded at Nile, 1798; defeated French and Spanish at Algeciras, 1801; commander in Baltic, 1808-13.

67. ORD/19. Letter to Orde, November 30, 1798.

68. William Cobbett, 1763-1835; essayist, politician, and agriculturalist; from 1804 wrote in the radical interest; member of Parliament for Oldham, 1832.

69. ORD/15.

70. ORD/19, November 12, 1798, and July 27, 1799.

71. ORD/15, November 12, 1798, ORD/19, July 29, 1799, and October 24, 1799.

72. Yorke Papers, Greenwich, YOR/13. The letter was a long one dated February 19 to Charles Yorke, 1764-1834, who was First Lord of the Admiralty, 1810-12.

73. *Laudator temporis acti*, literally "praiser of time passed."

74. This phrase, which originates in Shakespeare's *Henry V*, is usually used to describe Nelson and his captains. See *Henry V*, Act IV, Scene III.

75. BL, Add MSS 52780. To Edward Collingwood.

76. Adam Duncan, first Viscount Duncan, 1731-1804; admiral; at Havana, 1762; commander-in-chief, North Sea Fleet, 1795-1801; great victory at Camperdown against Dutch, 1797; a victory all the more creditable because of his disciplinary problems.

77. *Five Naval Journals* (June 26, 1800): 105.

78. BL, Add MSS 52780.

79. NEP/7.

80. Ibid.

81. Ibid.

82. Sir George Cockburn, 1772-1853; Admiral of the Fleet; in Mediterranean, 1793-1802; Admiral of the Fleet, 1851; his most significant service was in America, 1812-15. He was governor of St. Helena, 1815-16.

83. Sir Hyde Parker, 1739-1807; admiral, with Richard Howe at New York, 1778; commander-in-chief, Jamaica, 1796-1800, at Copenhagen, 1801, then recalled after unimpressive performance.

CHAPTER 5
NELSON: A HERO'S LIFE AND DEATH

1. Spenser Wilkinson, 1853-1937; barrister and journalist in Manches-

ter. He was subsequently first Chichele Professor of Military History at the University of Oxford, 1909-1923. His criticism of Alfred Mahan is in his *War and Policy* (New York: Dodd, Mead and Co., 1900), p. 126.

2. I hope these examples successfully illustrate the point I am making. Alfred Tennyson wrote about the search, and Algernon Swinburne wondered what they would do with it when they found the Holy Grail! Arthur was a real or legendary sixth-century king of Britain expected to return. Frederick Barbarossa, 1123?-90, Emperor Frederick I, 1152-90, is thought to be temporarily asleep in a Swabian Cave.

3. Emma, Lady Hamilton, 1761?-1815; mistress of Charles Greville and allegedly of George Romney, then mistress and later wife of Sir William Hamilton (see later note); gave birth to Horatia in 1801, who was later acknowledged by Nelson as his daughter.

4. George P. B. Naish, ed., *Nelson's Letter to His Wife and Other Documents 1785-1931* (London: Navy Records Society, 1958), p. 381.

5. Elizabeth Longford is the latest biographer of Wellington to relate this famous if brief meeting. She describes the encounter in *Wellington: The Years of the Sword* (London: Weidenfeld & Nicholson, 1969), pp. 110-11, and ventures the opinion that Nelson's style of leadership may have had an influence on Wellington.

6. Rev. James Stanier Clarke and John M'Arthur, *The Life of Admiral Lord Nelson KG from His Lordships Manuscripts*, vol. 1 (London: T. Cadell & W. Davies, 1809), p. 53.

7. Sir John Ross, *Memoirs and Correspondence of Admiral Lord de Saumarez from Original Papers in Possession of the Family*, vol. 1 (London: R. Bentley, 1838), pp. 227-28.

8. William Hotham, first Baron Hotham, 1736-1813; admiral; under Howe at relief of Gibraltar; second-in-command to Hood, 1793-94; commander in Mediterranean, 1795.

9. Sir Nicholas Harris Nicolas, *The Dispatches and Letters of Vice-Admiral Lord Viscount Nelson*, vol. 4 (London: H. Colburn, 1845), p. 90.

10. Naish, *Nelson's Letter*, p. 270.

11. With apologies to Matthew Arnold, 1822-88. See his poem *Shakespeare*.

12. Quoted in Spenser Wilkinson, "The War Training of Naval Officers," *Monthly Review*, October 1900. Reprinted as a pamphlet, no page reference.

13. Ann Parry, ed., *The Admirals Fremantle* (London: Chatto & Windus, 1971), p. 71.

14. Nicolas, *Dispatches and Letters*, vol. 2, p. 398.

15. Ibid., vol. 1, p. 120.

16. Ibid., vol. 1, p. 404.

17. Sir Thomas Masterman Hardy, first baronet, 1769-1839; vice-admiral;

flag captain of Nelson, 1799-1805; commander, South American station, 1819-1924; First Sea Lord, 1830.

18. Quoted in Nicolas, *Dispatches and Letters*, vol. 3, p. 49.

19. Sir John Barrow, *The Life of Richard Earl Howe KG* (London: John Murray, 1838), p. 374.

20. Collingwood Papers, Greenwich, COL/3. He continued, ". . . beyond all others shot will carry away the Masts and Yards of Friends as well as Foes. . . ."

21. Nicolas, *Dispatches and Letters*, vol. 6, p. 133.

22. Alfred Charles Dewar, 1875-1969; captain RN.

23. Kenneth Gilbert Balmain Dewar, 1879-1964; vice-admiral; assistant director of plan division, Naval Staff, 1917; deputy director, Naval Intelligence Division, 1925-27. The Dewars were brothers.

24. William Locker, 1731-1800; captain RN; at Quiberon Bay, 1759; commander, 1762; lieutenant commander of Greenwich Hospital, 1793-1800.

25. G. J. Marcus, *Heart of Oak. A Survey of British Sea Power in the Georgian Era* (London: Oxford University Press, 1975), p. 86.

26. Sir Richard Goodwin Keats, 1757-1834; admiral; one of Nelson's captains; highly thought of by Nelson, but missed Trafalgar.

27. John Creswell, *British Admirals of the Eighteenth Century* (Hamden, Conn.: Archon Books, 1972), p. 242.

28. Michael Howard, *The Times*, March 25, 1976.

29. Nelson Papers, BL, Add MSS 36610.

30. Clarke and M'Arthur, *The Life of Admiral Lord Nelson*, vol. 2, p. 31.

31. Maria Carolina, 1752-1814; married Ferdinand, king of Naples, 1768; a daughter of Maria Theresa and sister of Marie Antoinette. It is an interesting and curious coincidence that at the news of Nelson's victory at the Nile, Maria Carolina, Lady Hamilton, and Lord Spencer, the First Lord of the Admiralty, all swooned.

32. Sir William Hamilton, 1730-1803; diplomat and archaeologist; British plenipotentiary at the Court of Naples; became a close friend of Nelson.

33. Nicolas, *Dispatches and Letters*, vol. 3, p. 138.

34. Quoted in Wilkinson, *War and Policy*, p. 134.

35. Gilbert Elliot, first Earl of Minto, 1751-1814; viceroy of Corsica, 1974-96; minister at Vienna, 1799; governor-general of India, 1807-13.

36. Hugh Elliot, 1762-1830; minister at Naples, 1803. Hugh and Gilbert were brothers, sons of Sir Gilbert Elliot, 1722-77.

37. Elliot Papers, Greenwich. Nelson to Gilbert, ELL/138; Nelson to Hugh, ELL/303.

38. Captain Parker was later Sir William Parker.

39. This and the preceding quotation are from Rear-Admiral Augustus

Phillimore, *The Life of Admiral of the Fleet Sir William Parker Bart GCB*, vol. 1 (London: Harrison, 1876), pp. 258-59.

40. Alexander Davison, 1750-1829; government contractor and prize agent; a friend of Nelson from 1782 and acted as *homme d'affaires* for him. Davison made a large fortune from his contract work and was ultimately charged and found guilty of making illegal commissions at the expense of the government. He was imprisoned for this for a brief period in 1808.

41. Egerton Papers, BL, 2240.

42. Ibid.

43. St. Vincent Papers, Greenwich, JER/4.

CHAPTER 6
COLLINGWOOD: THE STOIC

1. Alfred Victor, comte de Vigny, 1797-1863; a leader of the French Romantic school; much influenced by Sir Walter Scott; officer in the French army, 1814-28.

2. See pages 169 and 176 of the *Military Condition* (Oxford: Oxford University Press, 1964). As is often the case, a translation cannot do full justice to de Vigny's style. For the French, see, for example, the edition edited by Gauthier-Ferrières (Paris: Larousse, 1913), in particular pages 147 and 150.

3. Ibid.

4. Quoted in *The Times* obituary notice of Field Marshal Montgomery, March 25, 1976.

5. Collingwood Papers, BL, Add MSS 52780. Letter, March 6, 1806.

6. Sir George Elliot, 1784-1863; admiral; second son of Gilbert, the first earl of Minto; served at St. Vincent and the Nile; commander, 1802; commander-in-chief, Cape of Good Hope, 1837-40; commander-in-chief and joint plenipotentiary with Sir Charles Eliot, China, 1840.

7. G. J. Marcus, *Heart of Oak. A Survey of British Sea Power in the Georgian Era* (London: Oxford University Press, 1975), p. 244.

8. The early forms of Sunday school provided fundamental instructions in the "3Rs," as well as religious instruction, for people whose labors during the rest of the week did not permit them any formal schooling.

9. Honoré Joseph Antonine, le comte Ganteaume, 1755-1818; wounded at the Battle of the Nile, 1798.

10. G. L. Newnham Collingwood, ed., *A Selection from the Public and Private Correspondence of Vice-Admiral Lord Collingwood Interspersed with Memoirs of his Life*, vol. 2 (London: J. Ridgway, 1828), p. 65.

11. Orde Papers, Greenwich, ORD/22.

CHAPTER 7
THE AGE OF NELSON—ALSO TAKING PART—
LESSER MORTALS

1. William James, *The Naval History of Britain* (London, 1822-1824), vol. 1, p. 84, and vol. 3, p. 79.

2. But the Temple, the prison in Paris, was nothing like a modern maximum security prison. There was a lot of unofficial coming and going. Sir Sidney Smith was incarcerated there in 1794-95.

3. Sir Nicholas Harris Nicolas, *The Dispatches and Letters of Vice-Admiral Lord Viscount Nelson*, vol. 2 (London: H. Colburn, 1845), p. 46.

4. Sir John Moore, 1761-1809; lieutenant-general; served in America, 1779-83; at Corsica, 1794; commander-in-chief in Portugal, 1808; died at Corunna during Peninsular War.

5. Percy Clinton Sydney Smythe, sixth Viscount Strangford and first Baron Penshurst, 1780-1855; envoy extraordinary at Portuguese Court in Brazil, 1808-15; ambassador at Constantinople, 1820. Claims were later made that Sir Sidney Smith rather than Strangford advised the Portuguese Regent to move his court from Portugal to Brazil.

6. Jean Baptiste Kléber, 1753-1800; left by Napoleon in Egypt, 1799; was dismissed after El Arish; assassinated in Cairo by a fanatic.

7. Nepean Papers, Greenwich, NEP/7.

8. NEP/5.

9. David Bonner Smith, ed., *Letters of Admiral of the Fleet the Earl of St. Vincent whilst First Lord of the Admiralty*, vol. 2 (London: Navy Records Society, 1921-26), p. 396.

10. Sir John Knox Laughton, *Letters of Charles Lord Barham, Admiral of the Red Squadron, 1758-1813*, vol. 3 (London: Navy Records Society, 1909), p. 162.

11. Keith Papers, Greenwich, KEI/L/23. Letter, January 4, 1800.

12. D. M. Schurman, *The Education of a Navy. The Development of British Naval Strategic Thought, 1867-1916* (London: Cassell, 1965), p. 25.

13. Leghorn, Italy, was a key port in the struggle between England and their friends in the Mediterranean, and the French.

14. Smith, *Letters of St. Vincent*, vol. 2, p. 322.

15. Rear-Admiral Augustus Phillimore, *The Life of Admiral of the Fleet Sir William Parker Bart GCB*, vol. 1 (London: Harrison, 1876), p. 137.

CHAPTER 8
THE LONG VICTORIAN PEACE

1. Sir Charles Napier, 1786-1860; admiral; with Portuguese navy, 1833;

commander in Baltic, 1854.

2. A. J. P. Taylor, *The Struggle for Mastery in Europe* (Oxford: Clarendon Press, 1954), p. 250.

3. Peter Karsten, *The Naval Aristocracy* (New York: Free Press, 1972), p. 277.

4. Sir James Robert George Graham, 1792-1861; Whig, then Conservative, then Peelite; First Lord of Admiralty, 1830-34, 1852-55; home secretary, 1841-46.

5. Sir Charles Frederick Alexander Shadwell, 1814-86; rear-admiral; president of Royal Naval College, Greenwich, 1878-81.

6. Philip Howard Colomb, 1831-99; vice-admiral; *Naval Warfare, Its Ruling Principles and Practice Historically Treated* (London: W. H. Allen, 1891); Essays on Naval Defense 1899. Sir John Charles Ready Colomb, 1838-1909, saw mixed naval and military service. *The Defence of Great and Greater Britain* (London: Edward Stanford, 1879).

7. Captain Charles Webley Hope, *The Education and Training of Naval Officers* (London, n.d.), no page reference. This pamphlet is in the Ministry of Defence Naval Historical Library, Earls Court, London.

8. Rear-Admiral G. C. Penrose Fitzgerald, *Life of Vice-Admiral George Tryon* (Edinburgh: W. Blackwood & Sons, 1897), tries to make out the best case for Tryon and his methods.

9. Sir Robert Stopford, 1768-1847; admiral; at relief of Gibraltar, 1781; with Richard Howe, 1794; with Nelson on chase to West Indies, 1805; in Rio and Copenhagen expeditions, 1806-07; commander-in-chief, Mediterranean Fleet, 1827-30, 1837-41; commanded operations against Mehemet Ali, 1840; governor of Greenwich Hospital, 1841-47.

10. Sir Archibald Berkeley Milne, second baronet, 1855-1938; Admiral second-in-command, Channel Fleet, 1908-9; commander-in-chief, Mediterranean Fleet, at outbreak of war; popular at court.

11. I am very grateful for the comments made to me on the navy before and during the First World War by Sir Angus Cunninghame Graham of Gartmore (born 1893; admiral, 1952).

12. Alfred, duke of Edinburgh, 1855-1900; commander-in-chief, Mediterranean, 1886-89; succeeded his uncle as duke of Saxe-Coburg and Gotha, 1893.

13. Charles William de la Poer Beresford, Baron Beresford, 1846-1919; admiral; Fourth Naval Lord, 1886-88; commander-in-chief, Mediterranean, 1905-7; commander-in-chief, Channel Fleet, 1907-9. "Charles B," as he was known, was a sparring partner of Sir John Fisher, especially after 1903.

14. Louis Alexander Battenberg, first marquess of Milford Haven, 1854-1921; admiral; at Alexandria, 1882; director of naval intelligence, 1902-5; First Sea Lord, 1912-14.

15. George V. 1865-1936; naval career, 1877-92; king of Great Britain and emperor of India, 1910-36.

16. Albert Victor Christian Edward, duke of Clarence and Avondale, 1864-1892; elder brother of George V; naval training from 1877; cruise around the world with his brother, 1879-82; subsequently in army; betrothed to Princess Mary, who married his brother George after his death.

17. Louis Francis Albert Victor Nicholas, first Earl Mountbatten of Burma, 1900-1979; Admiral of the Fleet; Supreme Allied Commander, Southeast Asia, 1943-46; viceroy of India, 1947, and governor-general, 1947-48; First Sea Lord, chief of defence staff, 1959-65. He said as a midshipman that he would be First Sea Lord one day, not an unexpected nor unattainable ambition, judging from his background. (From private source of information.)

18. Prince Philip, duke of Edinburgh, born 1921.

19. Prince Charles, born 1948.

20. Mrs. Worthington, an archetypal mother figure in the interwar years—harassed. See one of the lyrics of Sir Noel Coward, 1899-1973. The equivalent archetypal mother figure for the 1960s might be Mrs. Robinson (*The Graduate*).

21. The Cayzer family had a seat in Scotland at Gartmore Perthshire, and were founders of the Clan shipping line.

22. Marshall Field, 1843-1906. His business Marshall Field & Co. was at his death the largest wholesale and retail drygoods establishment in the world. His estate was valued at $125 million. His only daughter Ethel married Beatty as her second husband. She had an interest of at least $6 million under her father's will. She and Beatty married in 1904.

23. Holger Hervig, *The German Naval Officer Corps. A Political and Social History* (Oxford: Clarendon Press, 1973), p. 63. Jonathan Steinberg, "The Kaiser's Navy and German Society," *Past and Present*, July 1964, discusses the social outlook and education of the German navy.

24. Stafford Henry Northcote, first earl of Iddesleigh, 1818-87; president of Board of Trade; Chancellor of the Exchequer, 1874-80.

25. Sir Charles Edward Trevelyan, 1807-86; assistant secretary to the treasury, 1840-59. With Sir Stafford Northcote he published in 1853 *Report on the Organisation of the Permanent Civil Service*. These reforms, once much praised as a model, are now under criticism for their results. British decline in the world is said to date from then because it marks the date when British talent decided to go in for ruling rather than producing wealth. This view not surprisingly is unpopular in service and administrative circles. See Sir Peter Gretton's criticism of the historian Corelli Barnett in the July 1976 *Naval Review*, p. 272 and Barnett's reply in *Naval Review*, Jan. 1977, p. 74. It is suggested that the reforms channeled talent that should have been devoted to

creating wealth into government and administration and that the values of the administrators, increasingly dominated by Oxford and Cambridge, were inimical to creativity. Be that as it may, certainly the approach of the British Civil Service, as reformed, a defensive one, was far removed from that of the freewheeling spirit of the eighteenth-century aristocracy and merchant class or that of the energetic work-conscious northern and midlands industrial middle class who made Britain the greatest economic power in the world. Matthew Arnold's sweetness and light were bad for business.

26. HMS *Britannia*, training ship in the River Dart, 1863-1905.

27. Royal Naval Britannia College at Dartmouth, founded 1905.

28. Osborne. This was an additional college that existed from 1903-21.

29. Edward Thring, 1821-87; head master of Uppingham, 1853-87; founder of Head Masters Conference, 1869.

30. Samuel Butler, 1774-1839; head master of Shewsbury, 1798-1836.

31. Richmond Papers, Greenwich, RIC/12/3.

32. Sir Ernest Charles Thomas Troubridge, 1862-1926; admiral; entered navy, 1875; commander of cruiser squadron in Mediterranean, 1913; failed to intercept German battle cruisers *Goeben* (light cruiser) and *Breslau* on way to Dardanelles, 1914; exonerated by court-martial.

33. Henderson Papers, Greenwich, HEN/2/6. Letter dated July 4, 191(7?). It is an interesting if minor piece of crossword puzzle work to contemplate whom he had in mind when he wrote this. Lloyd George, Winston Churchill, and Louis Battenberg are obvious candidates. William the Conqueror might also be in mind, too!

CHAPTER 9
ENTERING THE WAR

1. See D. M. Schurman, *The Education of a Navy. The Development of British Naval Strategic Thought, 1867-1916* (London: Cassell, 1965), p. 91, for a comment on this example.

2. Unpublished memoirs of Admiral Sir Angus Cunninghame Graham.

3. Sir Sackville Hamilton Carden, 1857-1928; admiral; superintendent of the Malta dockyard, 1912; commander of Mediterranean squadron, 1914-15, in its attempt to silence Turkish forts at Dardanelles.

4. Sir John Michael De Robeck, 1862-1928; Admiral of the Fleet; succeeded Admiral Carden at Dardanelles; commander-in-chief, Mediterranean Fleet, 1919-22; commander-in-chief of Atlantic Fleet, 1922-26.

5. Keyes Papers, at the British Library, catalogued as Keyes/2/13. The subsequent quotation from the text is also from these papers. This quotation is from a letter of July 2, 1915, from Keyes to his wife.

6. Schurman, *Education of a Navy*, p. 16.

7. Peter Karsten, *The Naval Aristocracy* (New York: Free Press, 1972), p. 112.

8. At Tsushima on May 27-28, 1905, a Japanese fleet under Admiral Heihachiro Togo completely destroyed a Russian fleet under Admiral Z. P. Rozhdestvensky.

9. Sir Julian Stafford Corbett, 1854-1922; *The Campaign of Trafalgar* (London: Longman's, Green & Co., 1910).

10. Sir Winston Leonard Spencer Churchill, 1874-1965; First Lord of the Admiralty, 1911-15, 1939-40; prime minister, 1940-45, 1951-55.

11. Jellicoe Papers, BL, Add MSS 49007.

12. Nina Mary Benita Poore, duchess of Hamilton, 1878-1951; wife of the thirteenth duke.

13. BL, Add MSS 49007.

14. Maurice Paschal Alers Hankey, first Baron Hankey, 1877-1963; assistant secretary, Committee of Imperial Defence, 1908; secretary, Committee of Imperial Defence, 1912-38; secretary of War Cabinet, 1918-38; clerk to Privy Council, 1923-38; various ministerial appointments, 1939-42.

15. I am very grateful to Mrs. John Nutting, who on behalf of the trustees of the second Earl Beatty gave me access to the Beatty papers, which are as yet uncatalogued and held at Chicheley Hall, Buckinghamshire. This was a letter from Hankey to Beatty on Beatty's retirement as First Sea Lord, April 30, 1927.

16. Arthur J. Marder, ed., *Fear God and Dread Nought: The Correspondence of Admiral of the Fleet Lord Fisher of Kilverstone*, vol. 3 (London: Cape, 1952-59), p. 396.

17. BL, Add MSS 49035, July 28, 1913.

18. Sir Francis Charles Bridgeman, 1848-1929; Admiral of the Fleet; second-in-command to Charles Beresford in Channel, 1903-4; second-in-command to Beresford in Mediterranean, 1906-7; commander-in-chief, newly formed Home Fleet, 1907-9, and 1911; Second Sea Lord, 1910-11; First Sea Lord, 1911-12.

19. Marder, *Fear God and Dread Nought*, vol. 2. pp. 418-19.

20. John Alfred Spender, 1862-1942; Asquithian Liberal; journalist and author; editor of *Westminister Gazette*, 1896-1922.

21. Marder, *Fear God and Dread Nought*, vol. 2, p. 399. Letter dated October 25.

22. Ibid., vol. 2, p. 421. Letter to Mrs. Reginald McKenna.

23. Ibid., vol. 2, p. 424. Letter to Gerald Fiennes.

24. Ibid., vol. 2, p. 443. To Viscount Esher.

25. Sir Basil Henry Liddell Hart, 1895-1970; British military authority and

writer; military correspondent of *Daily Telegraph*, 1925-35, and *Times*, 1935-39.

26. John Frederick Charles Fuller, 1878-1966; major general and military writer; *Tanks in the Great War, 1914-18* (London: John Murray, 1920), and other writings.

27. A. C. Dewar and K. G. B. Dewar, "Naval Staff Appreciation of Jutland" (1922). It was prepared for the Admiralty but never released to the service or the public. Professor Arthur Marder believes that the Dewars were being deliberately controversial and their views should be regarded with some caution. See Arthur J. Marder, *From the Dreadnought to Scapa Flow. The Royal Navy in the Fisher Era*, vol. 3 (London: Oxford University Press, 1961-70), pp. viii-ix.

28. Tennant Papers, Greenwich, TEN/41/2. From notes for lecture on Jutland to the Royal Naval Staff College, 1931.

29. See footnote 27. K. G. B. Dewar was to write again on Jutland in *The Naval Review*, April 1969, p. 146.

CHAPTER 10
JELLICOE AND JUTLAND

1. Admiral Sir Reginald H. Bacon, *The Life of John Rushworth Earl of Jellicoe* (London: Hodder & Stoughton, 1936), p. 32. Jellicoe once hit a ball for eight runs.

2. Sir George Astley Callaghan, 1852-1920; Admiral of the Fleet; commanded naval brigade that relieved legations in Peking during Boxer uprising, 1900; second-in-command, Mediterranean, 1908; commander-in-chief, Home Fleet, 1911-14.

3. Sir William Robert Robertson, 1860-1933; field marshal quarter master general of the British Expeditionary Force, 1914; Chief of General Staff, 1915; Chief of Imperial General Staff, 1915-18; commander-in-chief, British Army of the Rhine, 1919-20;

4. Jellicoe Papers, BL, Add MSS 49037.

5. From notes made by Captain Oram quoted in Charles Owen, *No More Heroes—The Royal Navy in the Twentieth Century: Anatomy of a Legend* (London: Allen & Unwin, 1975), p. 64.

6. Beatty Papers.

7. Sir Charles Frederick Dreyer, 1878-1956; admiral; by 1907 recognized as the most accomplished gunnery officer of his time; flag commander to Jellicoe, 1910; Jellicoe's flag captain, 1915-16; director of Naval Ordnance, 1916-18; deputy chief of naval staff, 1930-31; commander-in-chief of China station, 1933-36.

8. Chatfield Papers, Greenwich, CHT/4/4.

9. Ibid.

10. A. Temple Patterson, ed., *The Jellicoe Papers, 1883-1916*, vol. 1 (London: Macmillan, 1966), p. 167.

11. Sir Cecil Burney, baronet, 1858-1929; Admiral of the Fleet; commander, Atlantic Fleet, 1911-12; second-in-command under Jellicoe, First Battle Squadron of Grand Fleet, 1914-16; Second Sea Lord, 1916-17.

12. Sir Lewis Bayly, 1857-1938; admiral, First Battle Squadron, 1914; commander-in-chief, Western Approaches, 1915-19.

13. Sir Frederic K. Charles Doveton Sturdee, 1859-1925; Admiral of the Fleet; chief of staff to Beresford in the Mediterranean, 1905-7; chief of war staff under Louis Battenberg, July 1914; Battle of Falkland Islands, 1914; in command of Fourth Battle Squadron, Jutland, 1916.

14. Sir George John Scott Warrender, seventh baronet, 1860-1917; admiral; in command of second Battle Squadron, 1914; commander-in-chief, Plymouth, 1915-16.

15. Patterson, *The Jellicoe Papers*, vol. 1, p. 177.

16. Sir Charles Edward Madden, first baronet, 1862-1935; Admiral of the Fleet; named by Fisher, October 1904, as one of the five best brains in the navy below the rank of admiral; Fourth Sea Lord, 1910-11, Chief of Staff under Jellicoe, 1914-16; commander of First Battle Squadron as second-in-command of fleet, 1916-19; commander of newly constituted Atlantic Fleet, 1919-22; First Sea Lord, 1927-30.

17. BL, Add MSS 49008.

18. Sir John Smyth, *Leadership in War, 1939-45* (Newton Abbot: David and Charles, 1974), p. 196.

19. Beatty Papers. Letter to his wife, December 5, 1916.

20. BL, Add MSS 49008. Letter dated March 26, 1915.

21. BL, Add MSS 49008.

22. Ibid.

23. Beatty Papers, Jellicoe was then, of course, First Sea Lord.

24. A. J. Marder, *Portrait of An Admiral—The Life and Papers of Sir Herbert Richmond* (London: Cape, 1952), p. 251.

25. Sir Arthur Knyvet Wilson, third baronet, 1842-1921; Admiral of the Fleet; in Crimean War and in operations against Alexandria; won VC at El Teb, 1884; commander-in-chief, Home and Channel fleets, 1903-7; First Sea Lord, 1910-12.

26. Peachey Papers, Greenwich, PCY/1. Contains typewritten extract of this letter to secretary of the admiralty.

27. Sir Alexander (Ludovic) Duff, 1862-1933; admiral; rear-admiral, Fourth Battle Squadron, 1914-16; experimented in defending ships against

mines, 1914; director of Anti-Submarines Division, 1916-17; assistant chief of naval staff, 1917-19; commander-in-chief, China station, 1919-22.

28. Duff Papers, Greenwich, DFF/15.

29. Patterson, *The Jellicoe Papers*, vol. 2, p. 156.

30. BL, Add MSS 48992.

31. Beatty Papers. Keyes and Chatfield to Beatty, August 4, 1922.

32. Alfred Charles William Harmsworth, Viscount Northcliffe, 1865-1922; journalist and newspaper proprietor; founded *Daily Mail* with brother Harold in 1896; baron, 1905; chief proprietor of *The Times*, 1908; director of propaganda in enemy countries, 1918; attacked in turn Kitchener, Asquith, Lloyd George, and many others.

33. Arnold White, 1848-1925; journalist; interested in the navy, its development, and its social problems; a friend of Fisher.

34. BL, Add MSS 48990.

35. Marder, *Portrait of An Admiral*, p. 351.

36. BL, Add MSS 49006.

37. BL, Add MSS 49007. Fisher to Jellicoe.

38. Arthur J. Marder, ed., *Fear God and Dread Nought. The Correspondence of Admiral of the Fleet Lord Fisher of Kilverstone*, vol. 3 (London: Cape, 1952-59), p. 443.

39. Ibid., vol. 3, p. 439. To David Lloyd George ca. March 14, 1917.

40. *Fear God and Dread Nought*, vol. 3, p. 151.

41. Ibid., vol. 3, p. 408. To Ernest B. Pretyman.

CHAPTER 11
AFTER THE BIG THING: BEATTY AND KEYES

1. Duff Papers, Greenwich, DFF/15.

2. Beatty Papers.

3. W. S. Chalmers, *The Life and Letters of David Earl Beatty* (London: Hodder & Stoughton, 1951), p. 262.

4. Jellicoe Papers, BL, Add MSS 49009. Letter dated December 19, 1916.

5. Ibid.

6. They were called soothsayers at the time. A more specific description would be fortune-tellers. One of them was a Mrs. Robinson.

7. Beatty Papers.

8. Ibid.

9. Ibid.

10. Ibid.

11. Cosmo Gordon Lang, 1864-1945; archbishop of York, 1909-28; arch-

bishop of Canterbury, 1928-42. He had visited the Grand Fleet in 1915 and continued solicitous for its welfare for the rest of the war.

12. Beatty Papers. There is a large amount of correspondence as yet unpublished between Beatty and his wife. Lady Beatty's comments to her husband are also very interesting because of the wide range of her acquaintances. A memoir of her would merit attention.

13. Ibid.

14. Ibid.

15. Ibid.

16. Ibid.

17. See comment in Arthur J. Marder, *From the Dreadnought to Scapa Flow. The Royal Navy in the Fisher Era*, vol. 4 (London: Oxford University Press, 1961-70), p. 36.

18. Hugh Montague Trenchard, first Viscount Trenchard, 1873-1956; known from 1912 as "Boom," Chief of Air Staff, 1919-29; chief of metropolitan police, 1931-35. He and Keyes (who was his brother-in-law) huffed and puffed at one another on more than one occasion.

19. Winston Churchill, who was First Lord at the time, must have had mixed feelings about this display.

20. This story is related both by Commander R. Travers Young and by Admiral J. H. Godfrey in the latter's *The Naval Memoirs*, vol. 1 (privately printed, 1964-66), p. 55. Whether the form of the story is apocryphal or not, it is evidence of the importance attached to being a member of the polo-playing set under Keyes.

21. Arthur J. Marder, ed., *Fear God and Dread Nought. The Correspondence of Admiral of the Fleet Lord Fisher of Kilverstone*, vol. 3 (London: Cape, 1952-59), p. 105. Churchill to Fisher.

22. Commander R. Travers Young, "Mischiefs in My Heart," unpublished memoir, Imperial War Museum. See pages 108 and 158.

23. Keyes Papers, British Library, Keyes/2/4.

24. Keyes/2/5.

25. Jellicoe Papers, BL, Add MSS 49006. On the same day Fisher made a similarly critical remark on Keyes to Beatty. Marder, *Fear God and Dread Nought*, vol. 3, p. 152.

26. A. Temple Patterson, ed., *The Jellicoe Papers, 1883-1916*, vol. 1 (London: Oxford University Press, 1966), p. 187.

27. Beatty Papers.

28. Sir Reginald Yorke Tyrwhitt, first baronet, 1870-1951; Admiral of the Fleet; commodore, Harwich Force, 1914-18; commander-in-chief, China station, 1927-29.

29. Keyes/2/9.

30. Keyes/2/9.

31. Keyes/2/13.

32. Keyes/2/15.

33. Unpublished papers of Commander R. Travers Young, Imperial War Museum, p. 107.

34. Sir Frederick Laurence Field, 1871-1945; Admiral of the Fleet; served during Boxer Rising, 1900; flag captain to Sir Martin Jerram at Jutland; Chief of Staff to Madden, November 1916 to April 1918; commander-in-chief, Mediterranean, 1928-30; First Sea Lord, 1930-33.

35. Sir Walter Henry Cowan, baronet, 1871-1956; admiral; at Jutland flag captain to Osmond Brock in *Princess Royal*; rear-admiral, 1918; appointed to Commandos in 1940 under his old friend and chief Sir Roger Keyes; prisoner of war, 1942. He gained a bar to his DSO in 1944. Despite all this action, like Rodney, he was never wounded.

36. Albert Victor, first Earl Alexander, 1885-1965; First Lord of the Admiralty, 1929-31, 1940-45, 1945-46; minister of defence, 1947-50.

37. Alexander Papers, Churchill College, AVAR 5/4.

38. Cunningham Papers, BL, Add MSS 52561.

39. Ibid.

40. BL, Add MSS 52569.

41. BL, Add MSS 52561.

42. Sir Philip Vian, 1894-1968; Admiral of the Fleet; boarded *Altmark* and rescued British seamen off Bergen, February 16, 1940. See his *Action This Day. A War Memoir* (London: F. Muller, 1960).

CHAPTER 12
INTERLUDE: BETWEEN THE WARS

1. In 1927 the director was Captain G. Blake.

2. Peachey Papers, Greenwich, PCY/1.

3. S. W. Roskill, *Naval Policy Between the Wars, II, 1930-39, The Period of Reluctant Rearmament* (London: Collins, 1976), p. 35, comments on the efforts of A. V. Alexander.

4. The Wincott Papers are at Churchill College. His reminiscences were published as Leonard Wincott, *Invergordon Mutineer* (London: Weidenfeld and Nicholson, 1974).

5. Wilfred Tomkinson, 1877-1971; vice-admiral; assistant chief of naval staff, 1929-31; in command of battle cruiser squadron, 1931-32.

6. Henderson Papers, Churchill College. See report letter of Tomkinson to the secretary of the admiralty, Sept. 24, 1931.

7. Edward Astley-Rushton, 1879-1935; rear-admiral; director of Royal Naval Staff College, 1922-25; director of Manning, Admiralty, 1928-30; commanded Second Cruiser Squadron, 1931-32. His words were received with scorn and derision by the men. Subsequently, at the Jubilee Review at Spithead in 1935, Astley-Rushton was passed over for decoration. He went to London afterward to protest at what he felt was a slight against the Naval Reserve and was killed in a car accident on his return journey from London.

8. Wincott Papers.

9. Quoted in S. W. Roskill, *The Art of Leadership* (London: Collins, 1964), p. 81.

10. Roskill, *Naval Policy Between the Wars*, vol. 2, pp. 101-102, discusses the claim by Wincott to have played a prominent part in the mutiny and casts doubt on this.

11. Roger Keyes protested in Parliament on July 31, 1934, at the way in which Wilfred Tomkinson had been treated. Tomkinson had served under Keyes in the Mediterranean. Thirty-six men, including Leonard Wincott, were discharged to the Royal Naval Barracks at Devonport soon after the event.

12. Beatty Papers. Letter from Field, September 22, 1931.

13. Sir (Joseph) Austen Chamberlain, 1863-1937, was First Lord of the Admiralty August-October 1931.

14. *The Times*, September 18, 1931.

15. Accusations of unfair bowling tactics were made by the Australians against the English team in the 1932-33 Test (international) series in Australia.

16. In February 1933 the Oxford Union passed, with a substantial majority, a resolution that "this House will not fight for King and Country."

17. Hannen Swaffer, 1879-1962; popular journalist and dramatic critic.

18. *What Would Nelson Do?* (London: Victor Gollancz, 1946).

19. Ib id., p. 62.

20. Sir Roger Roland Charles Backhouse, 1878-1939; Admiral of the Fleet; First Sea Lord, 1938-39.

CHAPTER 13
CUNNINGHAM: THE LESSONS OF THE GREAT WAR LEARNED AND THE SEARCH FOR ANOTHER NELSON CONCLUDED

1. Quoted in Viscount Cunningham of Hyndhope, *A Sailor's Odyssey. The Autobiography of Admiral of the Fleet Viscount Cunningham of Hynd-*

hope (New York: Hutchinson's, 1951), p. 459. Cunningham to Pound, March 19.

2. S.W.C. Pack, *Cunningham the Commander, 1883-1963* (London: B. T. Batsford, 1974).

3. Ernest Joseph King, 1878-1956; Fleet Admiral, 1944; commander-in-chief, U.S. fleet, December 1941; chief of naval operations, 1942.

4. Alan Francis Brooke, first Viscount Alanbrooke, 1883-1963; field marshal; commander-in-chief, Home Forces, 1940-41; Chief of Imperial General Staff, 1941-46.

5. Charles Frederick Algernon Portal, first Viscount Portal, 1893-1971; air chief marshal; Chief of Air Staff, 1940-46.

6. Cunningham Papers, BL, Add MSS 52558. He corresponded with these ladies for a few decades.

7. BL, Add MSS 52559. Letter of August 16, 1942.

8. James Edward Hubert Gascoyne-Cecil, fourth marquess of Salisbury, 1861-1947; Lord Privy Seal, 1903-5 and 1924-29.

9. Referred to in Alexander Papers, Churchill College, AVAR/5/5.

10. Bruce Austin, Baron Fraser, born 1888; Admiral of the Fleet; commander-in-chief, Home Fleet, 1943-44; commander-in-chief, British Pacific Fleet, 1944-46; First Sea Lord and Chief of Naval Staff, 1948-51.

11. John Cronyn, first Baron Tovey, 1885-1971; Admiral of the Fleet; vice-admiral and second-in-command, Mediterranean Fleet, 1940; commander-in-chief, Home Fleet, 1940-43.

12. AVAR/5/8.

13. Sir Geoffrey Oliver, born 1898; admiral; commanded HMS *Hermione*, 1940-42, Western Mediterranean; assistant chief of naval staff, 1947-48; president, Royal Naval College, Greenwich, 1948-50; commander-in-chief, East Indies station, 1950-52.

14. Cunningham Papers, Churchill College, Cunningham/2/1. Letter to Oliver Warner, December 28, 1965.

15. BL, Add MSS 52558.

16. Ibid. Letter of February 19, 1940. Many other opinions bear out the validity of Cunningham's judgment of Anthony Eden.

17. Ibid. Farouk, 1920-65; king of Egypt, 1936-52. In 1940-42 Farouk tried to maintain neutrality in the war. There had obviously been some decline in Cunningham's estimation of Farouk for on September 20, 1939, he described him as a "damned young rascal." Cunningham described him as a ruffian on August 2, 1940.

18. BL, Add MSS 52558. Letter dated February 10, 1941.

19. Randolph Frederick Edward Spencer Churchill, 1911-68; author and journalist; only son of Sir Winston; in 1940, on active service; in 1941, GSO on General Staff (Intelligence); GHQ, Middle East.

20. BL, Add MSS 52559. Letter dated July 7, 1941.

21. Leslie Hore-Belisha, 1893-1957; minister of transport, 1934-37; secretary of state for war, 1937-40. He aroused the ire of many military men, and this comment is occasioned by his removal from office. Cunningham's brother was General Sir Alan Gordon Cunningham, who was GOC, East Africa Forces, 1940-41. Perhaps Cunningham was here reflecting his brother's view of Hore-Belisha.

22. BL, Add MSS 52558. Letter dated January 7, 1940.

23. BL, Add MSS 52559. Letter of June 6, 1943. Eisenhower was at this time Supreme Allied Commander, North Africa.

24. Sir Algernon Usborne Willis, 1889-1976; Admiral of the Fleet; Chief of Staff, Mediterranean Fleet; HMS *Warspite*, 1939-41; Second Sea Lord, 1944-46; commander-in-chief, Mediterranean, 1946-48.

25. Algernon Willis, "War Memoirs of Admiral of the Fleet Sir Algernon Willis, 1939-45," Imperial War Museum, p. 4.

26. BL, Add MSS 52569. Letter of July 29, 1941.

27. BL, Add MSS 52561.

28. BL, Add MSS, 52559. Cunningham was in Washington during 1942.

29. BL, Add MSS 52560.

30. See Arthur J. Marder, *From the Dardanelles to Oran* (London: Oxford University Press, 1974), ch. 5. Force was used at Oran on July 3, 1940.

31. BL, Add MSS 52569, Signal 1355/28.

32. René Godfroy, born 1885; rear-admiral at Alexandria, 1940-43.

33. BL, Add MSS 52569.

34. Ibid. Vice-Admiral Tovey reported all this in a letter to Cunningham of October 17, 1940. The word *pussyfoot* was used in the letter.

35. BL, Add MSS 52560.

36. AVAR/5/5.

37. BL, Add MSS 52560.

38. BL, Add MSS 52561.

39. Ibid.

CHAPLTER 14
RECESSIONAL: ADMIRALS ALL FOR ENGLAND'S SAKE!

1. But we must not regard barbers as too lowly in the social pecking order; they had strong and historic affiliations with the surgeons.

2. Commander R. C. Parker, USN, "Leadership," *The Naval Review* 9 (1921): 226.

3. Comment was made to this effect on the services vote by the *Manchester Guardian* immediately after the results were announced. It was noted that

servicemen voted Labour in 1945 in overwhelming proportions. Nothing has been revealed since that time to contradict this view of the general feeling of the servicemen that it was time for a change.

4. John Cleveland (sometimes spelled Clevland); second secretary of the navy, 1746-51; first secretary, 1751-63.

5. Hawke Papers, Greenwich, HWK/16.

6. Ibid.

7. Sir Sidney Robert Fremantle, 1867-1958; admiral; 9th Cruiser Squadron, 1916; 2nd Crusier Squadron, 1917; deputy chief of naval staff, 1918-19; known as "Young Sid." His father, Sir Edmund Robert Fremantle, 1836-1929, had also been an admiral.

8. Alfred Von Tirpitz, 1849-1930; admiral and politician; secretary of state in the Imperial Navy Department; built up the German High Seas Fleet.

9. Alexander Papers, Churchill College AVAR/5/5. In his letter he included comments from Tirpitz.

10. The borough of Northampton has had a famous history, for example, in its repeated election of Charles Bradlaugh, 1833-91, the free thinker. Northamptonshire had both a strong landed interest and a significant nonconformist population. Rodney narrowly won a borough seat there in 1768 after a very expensive campaign which cost him at least 30,000 pounds and compounded his personal financial problems.

BIBLIOGRAPHY

I. ORIGINAL MATERIAL: GENERAL COLLECTIONS OF PAPERS (UNLESS OTHERWISE STATED)

A. At Churchill College, Cambridge

A. V. Alexander Papers. A mine of information. Includes letters from Winston Churchill and the earl of Halifax—in fact, from all the top people in the war. Useful light thrown on the contemporary assessment of Sir Andrew Cunningham's leadership.

A. B. Cunningham Papers. Contains letters sent to the naval historian Oliver Warner by friends and colleagues of Cunningham. Many memoirs of the man and the seaman.

Charles Daniel Papers. Very small collection of papers. Includes the diary of the Second Battle Squadron, 1914-16, by Admiral Sir Charles Saumarez Daniel 1894-. Useful for its sense of enthusiasm regarding the expected big battle with Germans.

G. C. Harper Diaries. Captain G. C. Harper RN, 1896-1962. Diaries contain memories of Admiral Jellicoe and life in the Grand Fleet.

A. R. Henderson Papers. Includes notes by the secretary to Admiral Tomkinson regarding the Invergordon Mutiny and copies of reports by Tomkinson to the Admiralty.

A. A. F. Macliesh Papers. Very small collection of papers. Includes a collection of diaries, letters, and photographs concerning Gallipoli made by Commander A. A. F. Macliesh.

Leonard Wincott Papers. Contains varied reminiscences of Invergordon. They are useful but not dispassionate evidence of lower-deck opinion at the time.

B. At Imperial War Museum (All Unpublished Materials)

Naval Memoirs of Admiral J. H. Godfrey. Also held by the University of California, Irvine. Covers many matters and are particularly useful for comment on the pre-First World War navy.

William Whitworth Papers. Letters and Papers of Sir William Whitworth when he was Second Sea Lord. Includes Cunningham correspondence.

Algernon Willis War Memoirs, 1939-45. Sir Algernon Willis was Chief of Staff to Cunningham in the Mediterranean. Memoirs contain some very useful material on Cunningham.

R. T. Young Papers. Includes comments by Commander Young on Jutland and Roger Keyes.

C. Papers in Private Possession

David Beatty Papers at Chicheley Hall, Newport Pagnell, Buckinghamshire. In the possession and ownership of the trustees of the second Earl Beatty. Have long awaited publication in the Navy Record series. Some already published; others, perhaps the majority, not yet published. Collection is uncatalogued.

Angus Cunninghame Graham Papers. Includes notes made by Sir Angus Cunninghame Graham on life in the Grand Fleet, 1914-17.

D. At Greenwich Museum Library (Catalogue Reference Included); Papers

Francis Austen (AUS). Collection of Sir Francis Austen (the brother of Jane Austen). Includes a good sample of everyday orders and letters regarding the conduct of a ship.

Sir Edward Berry (BER). Includes Nelson letters, and Nelson's comments on St. Vincent.

Sir Gilbert Blane, Bart (BLA). Dr. Gilbert Blane's career touched on naval history in the late eighteenth century, in so many different ways.

Bridport (Samuel Hood) (BRP). Includes some Nelson correspondence.

A. E. M. Chatfield (CHT). He was always a person on the inside track. Collection includes correspondence with Beatty, Dreyer, and many others.

Edward Codrington (COD). Includes a sea journal of the crucial year 1797.

Cuthbert Collingwood (COL). Collingwood is dealing in these papers with everyday work.

J. T. Duckworth (DUC). Collection is very useful regarding Richard Howe's leadership.

Sir Ludovic Duff (DFF). Duff, especially in his diaries, does not mince words about Jellicoe and Beatty.

Gilbert Elliot (ELL). Collection contains a lot of St. Vincent correspondence, much of it about Naples and Sicily, as is the Admiral Nelson part of the papers. Also contains correspondence of Hugh Elliot. Gives an invaluable picture of the challenge facing British naval leadership in the Mediterranean in the Napoleonic era.

Edward Hawke (HWK). Conveys Admiral Hawke's sense of drive.

W. H. Henderson (HEN). Many letters regarding the training of naval officers. Henderson was obviously very much of a paper tiger.

Viscount Hood (HOOD). Wide-ranging correspondence. Correspondence with Admiral Rodney is especially interesting. It includes much varied material.

John Jervis (JER). Gives us the full flavor of St. Vincent.

G. K. E. Keith (KEI). Includes much political correspondence of Viscount Keith. Gives a good sense of the diverse responsibilities of naval leadership of the time.

Augustus Keppel (KEP). Details the cares and concerns of Viscount Keppel—a good sense of the problems he faced as a naval leader.

Matcham (MAM). Collection of papers of the Matcham family. Includes Nelson correspondence.

Milne (MLN). Collection of the Milne family papers. Sir Alexander Milne (died 1896) had the most interesting career. Includes comments on the career prospects of a nineteenth-century naval officer.

Sir Evan Nepean (NEP). A lot of papers formerly catalogued under St. Vincent (JER) are now included in this collection.

Robert Dudley Oliver (BEL). General collection of naval papers. Includes the Order Book of Sir Richard King, commander-in-chief, Plymouth, during the troubled year of 1798.

John Orde (ORD). Very good collection of correspondence between Orde and the naval hierarchy of the time.

William Parker (PAR). Much useful information about his experiences as a midshipman.

A. T. G. C. Peachey (PEACHEY). Includes reflections by Peachey as a young officer at Jutland.

Pellew (Viscounte Exmouth) (PELLEW). Includes material on naval issues of his day, for example, prize money.

H. W. Richmond (RIC). Includes copious notes and cuttings on the themes of naval leadership and command.

William Tennant (TEN). Includes lectures on Jutland by Tennant.

Edward Vernon (VER). Shows Vernon's many naval interests, including improvement of the health and general welfare of the seamen.

Arnold White (WHI). Includes Sir John Fisher correspondence and many items of naval interest. White's journalist interests had a strong focus on the navy.

Wynne (WYN). Collection of family papers. Includes papers of Sir William Penn and Sir Charles Pole. Much detail concerning the 1797 mutinies. Also some St. Vincent correspondence.

Charles Yorke (YOR). Includes a complaining letter of Sir John Orde of 1811.

E. At Public Record Office

A. B. Cunningham War Diary, ADM/199/414 and 199/415. Reveals his anxieties and the wide-ranging nature of his responsibilities.

Edward Hawke, ADM/89, Part 2, and Letters of Hawke to John Cleveland, 1/89, Part I. Includes comment on Hawke's problems of command, especially in the year 1757.

Howe's Letters, ADM/1/99. Includes Richard Howe's letters about the Glorious First of June.

Out Letters of Evan Nepean, ADM/2/618, 1/580, and 2/617. Gives us the full flavor of Admiralty business during the St. Vincent and Nelson era.

F. At the British Library (BL) (Formerly British Museum)

George Anson, Additional Manuscripts (Add MSS) 14956 and 15957. Already much used in Sir John Barrow's *Life of George, Lord Anson*. (London: John Murray, 1839).

Edward Collingwood, Add MSS 52780 and 37425 E. Letters from Collingwood to his brother Edward describing the Battle of St. Vincent and other matters. Contains many useful items for the researcher.

A. B. Cunningham, Add MSS 52558-52563. Contains much unpublished material. Cunningham was a vigorous correspondent, who wrote vivid comments on many people including Admiral Ernest King. These comments give us a good sense of the man.

Egerton Collection, Add MSS 2240. Family collection of papers. Includes some interesting comment by Nelson in his correspondence with his agent, Davison. Nelson comments on St. Vincent, Keith, and others. Also includes Nelson's order book of 1798-99.

Hardwicke, Add MSS 35376, 35395, 36878, and 35898. Hardwicke family had many naval connections in the eighteenth century. Collection includes some Anson papers and copies of Hawke and Sidney Smith's letters.

J. B. Jellicoe, Add MSS 48990-49037. Much of this already published. But some unpublished nuggets for the researcher on naval leadership. Includes correspondence with Beatty.

John Jervis (St. Vincent), Add MSS 36708. Includes some correspondence with Nepean.

R. J. B. Keyes Papers (Keyes). Formerly at Churchill College. Part of these papers have already been published; most are letters by Keyes to his wife. He obviously had publication in mind when he made some of his comments.

Horatio Nelson, Add MSS 36608-37076. Includes interesting comments on health matters.

Journal of St. Vincent, Add MSS 31188. As was his wont, St. Vincent distributes praise and blame.

II. PRINTED COLLECTIONS OF LETTERS AND PAPERS

Barnes, G. R., and Owen, J. H., eds. *The Private Papers of John, Earl of Sandwich, 1771-82*. 4 vols. London: Navy Records Society, 1932-38. Collection gives the full flavor of Admiralty Administration at the time.

Collingwood, G. L. Newnham. *A Selection from the Public and Private Correspondence of Vice-Admiral Lord Collingwood Interspersed with Memoirs of His Life*. 2 vols. London: J. Ridgway, 1828. The style is succinct and Collingwood communicates the strength of his feelings by his restraint.

Corbett, Julian S., ed. *Private Papers of John, Second Earl of Spencer, 1794-1801*. 2 vols. London: Navy Records Society, 1913-14. As with the Sandwich Papers, gives a good idea of the sheer weight and variety of Admiralty work.

Erskine, David, ed. *Augustus Hervey's Journal*. London: William Kimber, 1953. Most entertaining. Gives a good sense of one aspect of the aristocratic style of naval leadership in the eighteenth century.

Gutteridge, H. C. *Nelson and the Neapolitan Jacobins—Documents Relating to the Suppression of the Jacobin Revolution at Naples*. London: Navy Records Society, 1903. Editor faults Nelson for advising Ferdinand IV of Naples to take the offensive against the French.

Halpern, Paul G., ed. *The Keyes Papers, Selections from the Private and Official Correspondence of Admiral of the Fleet Baron Keyes of Zeebrugge*. Vol. I. London: Navy Records Society, 1975. Editor is obviously trying to do full justice to Keyes and praises him for his work in the First World War. A reviewer in the *Naval Review* says that the evidence of this volume casts serious doubt upon the fact that Keyes lacked intellectual capacity. Keyes is not a wholly unsympathetic character, but we must be on our guard over the present-day fashion among historians for revision in all things. No historical character is safe these days from attempts at rehabilitation or overexaggeration of importance. The exercise gives historians employment. This is a welcome volume, as will be the second one, but the weight of evidence, from Fisher, Jellicoe and Beatty, Dudley Pound and Cunningham, down to lesser men, is as to Keyes's lack of intellectual capacity, although no doubt Churchill from the grave would put in a good word for Keyes.

Hannay, David, ed. *Letters Written by Sir Samuel Hood (Viscount Hood) in 1781-83.* London: Navy Records Society, 1895. Shows how much Viscount Hood detested Rodney.

Kemp, Lieutenant Commander P. K., ed. *The Papers of Sir John Fisher.* 2 vols. London: Navy Records Society, 1960-64. The official papers of Fisher up to 1907.

Laughton, Sir John Knox. *Letters and Papers of Charles, Lord Barham, Admiral of the Red Squadron, 1758-1813.* 3 vols. London: Navy Records Society, 1907-11. Some interesting vignettes of information, including the letters of Nauticus (Keith's secretary) to Charles Barham.

The Letters of Lord Nelson to Lady Hamilton with a Supplement of Interesting Letters by Distinguished Characters. London: T. Lovewell, 1814. Lady Hamilton's papers have suffered a fate even worse than Nelson's. This is one example.

Lloyd, C., Perrin, W. G., et al, eds. *The Keith Papers.* 3 vols. London: Navy Records Society, 1926, 1950, 1955. Gives us a good idea of the wide range of responsibilities of a commander-in-chief.

Marder, Arthur J., ed. *Fear God and Dread Nought. The Correspondence of Admiral of the Fleet Lord Fisher of Kilverstone.* 3 vols. London: Cape, 1952-59. Editor has a keen sympathy for Fisher, and Fisher's correspondence makes lively reading.

Naish, George P. B., ed. *Nelson's Letters to His Wife and Other Documents 1785-1831.* London: Navy Records Society, 1958. Useful material. The Nelson papers, as has already been noted, are unfortunately for the historian very dispersed.

Nicolas, Sir Nicholas Harris, ed. *The Dispatches and Letters of Vice-Admiral Lord Viscount Nelson.* 7 vols. London: H. Colburn, 1845-46. The magnum opus of Nelson studies. Very critical of Nelson's biographers Clarke and M'Arthur.

Parry, Ann, ed. *The Admirals Fremantle.* London: Chatto & Windus, 1971. Editor, using the Fremantle papers, has produced a discursive and readable, although by no means exhaustive work.

Patterson, A. Temple, ed. *The Jellicoe Papers*. vol. I 1883-1916. vol. II 1916-1935. 2 vols. London: Navy Records Society, 1966-68. Fundamental material for this study. Selection of the private and official papers with a relatively brief comment by Patterson.

Richmond, Captain H. W., ed. *Papers Relating to the Loss of Minorca in 1756*. London: Navy Records Society, 1911. Reinforces the impression of Admiral Byng's fatal incompetence on this particular expedition.

Smith, David Bonner, ed. *Letters of Admiral of the Fleet the Earl of St. Vincent Whilst First Lord of the Admiralty*. 2 vols. London: Navy Records Society, 1922-26. Includes much material regarding St. Vincent's struggle for administration reform.

Syritt, David, ed. *The Siege and Capture of Havana 1762*. London: Navy Records Society, 1970. Very informative about one of the many British successes in the Seven Years War.

Thursfield, Rear Admiral H. G., ed. *Five Naval Journals 1789-1817*. London: Navy Records Society, 1951. Peter Cullen's journal is the most useful for this study.

III. GENERAL HISTORY

Clowes, Sir William. *The Royal Navy: A History from the Earliest Times to the Present*. Vols. 4 and 5. London: Sampson, Low, Marston and Company, 1899-1900 (republished, New York: AMS Press, 1966). Volumes four and five are especially useful for the revolutionary and Napoleonic period, and they clearly cover less-well-known naval incidents omitted from other histories. The entire work is seven volumes in length.

Corbett, Sir Julian. *England in the Seven Years' War*. 2 vols. London: Longman's Green & Co., 1907. Particularly useful comment on Hawke.

James, William. *The Naval History of Britain*. 5 vols. London: Baldwin, Cradock & Joy, 1822-24. Detailed narrative. Index was provided for the work by the Navy Records Society, London, 1895.

Jenkins, E. H. *A History of the French Navy*. London: Macdonald's & Jane's 1973. Some useful comment on the French response to British naval development.

Kemp, Lt. Commander Peter. *Victory at Sea 1939-45*. London: Muller, 1957. Very readable narrative.

Lewis, Michael. *The Navy of Britain*. London: G. Allen & Unwin, 1948. First-rate introduction to naval history. The value of Michael Lewis's writing is that he integrates all aspects of naval history and sets it in its social background.

————. *A Social History of the Navy, 1793-1815*. London: Allen & Unwin, 1960. Invaluable for the background to the naval wars of the period and gives a useful interpretation of the statistics of the time.

————. *The Navy in Transition 1814-64. A Social History*. London: Hodder & Stoughton, 1965. Continues Michael Lewis's very interesting writing on the social history of the navy.

Marcus, G. J. *A Naval History of England. The Formative Centuries*. Boston: Little, Brown, 1961. Useful introduction to eighteenth-century naval history.

————. *The Age of Nelson. The Royal Navy 1793-1815*. New York: Viking Press, 1971. Recent general study of the period. Gives incisive comment on the great years of Nelson and also worthwhile comment on St. Vincent and Baron Collingwood.

————. *Heart of Oak. A Survey of British Sea Power in the Georgian Era*. London: Oxford University Press, 1975. Beautifully produced book that emphasizes that British shipbuilding stagnated in much of the eighteenth century.

Marder, Arthur J. *From the Dreadnought to Scapa Flow. The Royal Navy in the Fisher Era*. 5 vols. London: Oxford University Press, 1961-70. Best recent history of the Royal Navy in the First World War and the years immediately before.

————. *The Anatomy of British Sea Power. A History of British Naval Policy in the Pre-Dreadnought Era, 1880-1905*. Hamden, Conn.: Archon Books, 1964. (Originally New York: Alfred A. Knopf, 1940.) Deals with personnel, materiel, foreign policy, and Fisher in his top form.

Mathew, David. *The Naval Heritage*. London: Collins, 1944. General survey of British naval history with an optimistic tone to suit the year of publication.

Ralfe, J. *The Naval Chronology of Great Britain or An Historical Account of Naval and Maritime Events from the Commencement of the War in 1803 to the End of the Year 1816*. 3 vols. London: Whitmore and Fenn, 1820. The revolutionary and Napoleonic wars led to a number of similar chronological histories. This is one of them.

Roskill, Captain S. W. *The War at Sea 1939-45*. 3 vols. (In four parts.) London: H. M. Stationery Office, 1954-62. (Vol. 3 has two parts.) Official history, which suffers somewhat from lack of footnotes and attribution. But Roskill has no choice. A footnoted version exists but has not been published.

Wright, Quincy. *A Study of War*. Chicago: University of Chicago Press, 1965. Author appears to be trying to do for war what Arnold Toynbee attempted to do for civilization. The study includes some informative statistics on the duration of wars, and these statistics are referred to in the introduction to this work.

IV. MEMOIRS, AUTOBIOGRAPHY, AND BIOGRAPHY

Bacon, Admiral Sir Reginald H. *A Naval Scrap Book 1877-1900*. London: Hutchinson & Co., 1925. Includes a midshipman's eye view of Admiral Hornby (one of the Tryon school, no doubt) as "strict and severe."

———. *The Life of Lord Fisher of Kilverstone*. 2 vols. London: Hodder & Stoughton, 1929. Bacon was part of what might be called the Fisher-Jellicoe axis. Generally uncritical of Fisher.

———. *The Life of John Rushworth Earl of Jellicoe*. London: Cassell & Co., 1936. Bacon believed Jellicoe to be the greatest admiral of modern times. Interesting details of Jellicoe's life, but not a measured study.

Barnett, Corelli. *The Sword Bearers. Supreme Command in the First World War*. New York: Morrow, 1964. Includes a critical study of Jellicoe. Barnett believes, however, that Jellicoe's personal skill as an admiral delayed the final collapse of British seapower until 1945 and after.

Barrow, Sir John. *The Life of Richard Earl Howe KG*. London: John Murray, 1838. Helpful for its delineation of the influence of Howe on Hood and St. Vincent. The best biography so far of Howe.

———. *The Life of George Lord Anson*. London: John Murray, 1839. Nothing published since has wholly replaced this.

———. *The Life and Correspondence of Admiral Sir Sidney Smith GCB*. 2 vols. London: R. Bentley, 1848. Gives a good impression of the adventurous nature of Sir Sidney.

Baugh, Daniel A. *British Naval Administration in the Age of Walpole*. Princeton: Princeton University Press, 1965. A detailed and important study that shows the limitation of the scope of the authority at the Admiralty in naval administration.

Bennett, Geoffrey. *Charlie B.: A Biography of Admiral Lord Beresford of Metemmeh and Curraghmore*. London: Dawnay, 1968. An account of a popular and controversial character.

———. *Nelson the Commander*. London: B. T. Batsford, 1972. One of the latest and not the least in the long line of Nelson biographies.

Berckman, Evelyn. *Nelson's Dear Lord. A Portrait of St. Vincent*. London: Macmillan, 1962. Not a comprehensive life, but contains some percipient comment about St. Vincent. Has much about Nelson's relations with St. Vincent.

Beresford, Charles. *The Memoirs of Admiral Lord Charles Beresford Written by Himself*. 2 vols. London: Methuen & Co., 1914.

Bethune, Colonel Drinkwater. *A Narrative of the Battle of St. Vincent with Anecdotes of Nelson Before and After That Battle*. London: Saunders and Otley, 1840. A very clear account. Bethune, a military historian, was by happy accident an eyewitness of the battle.

Bourchier, Lady. *Memoir of the Life of Admiral Sir Edward Codrington*. 2 vols. London: Longmans, Green & Co., 1873. Interesting for its recital of Edward Codrington's naval experiences as a young man in the 1790s.

Bart, Sir Jahleel Brenton. *Memoir of Vice-Admiral Sir Jahleel Brenton Bart*. Reedited by his son, London: Longman & Co., 1855.

Brenton, Edward Pelham. *Life and Correspondence of John Earl of St. Vincent. GCP Admiral of the Fleet*. 2 vols. London: Henry Colburn, 1838. Gives a credible portrait of St. Vincent.

Buell, Thomas B. *The Quiet Warrior: A Biography of Admiral Raymond A. Spruance*. Boston: Little, Brown, 1974. Quotes, in appendix at page 437, a note by William Falconer on the duties and responsibilities of an admiral in *An Universal Dictionary of the Marine*.

Burney, William. *The Naval Heroes of Great Britain*. London: Richard Phillips, 1806. A patriotic and anecdotal work. Gives a good idea of the contemporary view of naval leaders at the time of publication.

Burns, James MacGregor. *Leadership*. New York: Harper & Row, 1978. Brave and ambitious attempt to categorize forms of leadership based on a lifetime study of the exercise of power. It does not always convince that the effort was worth making.

Campbell, Dr. J. et al. *Lives of the British Admirals*. 8 vols. London: C. J. Barrington, 1812-1817. Fed upon early authors and was fed upon in turn.

Camperdown, Earl of. *Admiral Duncan*. London: Longmans & Co., 1898. Much detail of the mutinies at Nore and Yarmouth and of the Battle of Camperdown in 1797.

Carver, Field Marshal Sir Michael, ed. *The War Lords: Military Commanders of the Twentieth Century*. Boston: Little, Brown, 1976. Includes essays by Temple Patterson on Jellicoe and Kemp on Cunningham. Temple Patterson suggests that Jellicoe's rigidity of outlook increased with the Great War.

Chalmers, W. S. *The Life and Letters of David Earl Beatty*. London: Hodder & Stoughton, 1951. Very favorable to Beatty—the equivalent of Admiral Bacon's Jellicoe.

Chatfield, Lord. *The Navy and Defence*. London: William Heinemann, 1942.
———. *It Might Happen Again*. London: William Heinemann, 1947. Chatfield was at Jutland and was subsequently very much a part of the naval establishment. He gives us a very good idea of the atmosphere in

leading naval circles between the wars. These two works form an autobiography.

Clarke, Rev. James Stanier, and M'Arthur, John. *The Life of Admiral Lord
Nelson KG from His Lordships Manuscripts.* 2 vols. London: T.
Cadell & W. Davies, 1809. All later serious historians of Nelson have
bitterly complained of the misuse of evidence and the changing of the
documents themselves for this life. Still, it is the first substantial life of
Nelson and worth quoting on occasions.

Copeman, Fred. *Reason in Revolt.* London: Glandford Press, 1948.

Cunningham of Hyndhope, Viscount. *A Sailor's Odyssey; The Autobiography of Admiral of the Fleet Viscount Cunningham of Hyndhope.*
New York: Hutchinson's, 1951. As to be expected from such a prolific
writer, one of the more readable of naval memoirs.

Dixon, Norman F. *On the Psychology of Military Incompetence.* London:
Cape, 1976. Among his selected disasters he has one naval one in
Camperdown.

Dundonald, Thomas, Eleventh Earl of, and Bourne, H. R. Fox. *The Life of
Thomas Tenth Earl of Dundonald.* 2 vols. London: Richard Bentley,
1869. Cochrane's unusual and ubiquitous career detailed. Useful view
of the fate of admirals after the Napoleonic wars.

Fisher, Lord. *Memories.* London: Hodder and Stoughton, 1919.
———. *Records.* London: Hodder and Stoughton, 1919. Fisher on Fisher
and others.

Fitchett, W. H. *Nelson and His Captains.* London: Smith, Elder & Co., 1902.
Title promises more than the book fulfills. Not enough about his captains.

Fitzgerald, Rear-Admiral C. C. Penrose. *Life of Vice-Admiral George Tryon.*
Edinburgh: W. Blackwood & Sons, 1897. Inevitably, interest is concentrated on the final disaster. A credible account.

Gabriel, Richard A., and Savage, Paul L. *Crisis in Command: Mismanagement in the Army.* New York: Hill and Wang, 1978. Criticism of U.S.
Army leadership with especial reference to Vietnam War.

Grimble, Ian. *The Sea Wolf: The Life of Admiral Cochrane.* London: Bond &
Briggs, 1978. An enthusiastic and lively biography.

Hall, Captain Basil. *The Midshipman.* London: Bell and Daldy, 1865. Discursive comments on life at sea in the period 1802-24.

Hamilton, Admiral Sir R. Vesey, and Laughton, John Knox. *1775-1814,
Recollections of James Anthony Gardiner Commander RN.* London:
Publications of the Navy Records Society, 1906.

Harrison, James. *The Life of The Right Honourable Horatio Lord Viscount
Nelson.* 2 vols. London: C. Chapple, 1806. Harrison was in such a rush

to get into print and catch the market that he did not have enough time to describe Nelson's funeral, which aroused much public interest and curiosity.

Hervig, Holger. *The German Naval Officer Corps: A Political and Social History.* Oxford: Clarendon Press, 1973. Study such as this one shows that the British navy was not alone in 1914 in the rigidity of its social attitudes and in its problems of education and acceptance of new technology.

Hood, Dorothy. *The Admirals Hood.* London: Hutchinson & Co., 1942. Careless book, full of misspellings. She comments on Hood being blamed for leaving so much to Sir Sidney Smith at Toulon in 1793.

Hoste, Lady Harriet, ed. *Memoirs and Letters of Captain Sir William Hoste.* 2 vols. London: R. Bentley, 1833. Hoste had been a protégé of Nelson.

Hough, Richard. *First Sea Lord. An Authorised Biography of Lord Fisher.* London: Allen & Unwin, 1969. Hough lacks Arthur Marder's fire and panache, but a useful work in that the information encourages the reader to speculate further about Fisher.

———. *Captain Bligh and Mr. Christian: The Men and the Mutiny.* London: Hutchinson, 1972. Hough sees Captain Bligh's career as an unfortunate example of how the patronage system worked in the eighteenth century.

James, Admiral Sir William. *Old Oak: The Life of John Jervis, Earl of St. Vincent.* London: Longmans, Green & Co., 1950. Readable and enthusiastic but by no means exhaustive treatment. Jervis needs a good modern biography.

Jellicoe of Scapa, Viscount. *The Grand Fleet 1914-16: Its Creation, Development and Work.* London: Cassell & Co., 1919. Jellicoe shows his belief in the fundamental importance of the fleet to the existence of the British Empire and his inevitable obsession with the preservation of the fleet.

Jordan, Gerald, ed. *Naval Warfare in the Twentieth Century 1900-1965.* London: Croom Helm, 1977. Essays in honor of Arthur Marder.

Karsten, Peter. *The Naval Aristocracy.* New York: Free Press, 1972. Shows how much the United States navy in the nineteenth century had in common with the British navy in its style and social attitudes.

Keppel. Hon., and Thomas, Revd. *Life of Augustus Viscount Keppel.* 2 vols. London: H. Colburne, 1842. Good naval biography in the nineteenth-century tradition, which did not stint length. Keppel was another good example of an aristocrat in the navy and a contrast in style to the life of Hervey.

Keyes, Admiral of the Fleet Sir Roger. *The Naval Memoirs.* 2 vols. London: Thornton Butterworth, 1934-35. Keyes writes on the period 1910-18.

————. *Adventure Ashore and Afloat*. London: G. G. Harran & Co., 1939. Reminiscences by Keyes of his early naval career at the end of the nineteenth century. Some good tales of interest for old China hands.

Laughton, J. Knox, ed. *From Howard to Nelson*. London: Lawrence & Bullen, 1899. Articles by different contributors on famous seamen, for example, by S. I. Fremantle on Lord Hawke. Book lacks a unifying theme.

Mackaness, George. *The Life of Vice-Admiral William Bligh*. Sydney: Angus & Robertson, 1951. A case can be made out for almost anyone, and Mackaness does his best for Bligh.

Mackay, Ruddock, F. *Admiral Hawke*. Oxford: Clarendon Press, 1965. Most modern study of Hawke. Still, a very difficult person to depict. Lavish praise for Hawke not always supported from the evidence in the text.

————. *Fisher of Kilverstone*. Oxford: Clarendon Press, 1973. Some useful comments on Fisher's early years.

Mahan, Alfred, *The Life of Nelson, the Embodiment of the Sea Power of Great Britain*. London: Sampson, Low & Co., 1897. Nelson was the hero par excellence for Mahan and his ilk.

Marder, A. J. *Portrait of an Admiral—The Life and Papers of Sir Herbert Richmond*. London: Cape, 1952. Relatively early Marder. Richmond was an inveterate critic of Jellicoe and favored Beatty. Includes many interesting comments on other personalities.

Mundy, Godfrey Basil, Major-General. *The Life and Correspondence of the Late Admiral-Lord Rodney*. 2 vols. London: J. Murray, 1830. Portrays Rodney's ups and downs and deals with the vexatious question about who first suggested breaking the enemy's line.

Napier, Elers, Major General. *The Life and Correspondence of Admiral Sir Charles Napier KCB*. 2 vols. London: Hurst & Blackett, 1862.

Nicol, John. *The Life and Adventures of John Nicol Mariner*. Edinburgh: W. Blackwood, 1822. Purported reminiscences of the Nelson period.

Oglander, C. Aspinall. *Roger Keyes*. London: Hogarth Press, 1951. Authorized life of Keyes. The present publication of Keyes papers is obviously putting this more in perspective and dating it.

Oman, Carola. *Nelson*. London: Hodder & Stoughton, 1947. Very readable and popular biography of Nelson. She has a useful note on the chequered fate of the papers of Nelson and Lady Hamilton.

Osler, Edward. *The Life of Admiral Viscount Exmouth*. London: Smith, Elder & Co., 1835. After 1816, Exmouth's life was relatively uneventful. Gives a good idea of the relative tranquility and stagnation of the navy after the Napoleonic period.

Pack, S. W. C. *Admiral Lord Anson*. London: Cassell, 1960.

————. *Cunningham the Commander, 1883-1963*. London: B. T. Batsford, 1974. Pack's best naval biography. He served under Cunningham and gives a very credible and creditable character portrait.

Parsons, G. S. *Nelsonian Reminiscences. Leaves from Memory's Log.* London: Little & Brown, 1843. Very discursive and anecdotal. Includes a defense of Lady Hamilton.

Patterson, A. Temple. *Jellicoe: A Biography.* London: Macmillan, 1969. Patterson is an authority on Jellicoe, and he has also edited the Jellicoe Papers for the Navy Records Society. Useful balance to the more enthusiastic advocates of Jellicoe such as Sir Frederic Dreyer and Bacon.

Pettigrew, Thomas Joseph. *Memoirs of the Life of Vice-Admiral Lord Viscount Nelson KB.* 2 vols. London: T. & W. Boone, 1849. Includes some arguable details about Lady Hamilton's life.

Phillimore, Rear-Admiral Augustus. *The Life of Admiral of the Fleet Sir William Parker Bart GCB.* 3 vols. London: Harrison, 1876-80. Very useful work. Parker had contact as a young man with many of the famous seamen of Nelson's time, including Nelson, himself. Good for views of more junior officers at the time.

Ralfe, J. *The Naval Biography of Great Britain.* 4 vols. London: Whitmore & Fenn, 1828. Many biographies were written about eminent naval persons at the end of the eighteenth century and in the first part of the nineteenth century. They often fed on one another for details and anecdotes, but the relative attention given to different figures gives us some idea of their contemporary regard.

Ross, Sir John. *Memoirs and Correspondence of Admiral Lord de Saumarez from Original Papers in Possession of the Family.* 2 vols. London: R. Bentley, 1838. Detailed account of an important career.

Sainty, J. C. compiler. *Admiralty Officials 1660-1870.* London: Athlone Press, 1975. Invaluable reference work.

Sherrard, O. A. *A Life of St. Vincent.* London: G. Allen & Unwin, 1933. Quality of writing is poor. Sherrard makes the point that St. Vincent's common sense has deterred biographers.

Southey, Robert. *The Life of Nelson.* 2 vols. London: John Murray, 1814. Despite its casual use of evidence, it still remains read and was very popular in the nineteenth century, being regarded as a classic. It no doubt played a significant part in fostering the cult of Nelson.

Spinney, David. *Rodney.* London: Allen & Unwin, 1969. Best modern biography and very readable. Shows him warts and all. It has done quite a deal for the modern revival of Rodney's reputation.

Tucker, Jebediah Stephens. *Memoirs of Admiral the Right Hon. Earl of St. Vincent.* 2 vols. London: R. Bentley, 1844. Father of the author was private secretary to the earl of St. Vincent for many years. Classic of naval biography.

Vian, Admiral of the Fleet Sir Philip. *Action This Day. A War Memoir.* London: F. Muller, 1960.

Walder, David. *Nelson.* London: Hamish Hamilton, 1978. Well written though suffers from insufficient references.

Warner, Oliver. *Admiral of the Fleet Cunningham of Hyndhope.* Athens: ʿnio University Press, 1967. Not meant to be a comprehensive biogrʿ phy. Concentrates on Cunningham's period in the Mediterranean.

——. *The Life and Letters of Vice-Admiral Lord Collingwood.* London: Oxford University Press, 1968. Collingwood is not the type of person who easily comes alive in biography. Warner does his best.

——. *Command at Sea: Great Fighting Admirals from Hawke to Nimitz.* London: Cassell, 1976. Series of portraits. Includes a particularly sensitive study of Collingwood.

V. SPECIAL STUDIES ON LEADERSHIP AND OTHER THEMES

Abott, William Shirower. "Creative Command—Bonaparte at Headquarters." *Military Review*, October 1968. It is stimulating in reading this to think at the same time of Nelson's equally creative approach to the question of command.

An Act for Amending, Explaining and Reducing into One Act of Parliament The Laws Relating to the Government of His Majesty's Ships, Vessels and Forces by Sea. London, 1970.

Adair, J. E. "New Trends in Leadership and Management Training." Lecture given at the Royal United Services Institution on April 9, 1967, and published separately as a pamphlet. Interesting review of work in the field of leadership. Theme is that you cannot teach leadership.

An Answer to Mr. Pitt's Attack upon Earl St. Vincent, and the Admiralty, in his Motion for an Enquiry into the State of the Naval Defence of the Country on the 15th of March, 1804. London: H. Ebers, 1804. St. Vincent's troubles at the Admiralty caused quite a spate of pamphleteering. This is an example.

An Authentic Narrative of the Proceedings of His Majesty's Squadron under the Command of Rear-Admiral Sir Horatio Nelson from its sailing from Gibraltar to the Conclusion of the Glorious Battle of the Nile. Drawn up from the Minutes of An Officer of Rank in the Squadron. 2nd. ed. London: T. Cadell & W. Davies, 1798.

Barclay, Brigadier C. N. "Military Leadership. Is it inherent or acquired?" *British Army Review*, 1974.

Barnett, Corelli. "Leadership in Perspective." *British Army Review*, December 1971. Interesting comment on the army in the nineteenth and twentieth centuries.

Bartlett, C. J. *Great Britain and Sea Power, 1815-53*. Oxford: Clarendon Press, 1963. Useful study on themes such as the depoliticization of the Board of Admiralty, manning problems, and declining local initiative on the period.

de Belot, Raymond. *The Struggle for the Mediterranean 1939-45*. Princeton: Princeton University Press, 1951. Includes useful comment on Cunningham from the French point of view.

Bidwell, Shelford. *Modern Warfare*. London: Allen Lane, 1973. Challenging and provocative. Believes war to be a form of mental illness.

Brenton, Rear Admiral Sir Jahleel. *The Hope of the Navy or The True Source of Discipline and Efficiency*. London: J. Nisbet & Co., 1839. A moral sermon.

Bush, Captain Eric. *How to Become A Naval Officer* London: George Allen & Unwin, 1963. Conventional list of leadership qualities. Much republished book.

Campbell, D. T., and Thelma H. McCormack. "Military Experience and Attitudes Towards Authority." *American Journal of Sociology*, March 1957, pp. 482-90.

A Candid and Impartial Narrative of the Transactions of the Fleet Under the Command of Lord Howe. London, n.d. Narrative of the revolutionary wars.

Captain Foote's Vindication of His Conduct When Captain of His Majesty's Ship Sea Horse and Senior Office in the Bay of Naples in the Summer of 1799. London: J. Hatchard, 1810. Emphasizes the importance of character in an officer.

Cattell, J. McKeen. "Statistical Study of Eminent Men." *Popular Science Monthly*, 1903, p. 359. Published at a period when there was a rising confidence that a science of leadership was possible.

Chaplin, Denis. "The East German Army Concept of Discipline." *British Army Review*, 1974. This is an interesting study of the concept of co-responsibility. Frederich Engels, who wrote, among other subjects, on military themes, gets great attention from the East Germans.

Clarke, Richard. *Plans for Increasing the Naval Force of Great Britain*. London: Richardson, Whites, Egerton, Debrett, 1795. Plan for voluntary recruitment.

Clerk, John of Eldin. *An Essay on Naval Tactics Systematical and Historical with Explanatory Plates*, 2nd ed. Edinburgh: A. Constable & Co., 1804. Important thesis on naval tactics, although Clerk overrated his own influence on naval leaders.

Cope, Rear Admiral Harley F. *Command at Sea.* Annapolis: United States Naval Academy, 1967. Emphasizes the personal factor in command.

Corbett, Julian S. "Education in the Navy." *Monthly Review,* 1902.

———. *The Campaign of Trafalgar.* London: Longmans, Green & Co., 1910. A standard work.

Creswell, John. *British Admirals of the Eighteenth Century.* Hamden, Conn.: Archon Books, 1972. Thesis is that there was no straitjacket of Fighting instructions. They were obeyed as a matter of convention.

———. *Generals and Admirals: The Story of Amphibious Command.* Reprint. Westport, Conn.: Greenwood Press, 1976. Discursive study of these officers, from the late seventeenth century onwards.

Crowley, Rear-Admiral G. C. "The Greatest Single Factor of Officer and Rating." *RUSI Journal,* 1968, p. 210.

Dewar, A. C., and Dewar, K. G. B. "Naval Staff Appreciation of Jutland." Printed in 1922 but not issued.

Dictionary of National Biography. Invaluable for its articles on lesser known eighteenth- and early nineteenth-century figures. On occasions the details could be more precisely stated; for example, dates are given when office was taken up but not always included when office was relinquished. A good number of articles were written by Sir John Knox Laughton (1830-1915), who does not hesitate to put forth his own strong opinions. For example, he has a much lower view of Collingwood than the author of this study has and many of Collingwood's contemporaries had. Piers Mackesy (see bibliography note on Mackesy) gives strong support to Collingwood.

Dreyer, Sir Frederic C. *The Sea Heritage: A Study of Maritime Warfare.* London: Museum Press, 1955. Particularly useful regarding Jutland. Contains much praise of Jellicoe.

Drinkwater, John. *A History of the Siege of Gibraltar, 1789-93.* London: J. Murray, 1844. Another work by John Drinkwater Bethune. Straightforward narrative. Gibraltar was a good testing ground for many of the great naval leaders of the 1780s and 1790s.

Dugan, James. *The Great Mutiny.* New York: Putnam, 1965. About 1797, but does not supersede the G. E. Manwaring and Bonamy Dobrée book. (See later bibliography entry on Manwaring and Dobrée.)

Eccles, Henry E. *Military Concepts and Philosophy.* New Brunswick, N.J.: Rutgers University Press, 1965. Traditional comments on leadership demands.

Edwards, Kenneth. *The Mutiny at Invergordon.* London: Putnam, 1937. Very right-wing tone. Little understanding of the British Left, but otherwise a reasonable factual account and not without sympathy for the predicament of the men.

Ekins, Rear Admiral Charles. *Naval Battles from 1744 to the Peace in 1814, Critically Reviewed and Illustrated*. London: Baldwin Cradock & Joy, 1824.

Elias, Norbert. "Studies in the Genesis of the Naval Profession." *The British Journal of Sociology* 1 (1950). Three parts of this study were promised but apparently only one appeared. Worthwhile, but overly brief, consideration of the professional traits in the seventeenth-century navy.

Fiedler, F. E. *A Theory of Leadership Effectiveness*. New York: McGraw Hill, 1967. Fairly recent and important, but controversial, contribution to social science studies on the theme of leadership. Puts forward a theoretical model of leadership effectiveness.

Ford, Colonel James. "Coefficients of Leadership, Discipline, Morale, Efficiency." *United States Military Review*, July 1968.

Glascock, Captain. *The Naval Service or Officers' Manual*. London: Saunders & Otley, 1836.

de la Gravière, Captain E. Jurien. *Sketches of the Last Naval War*. Translated by Hon. Captain Plunkett RN. London: Longman, Brown, Green & Longmans, 1848. Another French view. Includes interesting comment on the decline of the French fleet during the revolutionary and Napoleonic wars.

Greer, F. L. "Leader Indulgences and Group Performance." *Psychological Monographs*, 1961.

Grenfell, Commander Russell. *The Art of the Admiral*. London: Faber & Faber, 1937. Mixture of historical comment and generalization—critical of the conduct of Jellicoe.

Groos, Captain O. *The Battle of Jutland (The German Official Account) From Der Kreig Zur See 1914-18 North Sea*. Translated by Lt-Commander W. T. Bagot RN. London: H.M.S.O., 1926 Ventures belief in superior German performance during the battle and pays tribute to the weight of Jellicoe's responsibilities.

Hackett, Lt-General Sir John Winthrop. *The Profession of Arms—The 1962 Lees Knowles Lectures*. London: Times Publishing Co., 1963. Hackett, both a professional soldier and academic, gives historical reflections on military leadership trends.

Hamilton, Sir Ian. *The Soul and Body of an Army*. New York: George H. Doran Co., 1921. Purports to be about leadership. Reveals a good deal of Hamilton's prejudices. Anti-Semitic in outlook and antibusiness.

Hays, Colonel Samuel H., and Lt-Colonel William N. Thomas, eds. *Taking Command: The Art and Science of Military Leadership*. Harrisburg, Pa.: Stackpole Books, 1967. Title is more impressive than the contents. One learns to lead through leading is the message.

Henderson, Admiral W. H. *Historical Abstract of Ages of Entry at the Navy.* London, 1914. Part of the continual debate about the best form of naval education.

————, and Gray, H. B. *The Training of Naval Officers, An Imperial Question.* London, n.d. Advocated the state defraying all the cost of training for the navy.

The History of the Mediterranean Fleet from 1741-44. With the Original Letters ETC that Passed Between the Admirals Mathews and Lestock. London: J. Millan, 1745. Justification for the line-of-battle doctrine.

Hoefling, Colonel John A. "Leadership, There Is No Right Way." *Army,* July 1970. Discusses personality traits necessary for leadership.

Hollingsworth, T. H. "A Demographic Study of the British Ducal Families." *Population Studies* 2 (July-March 1957-58).

Hope, Captain Charles Webley. *The Education and Training of Naval Officers.* Edinburgh, 1869. In the decade of the 1870s there was much concern about naval training.

Hough, Richard. *Admirals in Collision.* New York: Viking Press, 1959. Speculates about the intentions of Admiral Tryon before his final disaster. Interesting book, although the narrative format might have been clearer.

Illing, Brigadier H. C. "Leadership and the Commanding Officer." *British Army Review,* August 1975.

An Impartial and Authentic Account of the Life of Richard Parker, President of the Delegates at the Nore. London: J. Fairburn, 1797. Nore sensation led to much curiosity about the life of one of the leading mutineers.

Impressment of Seamen and a Few Remarks on Corporal Punishment Taken from the Private Memoranda of a Naval Officer. London: Roake & Varty, 1834. Favors retention of the power, but discontinuance of the practice, of impressment.

A Key to the Papers Which Have Been Presented to the House of Commons Upon the Subject of the Charges Preferred Against the Earl of St. Vincent. London, 1806.

Kingston-McCloyhry, Air Vice Marshal E. J. "Leadership with Special Reference to World War II." *RAF Quarterly,* Winter 1967.

Kohs, S. H., and Irle, K. W. "Prophesying Army Promotion." *Journal of Applied Psychology* 4 (1920): 73-87.

The Late Glorious Victory. Journal of the Proceedings of His Majesty's Fleet under the Command of Sir John Jervis KB on the 14th February 1797. n.d.

Lloyd, Christopher, ed. *The Health of Seamen.* London: Navy Records Society, 1965. Well-selected extracts from the writings of naval physicians

such as Dr. James Lind, Sir Gilbert Blane, and Dr. Thomas Trotter.
———, and Coulter, Jack L. S. *Medicine and the Navy, 1200-1900*. Vol. 3, 1714-1815. Edinburgh: E & S Livingstone, 1961-63. Standard work. Especially valuable, since it takes a broad view of the subject.

Mackesy, Piers. *The War in the Mediterranean, 1803-1810*. Cambridge, Mass.: Harvard University Press, 1957. Powerful argument in favor of Collingwood's reputation as opposed to the criticism of him by Alfred Mahan or J. Knox Laughton. Also worthwhile for its comments on Sir Sidney Smith and Sir John Duckworth.

Mahan, Alfred T. *Types of Naval Officers*. London: Sampson, Low, Marston, 1902. Mahan used the exploits of leading figures such as Hawke to illustrate variations of naval leadership. Series of biographical studies.

Manwaring, G. E., and Dobrée, Bonamy. *The Floating Republic*. London: Goeffrey Bles, 1937. Sympathetic and well-written account of the mutinies of 1797.

Marazek, Colonial James. *The Art of Winning Wars*. New York: 1968. Talks much about creativity and intuition as the keys to leadership.

Marder, Arthur J. *From the Dardanelles to Oran*. London: Oxford University Press, 1974. Particularly interesting from the point of view of this work for his study of the Oran issue. Reader can make comparison with Cunningham at Alexandria.

Mariner's Mirror, 1911-. Does not have many articles on naval leadership, but it does include from time to time studies of particular incidents such as the 1797 Naval Mutinies.

McElwee, William Lloyd. *The Art of War: Waterloo to Mons*. London: Weidenfeld and Nicholson, 1974. Points out that Tsushima may have misled naval experts, for sinking ships by long-range gunfire was a difficult tactic.

Moncreiff, John. *Three Dialogues on the Navy Containing: 1. A plan of education for officers. 2. The plan of a standing force by Sea. 3. A scheme of Discipline and Government*. London, 1759. Advocates improvements in naval education such as the study of history.

Montgomery of Alamein, Field Marshal Viscount. *The Path to Leadership*. London: Collins, 1961. Another very general study.

Moran, Lord. *The Anatomy of Courage*. London: Constable, 1966. Famous general practitioner, one of whose patients was Churchill, gives a sensitive study of courage and leadership, citing evidence from his own experience. His comments on army leadership in the First World War are an interesting comparison with the style of naval leadership.

Morgan, Charles L. *The Gunroom*. London: A & G Black, 1919. Morgan is better known as a fine general novelist, but writes with great interest on wartime service.

Moseley, Sidney A. *The Fleet from Within*. London: Sampson, Low, Marston & Co., 1919. General picture of sea life by an R.N.V.R. officer.

Nauticus. "The Children of Nelson," *The New Review*, February 1894. A discussion of Nelson's influence. Nauticus was probably Admiral Henderson.

Naval Anecdotes: Illustrating the Character of British Seamen, and Recording the Most Impressive Examples of Their Skill, Valour, Fortitude and Magnanimity, which have occurred at Various Periods, in Every Quarter of the Globe. London: James Cundee, 1806.

Naval Anecdotes for the Years During Which the Right Hon. The Earl of St. Vincent KB Presided at the Board of Admiralty by a Recorder of the Facts. London: R. Ogle, 1805. Anti-St. Vincent.

The Naval Chronicle, 1799-1818. Regular periodical. Replete with reminiscences exploiting the considerable public interest of the time in naval matters. Interesting for comment on less well-known but highly idiosyncratic characters such as Rear Admiral John Willett Payne.

Naval Leadership. With Some Hints to Junior Officers and Others. Annapolis: United States Naval Institute, 1939. Older version of the 1964 publication, but neither is intellectually demanding. Tells us that it is impossible for a liar to be a gentleman, or for a gentleman to be unintentionally offensive!

The Naval Review, 1912-. Journal catering to the naval profession and naval historians. Has contained throughout the years a large number of articles on the theme of leadership, some signed; others initialed. Also includes historical studies of prominent naval figures.

A few other recent articles from the *Naval Review*, which were consulted are:

Dibble, R. K. "Leadership, A Comparative Approach." January 1972.

"Droxford." April 1975.

"Idealism, Ambition and Leadership." April 1975.

"Leadership." July 1951.

"Leadership for Young Officers." January 1977.

Marder, A. J. "Nelson: A Case Study." April 1961.

"Onlooker." July 1951.

"Oboe." January 1977.

Pursey, H. "Invergordon, First Hand—Last Word," April 1976.

Roskill, S. W. "Truth and Criticism in History and Jutland." April 1957.

———. "More Thoughts on Leadership." October 1959. Roskill is here emphasizing the importance of tradition.

Taylor, A. H. "Trafalgar 21st October 1805," November 1955.

The Naval Songster or Jack Tar's Chest of Conviviality for 1799: Containing a collection of Celebrated Sea Songs. London: J. Fairburn, 1799(?). Song of praise for St. Vincent included.

Neale, William Johnson. *History of the Mutiny at Spithead and the Nore with an Enquiry into its Origins and Treatment and Suggestions for the Prevention of Future Discontent in the Royal Navy.* London: Thomas Tegg, 1842.

Newman, Major-General A. S. "What Are Generals?" *Army*, July 1969. Describes but does not really define.

O'Conor, Captain Rory. *Running a Big Ship on Ten Commandments.* Portsmouth: Gieves, 1937. Has the intellectual content of a restaurant menu, but was popular reading in its day with serving officers.

Official Documents and Interesting Particulars of the Glorious Victory Obtained Over the French Fleet on Sunday June 1st 1794, By the British Fleet under the Command of Admiral Earl Howe. London: J. Debrett, 1794.

Owen, Charles. *No More Heroes—The Royal Navy in the Twentieth Century: Anatomy of a Legend.* London: Allen & Unwin, 1975. A mixture of shrewd comment and sentiment.

Pack, S. W. C. *Britannia at Dartmouth.* London: Redman, 1967. Discursive and sentimental study with some interesting glimpses of naval training over the years.

————. *Sea Power in the Mediterranean.* London: Barker, 1971. General history of British sea power set around leading figures.

————. *Night Action off Cape Matapan.* Annapolis: Allan, 1972. Concentrates on Cunningham's great battle action. Clear and succinct presentation.

Principles and Problems of Naval Leadership. Washington, D.C.: U.S. Bureau of Naval Personnel, 1964. Many general statements. Concentrates on relatively lower-rank problems.

A Proposal for the Encouragement of Seamen to Serve More Readily in His Majesty's Navy for Preventing of Desertion. London: A. Millar, 1758. Part of the growing interest in amelioration of seamen's circumstances. Suggested that houses should be provided for married seamen.

Ranft, Bryan, ed. *Technical Change and British Naval Policy 1860-1939.* London: Hodder and Stoughton, 1977. Contains essays on technology and British naval Policy in the period.

Richmond, Sir Herbert. *Command and Discipline.* London: E. Stanford Ltd., 1927. *Naval Training*, below, seems largely based on this.

————. *Naval Training.* London: Oxford University Press, 1933. Emphasizes his view that a well-educated man makes the best officer.

————. *Statesmen and Sea Power.* Oxford: The Clarendon Press, 1947. General comment on strategy and the politics of seapower.

The Rights of the Sailors Vindicated in Answer to a Letter of Junius on the 5th of October Wherein He asserts the Necessity and Legality of Pressing Men in to the Service of the Navy. London, 1772.

Roskill, S. W. *The Strategy of Sea Power*. London: Collins, 1962. Concentration on the nineteenth- and twentieth-century British navy.

———. *The Art of Leadership*. London: Collins, 1964. Title suggests Roskill's view of the question. It was written with official encouragement and approval.

———. *Naval Policy Between the Wars. I. 1919-29. The Period of Anglo-American Antagonism*. London: Collins, 1968. As far as this study is concerned, very useful for its comments on Beatty, Field, and Keyes after the war.

———. *Naval Policy Between the Wars, II, 1930-39, The Period of Reluctant Rearmament*. London: Collins, 1976. Devotes a chapter to the Invergordon Mutiny. He would have prefered Chatfield to Pound as First Sea Lord during the Second World War.

———. *Churchill and the Admirals*. London: Collins, 1977. Discusses relations of Churchill and the Admiralty in the First and Second World wars.

Royal Naval College Pamphlet on "Leadership." n.d. Strong emphasis on the humane and ethical.

Shurman, D. M. *The Education of a Navy. The Development of British Naval Strategic Thought, 1869-1914*. London: Cassell, 1965.

Selected Readings in Leadership. Annapolis, 1960. Very traditional comments on leadership.

Slim, Field Marshall Sir William. *Courage and Other Broadcasts*. London: Cassell, 1957.

———. "Leadership in Management." *Australian Army Journal*, November 1957.

Smyth, Sir John. *Leadership in War: 1939-45*. Newton Abbot: David & Charles, 1974. Presents a similar approach to Roskill's. Interest is due to Smyth's combination of military and political experience.

———. *Leadership in Battle 1914-18*. Newton Abbot: David & Charles, 1975. Comment on leadership qualities of First World War army commanders.

Spear, J. W. Edwin. "British Naval Reform." dissertation, University of California, Riverside, 1974. About the reforms of the Anson era. Very thorough, but at times pedestrian, survey of Anson's reforms and improvements in the period 1745-63. Strong advocacy, to the point of special pleading, on behalf of Anson.

Steinberg, Jonathan. "The Kaiser's Navy and German Society." *Past and Present*, July 1964.

Stogdill, Ralph M. *Handbook of Leadership. A Survey of Theory and Re-*

search. New York: Free Press, 1974. Very useful and comprehensive survey of social science research throughout this century on leadership.

Swaffer, Hannen. *What Would Nelson Do?* London: Victor Gollanez, 1946. Great popular journalist concentrates on lower deck grievances.

Taylor, Rev. Gordon. *The Sea Chaplains: A History of the Chaplains of the Royal Navy*. Oxford: Oxford Illustrated Books, 1978. A readable and informative history.

The Trial of the Honourable Admiral John Byng at a Court Martial as taken by Mr. Charles Fearne, Judge Advocate of His Majesty's Fleet. London: R. Marby, 1757. Byng's defense makes worthwhile reading.

Tuchman, Barbara. "Generalship." Address at U.S. Army War College, 1973. Lecture was of general interest by a popular historian talking to military men. She says of Nelson, "If there were more Lady Hamiltons there would be more Nelsons." No doubt the reverse would be true as well.

Van Gils, M. R., ed. *The Perceived Role of the Military*. The Hague: Rotterdam University Press, 1971. Contains a number of interesting articles on leadership, including one by F. E. A. Fiedler, "Do leaders really learn leadership?"

Vernon, Philip E., and Parry, John B. *Personnel Selection in the British Forces*. London: University of London Press, 1949. Useful as describing attempts to measure ability for the forces and reflecting the state of social psychology at the time.

A View of the Naval Force of Great Britain by an Officer of Rank. London: J. Sewell, 1791. Officer of rank was Sir J. B. Warren. He was advocating more justice for seamen in matters of prizes and wages.

de Vigny, Alfred. *Servitude et Grandeur Militaires*. Paris: Larousse, 1913. Curious book, difficult to categorize. But it is worth studying for its place in the history of literature, especially with respect to the Romantic movement and for its tribute to Collingwood.

Vroom, Victor H., and Yetton, Philip W. *Leadership and Decision Making*. Pittsburgh: University of Pittsburgh Press, 1973. Investigation of and discussion of styles of leadership. They are critical of F. E. A. Fiedler.

Walder, David. *Nelson*. London: Hamilton, 1978.

Wall, Sir Robert. *Suggestions for the Establishment of a Naval University with some observations on the Formation of a Corps of Naval Engineers*. London, 1831.

Wilkinson, Spenser. *The War Training of Naval Officers*. n.d. Reprint of an article in the *Monthly Review* of October 1900. Spenser Wilkinson was an important military thinker.

————. *War and Policy*. New York: Dodd, Mead and Company, 1900. Penetrating comment on war and on other writers on war such as Mahan.

Williams, Glyndwr, ed. *Documents Relating to Anson's Voyage 1740-44*. London: Navy Records Society, 1967. Casts a little, although not much, light on the character of Anson.

Wincott, Leonard. *Invergordon Mutineer*. London: Weidenfeld and Nicholson, 1974. Wincott has been taken to task by Roskill but it is, whatever the facts in dispute may be, an excellent book in giving the flavor of lower deck life between the wars. Wincott loved the navy even if he disliked the social structure of command.

Wolfe, Malcolm E. et al. *Naval Leadership*. Annapolis: Naval Institute, 1964. Series of essays giving views of senior officers on the necessary ingredients of leadership. Unfortunately, the essays abound with banality, for example, unilluminating phrases, unexplained, such as the "moral power of free men!"

INDEX

Aboukir, 69
Acre, 84, 104, 159
Addington, Henry (Viscount Sidmouth), 41, 49
Admiralty, 13, 16, 17, 18, 24, 28, 31, 42, 49, 58, 59, 73, 86, 94, 95, 98, 108, 109, 116, 117, 122, 129, 137, 138, 140, 141, 144, 162, 163
Admiralty Committee, 92
Alanbrooke, Alan (viscount), 150
Albermarle, earl of. *See* Keppel, George; Keppel, William
Alexander, Albert (A.V.) (earl), 140, 144, 151
Alexander, Harold (earl), 168
Alexandria, 94, 154, 157, 160
Algiers, 94
Allied Powers, 5
American Navy, 105
American Revolution, 3, 22, 43
Americans, 144, 150
Anson, George (baron), 23, 27, 29, 31, 32, 39, 41, 42, 48, 168
Arab-Israeli War of 1973, 168
Argentina, 145

Arnold, Benedict, 35
Arnold, Thomas, 101
Art of the Admiral (Grenfell), 20
Asquith, Herbert (earl of Oxford and Asquith), 119, 120, 121
Astley-Rushton, Edward, 145
Atkinson, L., 153
Atlantic Fleet, 144
Attlee, Clement (earl), 137
Australia, 146
Australian Colonies, 88
Austrian Succession, War of, 31
Axis, The, 5

Backnouse, Sir Roger, 146
Bacon, Sir Reginald, 116, 140
Baldwin, Stanley (earl), 137
Balfour, Arthur (earl), 119, 121
Ball, Sir Alexander, 65
Baltic, 84, 88, 94
Bank of England, 146
Barbados, 35
Barfleur, battle of, 29
Barham, Charles (baron), 17, 18, 28, 29, 74, 86, 93

Bass, George, 23
Bastia, siege of, 68
Battenberg, Prince Louis of, 100, 103, 108, 113
Baugh, Daniel, 25
Bayly, Sir Lewis, 115
Bazaine, François, 168
Beatty, David (first earl), xiii, 77, 100, 102, 109, 110, 114, 115, 116, 118, 120, 122, 123, 124, 137, 142, 145, 162; compared to Jellicoe, 127-130, 132, 133; family pressures on, 131; gains earldom, 127; leadership qualities of, 129-134; personality, 129-130; and the press, 133; at Scapa Flow, 127
Beatty, David (second earl), 127
Beatty, Ethel (countess), 117, 129, 130, 133
Bedford, duke of. *See* Russell, John
Bennett, Goeffrey, 9, 158
Bentham, Jeremy, 28
Bentham, Sir Samuel, 28
Beresford, Charles (baron), 100, 101, 106
Berkeley, George (baron), 53
Berry, Sir Edward, 48, 69
Berwick (ship), 34
Bey of Algiers, 80
Bey of Tunis, 80
Birmingham (ship), 152
Blake, Robert, 12
Blane, Gilbert, 15, 24, 34
Boer War, 111
Boscawen, Edward, 33
Boulogne expedition, 70
Bourchier, Jane (lady), 41
Boxer Rebellion, 113, 134
Boyle, Roger (earl of Orrery), xii
Bradley, Omar, 9
Brenton, Edward, 9
Brest, 43, 50
Bridgeman, Sir Francis, 107, 108
Britannia (ship), 101
British Navy, 25, 29, 46; post-Victorian, 120; pre-First World War, 98. *See also* Royal Navy
Brittany, 30, 37

Bruce, Andrew (Viscount Cunningham). *See* Cunningham, Sir Andrew
Bruges, 139
Buenos Aires, 85
Burney, Sir Cecil, 115, 118
Burns, James, 6
Butler, Samuel, 101
Byng, John, xii, 30, 34, 169

Cadiz, 73, 77
Calabria, 86
Calder, Sir Robert, 54, 66
Callaghan, Sir George, 113, 115, 162
Camperdown (ship), 98
Cape of Good Hope, 87
Carden, Sir Sackville, 104, 138
Caribbean, 166, 169
Carlyle, Thomas, 3
Cartagena (Carthagena), 17, 25
Cartagena expedition, 25, 41
Cayzer, Gwendoline, 100. *See also* Jellicoe, Gwendoline (countess)
Chadwick, Edwin, 28
Chamberlain, Sir Austen, 146
Chamberlain, Neville, 136
Channel Fleet, 49, 54, 88, 169
Channel Islands, 84
Charles (prince of Wales), 100
Chatfield, Alfred (baron), 16, 17, 114, 120
Chilean Navy, 91
China, 102, 134, 166
Churchill, Randolph, 152
Churchill, Sir Winston, 72, 103, 106, 107, 119, 122, 137, 140, 151, 152, 161
Church of England, 25, 27
Civil Service, 101, 102
Clapham Junction, 114
Clarence, duke of (William IV, king of England), 15, 18, 36, 64, 74, 77, 78, 140
Clarke, Reverend James, 71
Cleveland, John, 166
Cobbett, William, 58
Cochrane, Thomas (earl of Dundonald), 40, 91
Cockburn, Sir George, 60
Codrington, Sir Edward, 40, 41, 92

Coffin, Isaac, 37

Collingwood, Cuthbert (baron), xiii, 41, 42, 46, 50, 58, 59, 64, 69, 82, 85, 92, 93, 102, 125, 159, 161; battle record of, 79; as commander of Mediterranean, 80; compared to Jellicoe, 77, 81; compared to Nelson, 77, 78, 79, 81; humanitarianism of, 78-79; letters of, 77; personality, 77; political sense, 80; Romantic appeal, 76

Colomb, Sir John, 96

Colomb, Philip, 96

Constantinople, 88, 89, 118

Cook, James, 23

Copenhagen, battle of, 88

Corbett, Sir Julian, 95, 106

Corsica, 72

Cowan, Sir Walter, 140, 141

Crete, 153, 157

Crimean War, 94

Cromwell, Oliver, 3, 10, 106

Cuba, 106

Cullen, Peter, 13, 59

Cunningham, Sir Alan, 204

Cunningham, Sir Andrew, xii, xiii, 42, 50, 77, 121, 141, 147, 161, 164, 165, 168; leadership qualities of, 148, 150-158; at Matapan, 155-157; in the Mediterranean (1939-1942), 148, 150, 154; Nelsonian quality of, 157-158; personality, 152; relations with Sir Winston Churchill, 151; at Tobruk, 153

Danes, 72, 73

Dardanelles Commission, 123

Dardanelles expedition, 89, 104, 136, 138, 150

Dartmouth (naval college), 101

Davis, Evan, 68

Davison, Alexander, 73

de Gaulle, Charles, 153

De Robeck, Sir John, 104, 105, 108

Devon, 100

Dewar, Alfred, 70, 110

Dewar, Kenneth, 70, 110

Dogger Bank, 122

Dominica, 81

Douglas, Sir Charles, 23, 36

Douglas, Sir Howard, 36

Dover Patrol, 137, 140

Dover, Straits of, 139, 140

Dreadnoughts, 164

Dreyer, Sir Charles, 114, 115

Duckworth, Sir John, 20, 58, 60, 61, 88

Duff, Sir Alexander, 118, 127

Duff, George, 13

Duncan, Adam (viscount), 60

Dundas, Henry (Viscount Melville), 53

Eden, Anthony (earl of Avon), 152

Egypt, 102, 150, 157

Eisenhower, Dwight, 153, 168

El Arish, 85

Elliot, Sir George, 78

Elliot, Gilbert (earl of Minto), 72, 88

Elliot, Hugh, 72

England. See Great Britain

Eton (College), 101

Europe, 5, 163

Falconer, William, 19, 24

Ferdinand IV (king of Naples), 71

Field, Sir Frederick, 140, 145

Finesterre, battle of, 29

First World War, 5, 14, 91, 92, 102, 104, 106, 111, 125, 131, 134, 136, 142, 143, 146, 147, 148, 150, 156, 157, 164. See also Great War

Fisher, John (viscount), 8, 60, 91, 94, 100, 101, 103, 105, 106, 107, 108, 113, 118, 119, 120, 121, 122, 133, 134, 137, 152, 159, 165, 169

Flanders, 14

Flinders, Matthew, 23

Foudroyant (ship), 50

France, 19, 37, 43, 113, 154, 156, 161, 168; and evacuation of Egypt, 85; fall of, 154; and naval leadership of, xiii, 22-23, 46; ships of, 25, 43, 155

Franco-German War, 106, 108

Fraser, Bruce (baron), 151

Frederick Barbarossa (emperor), 63

Frederick II (the Great) (king of Prussia), 3, 30

Frederick William I (king of Prussia), 30

Fremantle, Sir Sidney, 167

Fremantle, Sir Thomas, 48, 60, 67

French Fleet, 80, 124, 154

French Navy, 166

French Revolution, 3, 7

French revolutionary wars, 87

French, Sir John, 113

Gaeta, 86

Ganteaume, Joseph, 79

Gardner, Alan, 53

George II (king of England), 32

George III (king of England), 18, 37, 58, 87

George V (king of England), 100, 132, 140

German Navy, 109

Germans, 129, 132, 139, 154

Germany, 109, 113, 154; aircraft of, 148; and First World War, 106, 109, 139

Gibbon, Edward, 12, 49

Gladstone, William, 101

Godfroy, René, 155

Graham, Sir James, 95

Grand Fleet, 76, 88, 105, 107, 113, 114, 115, 116, 118, 121, 122, 127, 128, 129, 130, 132, 134

Graves, Thomas (baron), 37

Great Britain, 49, 113, 143, 147, 148, 154, 160

Great War, 133, 134, 136, 150, 151, 167. See also First World War

Greenwich, 95

Greenwich Naval College, 51

Grenfell, Russell, 19

Grenville, James, 35

Haig, Douglas (earl), 14, 113, 127

Hallowell, Sir Benjamin, 16

Hamilton, Emma (lady), 64, 65-66, 71, 108

Hanbury, Sir Charles, 32

Hankey, Maurice (baron), 106, 133

Hardy, Sir Thomas, 68, 79

Harper, John (vice-admiral), 128

Harrow (school), 101

Hawke, Edward (baron), xii, 23, 27, 29, 30, 31, 32, 33, 37, 39, 50, 92, 166, 168, 172

Henderson, Sir William Hannam, 8, 102

Hermione (ship), 39

Heroes and Hero Worship (Carlyle), 3

Hervey, Augustus (earl of Bristol), 40

Hitler, Adolf, 162

Hobbs, John ("Jack"), 125

Hood, Alexander (first Viscount Bridport), 39, 58

Hood, Sir Samuel, 60

Hood, Samuel (viscount), 15, 23, 31, 35, 48, 52, 58, 66, 72, 85, 87, 88, 92, 93, 166, 168

Hore-Belisha, Leslie, 152

Hornby, Sir Thomas, 104

Hotham, William (baron), 65, 66, 73

Howe, Richard (earl), 10, 23, 27, 31, 32, 34, 37, 39, 40, 41, 58, 92, 93

Howes, H. L., 114

Industrial Revolution, 3, 22, 23, 28, 74

Invergordon Mutiny, 144, 145, 146

Ireland, 131

Italian Fleet, 157

Italian peninsula, 72

Italian torpedo boats, 148, 157

Italy, 5, 72

Jamaica, 32, 34

Jamaica Assembly, 89

Japanese, 144

Jellicoe, Gwendoline (countess), 130, 131. See also Cayzer, Gwendoline

Jellicoe, John Rushworth (earl), xi, xiii, 13-14, 16, 42, 50, 74, 76, 77, 81, 94, 98, 100, 102, 105, 106, 107, 108, 109, 110, 148, 150, 151, 153, 154, 160, 162, 165, 168, 169; compared to Beatty and Keyes, 125, 127, 129-130, 131, 132, 133, 134, 137, 142; criticized by Fisher, 121, 124; at Jutland, 116, 117, 128; leadership of, 113-124; personality, 111;

pessimism of, 118-119; and the press, 120-121; and rapport with subordinates, 113-115; and Sir Winston Churchill, 122
John (king of England), 40
Jutland, battle of, 50, 109, 111, 113, 116, 117, 119, 120, 127, 128, 143, 155, 157, 160, 162, 165, 169

Keats, Sir Richard, 70
Keith, George (viscount), 42, 65, 72, 73, 74, 85, 86, 87, 89
Keppel, George (third earl of Albemarle), 43
Keppel, William (second earl of Albemarle), 42
Keyes, Eva (lady), 130
Keyes, Roger (baron), xiii, 84, 87, 104, 120, 125, 127; at the Dardanelles, 136, 138; leadership qualities of, 137-142; personality, 136, 137; and Sir Winston Churchill, 136, 140; at the Zeebrugge raid, 136, 139, 140
King, Ernest, 120
King, Sir Richard, 55
King and Country Resolution, 146
Kléber, Jean, 85

Labour (party), 146
Ladybird (ship), 153
Lang, Cosmo, 132
Laughton, Sir John, 93
Lestock, Richard, 29, 30, 98, 169
Liddell Hart, Sir Basil, 109
Lind, James, 24
Lisbon, 71, 73
Lloyd George, David (earl), 63, 103, 118, 120, 127, 139
Lochinvar (ship), 140
Lock, Charles, 67
Locker, William, 70
London, 17, 88, 89

MacArthur, Douglas, 168
M'Arthur, John, 71

Macclesfield, earl of. See Parker, Thomas
McClintock, John, 102
Mackay, Ruddock, 33
McKenna, Reginald, 132
Madden, Sir Charles, 115, 127, 128, 129, 140
Mahan, Alfred, 8, 33, 63, 93
Malta, 136
Malthus, Thomas, 28
Man, Robert, 55
Manila, 32
Marder, Arthur, 9
Maria Carolina (queen of Naples), 71, 86
Marlborough (ship), 128
Mars (ship), 13, 51
Marshall, George, 168
Martinique, 35
Matapan, battle of, 148, 151, 154, 155-157, 164, 165
Mediterranean, 11, 16, 42, 50, 58, 59, 67, 71, 77, 79, 80, 81, 85, 87, 88, 94, 104, 131, 137, 141, 142, 148, 150, 151, 153, 154, 169
Mediterranean fleet, 54, 136, 151, 154, 169
Merchant Navy, 24, 100
Mill, James, 28
Milne, Sir Berkeley, 98
Minorca, 72
Minto, earl of. See Elliot, Gilbert
Moncreiff, John, 8
Monk, George (duke of Albemarle), 12
Montagu, William, 39
Montgomery, Bernard (viscount), 9, 20, 70, 77, 99, 131, 168
Monthly Review, 95
Moore, Sir John, 84
Moran, Charles (baron), 14
Mordaunt, Sir John, 30
Mountbatten, Louis (earl), 100, 101, 103
Mutinies, naval, 17, 32-55
My Memoirs (Von Tirpitz), 167

Napier, Sir Charles, 91, 94, 98
Naples, 67, 71, 72
Naples, Kingdom of, 71-72

Napoleon, 7, 10, 18, 66, 71, 72, 84, 106, 119
Napoleonic Wars, 25, 87
Naval Chronicle, 8, 9, 18
Naval Review, 4, 121, 145
Naval mutinies. *See* Mutinies, naval
Navy Board, 95, 169
Nelson, Horatio (viscount), xi, xiii, 7, 10, 13, 15, 16, 17, 22, 23, 24, 27, 29, 33, 35, 37, 41, 46, 47, 48, 49, 50, 54, 56, 57, 59, 60, 76, 77, 78, 79, 80, 81, 82, 84, 87, 89, 90, 92, 93, 95, 102, 105, 106, 107, 108, 109, 110, 111, 113, 118, 119, 121, 122, 123, 124, 125, 131, 134, 139, 145, 148, 150, 151, 153, 157, 158, 160, 161, 165, 166, 168, 169, 170; administrative ability of, 65; at battle of the Nile, 57, 65, 69; egotism of, 85; insubordination of, 72-73; lack of professional discipline, 65; leadership of, 62, 64, 67-75; legacy of, 91; liaison with Lady Hamilton, 64, 65, 66, 71; morality of, 64-65; morbidity of, 15-16; personality, 64, 67, 70, 72; relationship with subordinates, 68, 69
Nelson the Commander (Bennett), 9
Nepean, Sir Evan, 20, 29, 48, 54, 57, 60, 86
New Zealand, 120
Nicholls, Sir Henry, 15
Nile, battle of the, 65, 66, 69, 74
Nore mutinies, 52, 53
Northampton, 169
Northcliffe, Alfred (viscount), 107, 120
Northcote-Trevelyan Reforms, 101
North Sea, 88, 109, 118
Norway, 141
Nugent, James, 25

Ocean (ship), 79
Oglander, Aspinall, 139
Oliver, Sir Geoffrey, 152
Oram, Harry, 144
Orde, Jane (lady), 57
Orde, Sir John, 49, 51, 56, 57, 58, 59, 60, 61, 73, 81, 87, 106

Orkneys, 88
Orrery, earl of. *See* Boyle, Roger
Ostend, 139
Oxford, 101

Parker, Sir Hyde, 60, 65, 72, 73, 88
Parker, Sir Peter, 48, 77
Parker, Thomas (earl of Macclesfield), 32
Parker, Sir William, 49, 73, 88, 92
Patton, George, 168
Patton, Philip, 52, 53
Peel, Sir Robert, 101
Pégase (ship), 50, 156
Pelham-Holles, Thomas (duke of Newcastle), 31
Pellew, Sir Edward (Viscount Exmouth), 49, 92, 94
Peninsular War, 79, 84
Pepys, Samuel, 32
Pettet, Robert, 70
Pitt, William (the Elder), 17, 33
Pitt, William (the Younger), 49, 53
Pocock, Sir George, 43
Pole, Sir Charles, 15, 53, 55
Pompée (ship), 85
Porcupine (ship), 48
Portal, Charles (viscount), 150
Port Royal, Jamaica, 32
Portsmouth, England, 16, 17, 28
Portuguese Navy, 91
Pound, Sir Dudley, 16, 17, 140, 141, 150, 151, 153, 154, 157, 168
Prickett, Cecil, 145
Pursey, Harry, 145

Queen Elizabeth (ship), 138

Radar, 148, 156
Richmond, Sir Herbert, 8, 9, 70, 78, 94, 117, 120, 121, 127, 132, 134
Robertson, Sir William, 113
Rodney, George (baron), 15, 17, 23, 24, 31, 34, 35, 40, 41, 77, 92, 93, 103, 161, 166, 168
Roosevelt, Franklin, 154

Roskill, Stephen, 4, 6, 8, 9, 10, 142, 144, 146

Rosyth, 88, 118, 130

Royal Air Force, 136, 157

Royal Naval College (Dartmouth), 9, 104

Royal Naval Staff College, 143

Royal Navy, xii, xiii, xiv, 9, 96, 99, 156, 157, 158, 162, 166, 168; between the world wars, 143-147; compared to British Army, 17-19; compared to French Navy, 43; continuity in, 163; in the eighteenth century, 22-46; medical treatment in, 25; and mental stress of officers, 14-16; qualities of superior officers, 19-20; and tradition of career professionalism, 18-19

Russell, John (duke of Bedford), 31, 33

Russia, 72, 94, 162

Russian Fleet, 105

Russian Navy, 28, 105

St. Nicholas (ship), 50

Saints, battle of the, 15, 29, 35, 36

St. Vincent, battle of, 50, 64, 74, 108, 124, 168

St. Vincent, John Jervis (earl of), xiii, 19, 20, 22, 23, 27, 28, 30, 37, 39, 41, 43, 46, 66, 67, 72, 73, 74, 76, 77, 79, 82, 84, 88, 92, 93, 95, 99, 102, 105, 109, 121, 125, 145, 148, 150, 152, 156, 159, 161, 163, 164, 166, 169; at battle of St. Vincent, 50, 51; becomes First Lord of the Admiralty, 49; compared to Nelson, 47-48; favoritism of, 60; leadership qualities of, 48-49, 54, 61; on naval discipline, 55-56; on other admirals, 60-61; personality of, 48-49; and Sir John Orde, 51, 56-59; unpopularity of, 54

San Josef (ship), 50

Santa Cruz expedition, 70, 71

Santo Domingo Bay, 89

Saumarez, James (lord de Saumarez), 58, 60, 64, 65, 79, 84, 92

Saumarez, Philip, 32

Saunders, Sir Charles, 32, 33, 42, 48

Saxe, comte de, 20

Scapa Flow, 88, 114, 115, 118, 119, 120, 127, 130, 133, 143, 169

Schröder, Ludwig, 101

Scurvy, 52

Second World War, xii, 5, 100, 124, 134, 136, 143, 147, 150, 161, 164

Seven Years War, 24

Seymour, Lord Hugh, 53

Shipbuilding: British, 23; French, 23

Sicily, 79, 85

Slave trade, 27, 54, 68, 94

Smith, Adam, 22, 28

Smith, Charles, 85

Smith, Sir Sidney, 12, 60, 61, 71, 72, 79, 82, 84, 85, 86, 87, 89, 136, 159, 166

Smyth, Sir John, 9, 115

Somme, battle of the, 109

Spain, 5, 43, 78, 79, 168

Spanish Fleet, 43, 50, 124

Spanish Navy, 43, 89; warships, 23

Spencer, George (earl), 28, 29, 52, 57, 65, 74

Spencer, Lavinia (countess), 64

Spender, John Alfred, 108

Spithead, 52, 53, 166

Stopford, Sir Robert, 98

Straits of Gibraltar, 73

Strangford, Percy (viscount), 85

Sturdee, Sir Frederic, 115

Sudan, 102

Suffren, Pierre de, 43

Sunday Schools, 79

Sutcliffe, Herbert, 125

Swaffer, Hannen, 146

Sweden, 72

Taylor, A. J. P., 94

Tennant, Sir William, 51, 110

Termagent (ship), 70

Thompson, Sir Charles, 54

Thompson, Edward, 25

Thornborough, Edward, 101

Three Dialogues on the Navy (Moncreiff), 8

Thring, Edward, 101

Tobruk, 153

Tolstoy, Leo (count), 161
Tomkinson, Wilfred, 144, 145
Tory, 41, 58
Toulon, 72, 79, 85, 160
Toulon, battle of (1744), 29, 33, 36, 43
Tovey, John (baron), 151, 155
Trafalgar, battle of, 35, 67, 70, 71, 79, 80, 89, 92, 108, 109, 113, 157, 160, 161, 165
Treatise of the Scurvy (Lind), 24
Trenchard, Hugh (viscount), 136
Trotter, Thomas, 24
Troubridge, Sir Thomas (1758-1807), 49, 60, 163
Troubridge, Sir Thomas (1862-1926), 102, 103
Tryon, Sir George, xii, 88, 96, 98, 99
Tsushima, battle of, 105
Turkey: defeat of, 138; sultan of, 74; Turks, 89
Turkish Navy, 89

Union Club, 136
United Irishmen movement, 55
United Provinces, 87
United States of America, 5, 41, 133; Navy, 95, 105, 150; privateers, 166; seamanship, 92; and war of 1812, 24, 92
Universal Dictionary of Marine, An (Falconer), 19
Ushant, battle of, 41
Utilitarianism, 28

Vanguard (ship), 73, 74
Vernon, Edward, 14, 23, 30, 31, 39
Vian, Sir Philip, 141
Vichy, 155
Victoria (ship), 98
Victorian England, 120
Victorian Navy, 93, 134, 167
Victory (ship), 164
Vienna, 88

Ville De Paris (ship), 53
Villeneuve, Pierre de, 8, 166
Vittorio Veneto (ship), 156
Von Clausewitz, Karl, 20
von Moltke, Helmuth (count), 168
Von Tirpitz, Alfred, 167

Wallis, Provo (admiral), 15
Walpole, Horace, 37
War Council, 122
War of 1812 (American), 24, 92
War Office, 18, 141
Warrender, Sir George, 115
Warspite (ship), 156
Washington, D.C., 150, 151
Washington, George, 105
Waugh, Evelyn, 141
Wavell, Archibald (earl), 4, 10, 151
Wellesley, Arthur. *See* Wellington, duke of
Wellington, duke of, 6, 14, 64
West Indies, 35, 41
Westminster, 103, 141, 163
What Would Nelson Do? (White), 146
Whig, 41, 50, 54, 58
White, Arnold, 120, 146
Whitehall, 103, 119, 133, 155, 169
Wilkinson, Spenser, 63, 68, 94
William IV (king of England). *See* Clarence, duke of
Willis, Sir Algernon, 153
Wilson, Sir Arthur, 117, 145
Wolfe, James, 33
World War I. *See* First World War
World War II. *See* Second World War

York, Philip (earl of Hardwicke), 32, 41
Young, Robert Travers, 137

Zeebrugge Raid, 127, 136, 139, 140
Zhukov, Georgy, 10

About the Author

JOHN HORSFIELD, as well as being a professor of history in the United States, is an English lawyer. He specializes in naval history, the history of sport, working class and urban history, and English constitutional law. He has also served in the armed forces where he received a first-hand impression of the stresses and demands of military leadership.